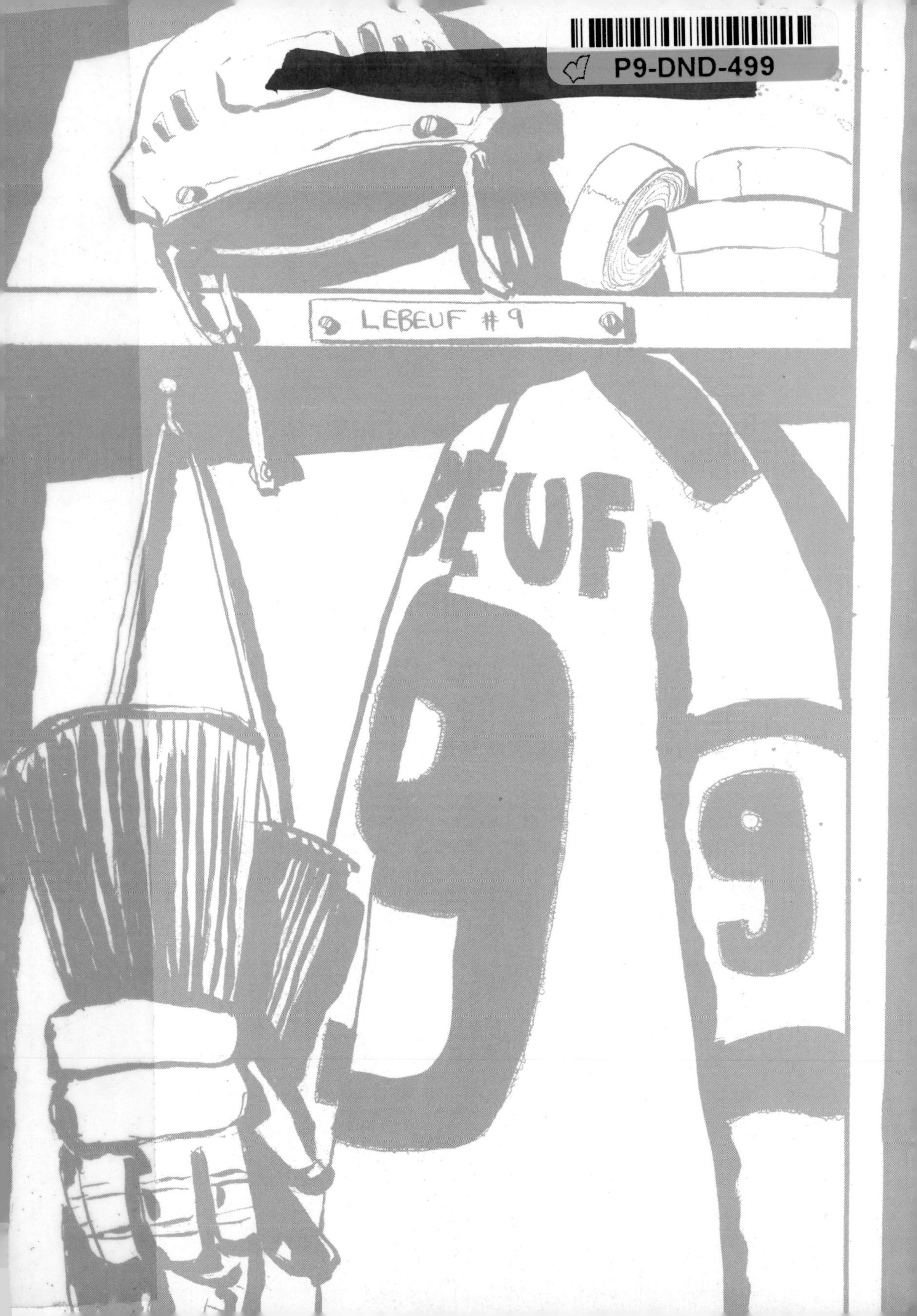
LEBEUF # 9
9
9

Other graphic novels by Jeff Lemire:

• Essex County (Vol 2): Ghost Stories
        ISBN:978-1-891830-94-5
• Essex County (Vol 3): The Country Nurse
        ISBN 978-1-891830-95-2

"Lester's Comic" by Jeff Lemire — Age 9

ISBN 978-1-891830-88-4
1. Farm Life
2. Hockey
3. Super-Heroes
4. Graphic Novels

Visit Jeff Lemire at www.jefflemire.com/.

Second Printing, February 2008. Printed in Canada.

ESSEX COUNTY VOL.1:
TALES FROM THE FARM

BY JEFF LEMIRE

Top Shelf Productions
Atlanta / Portland

SUMMER

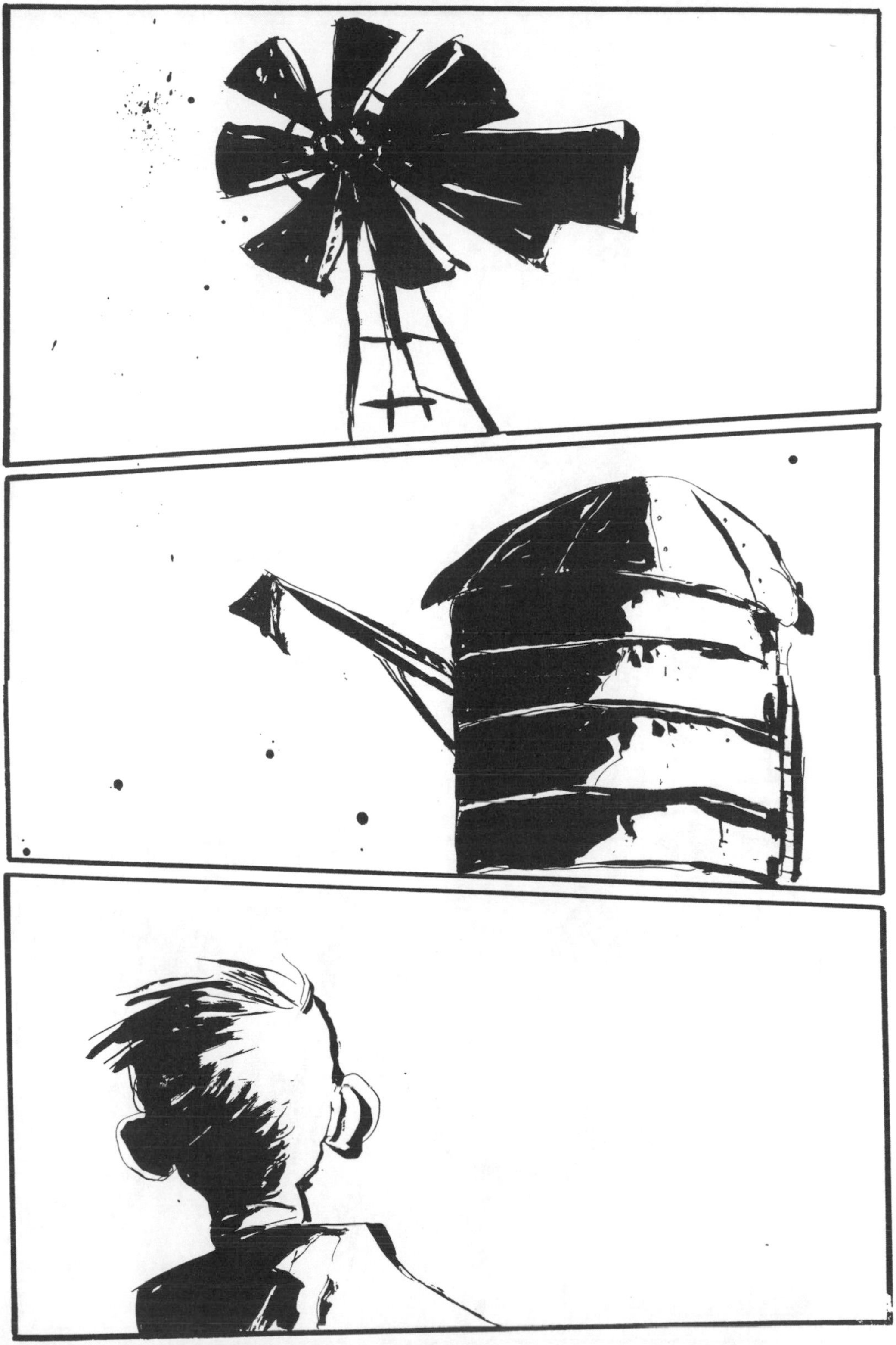

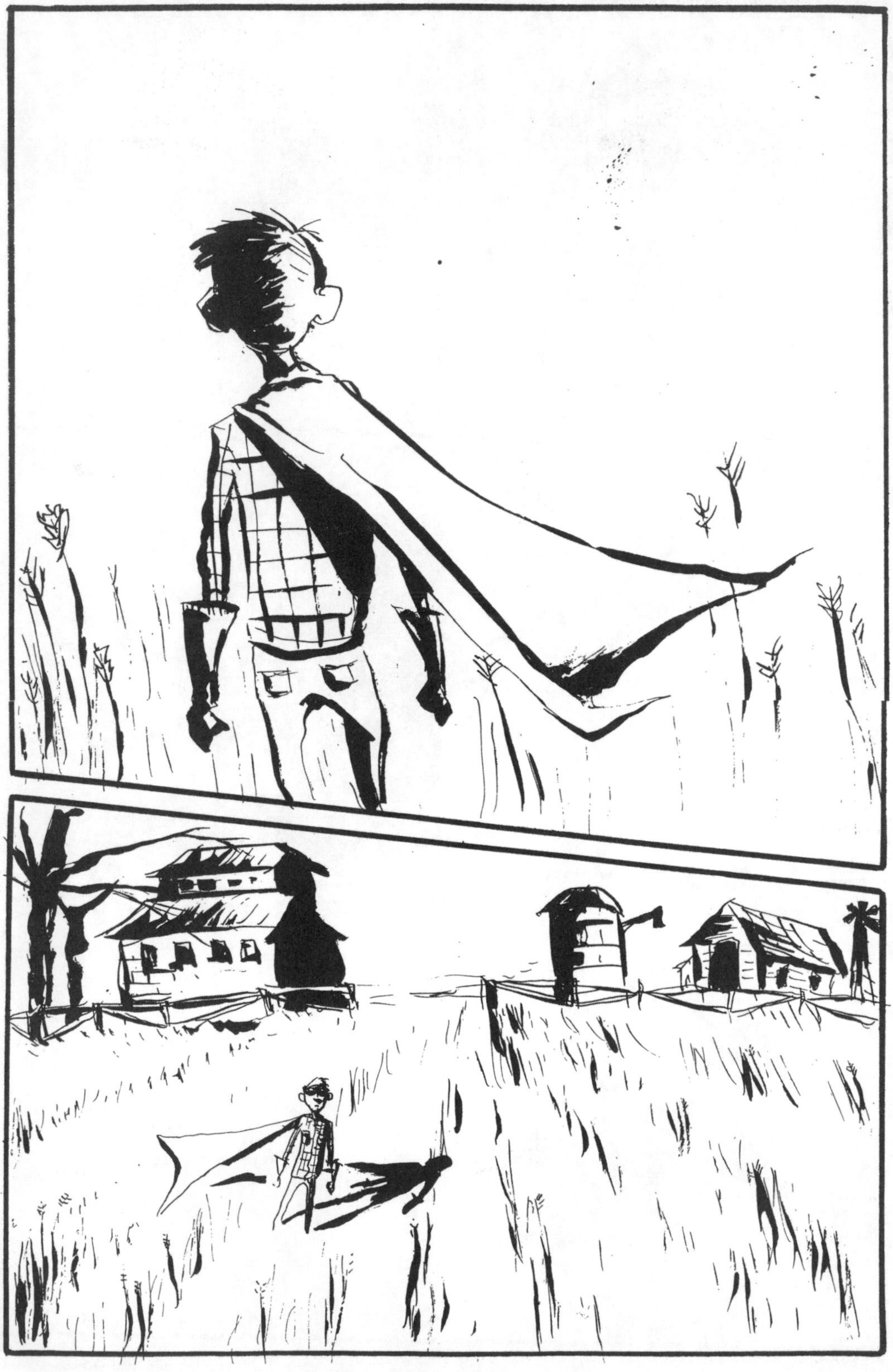

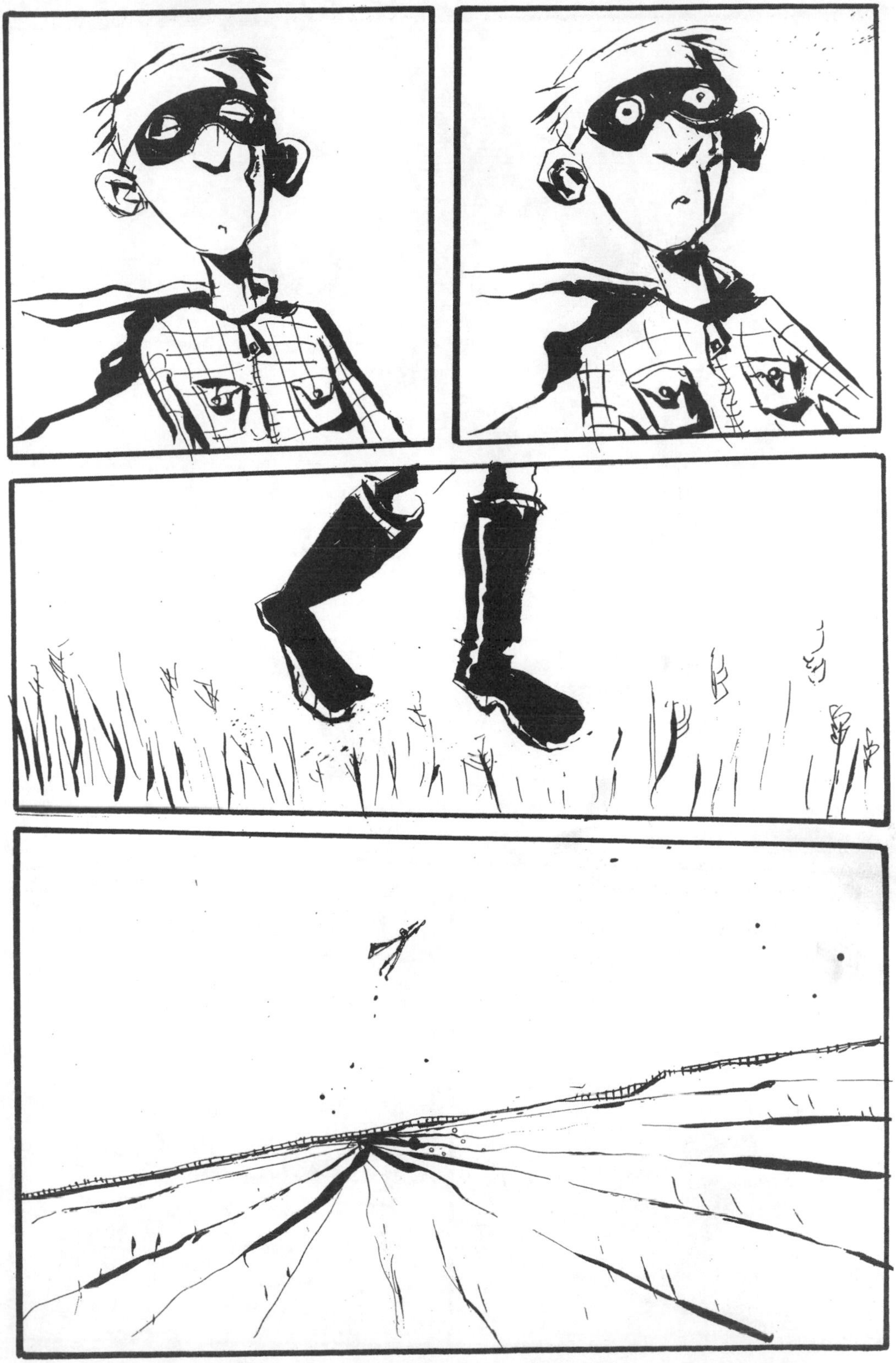

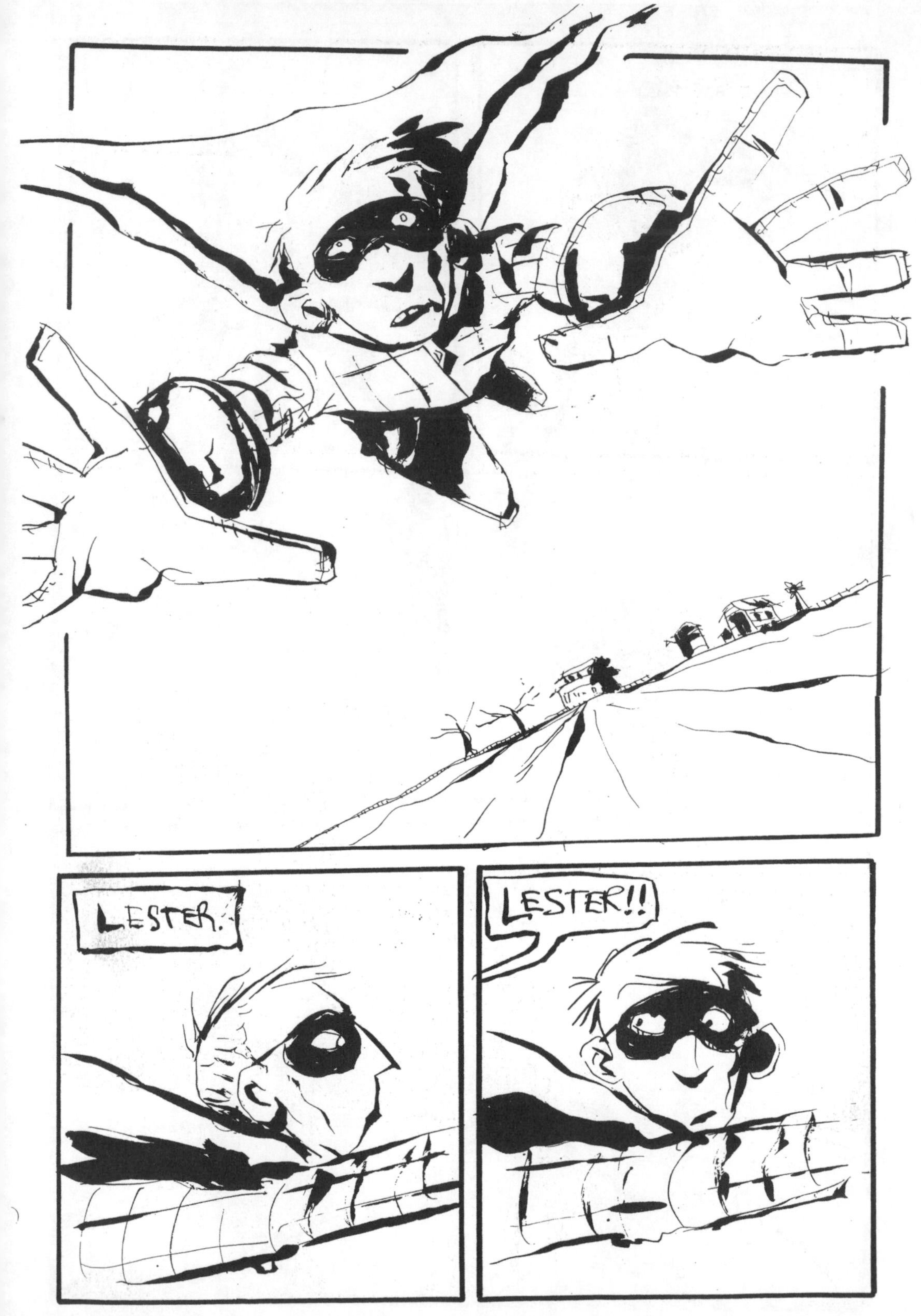
LESTER.
LESTER!!

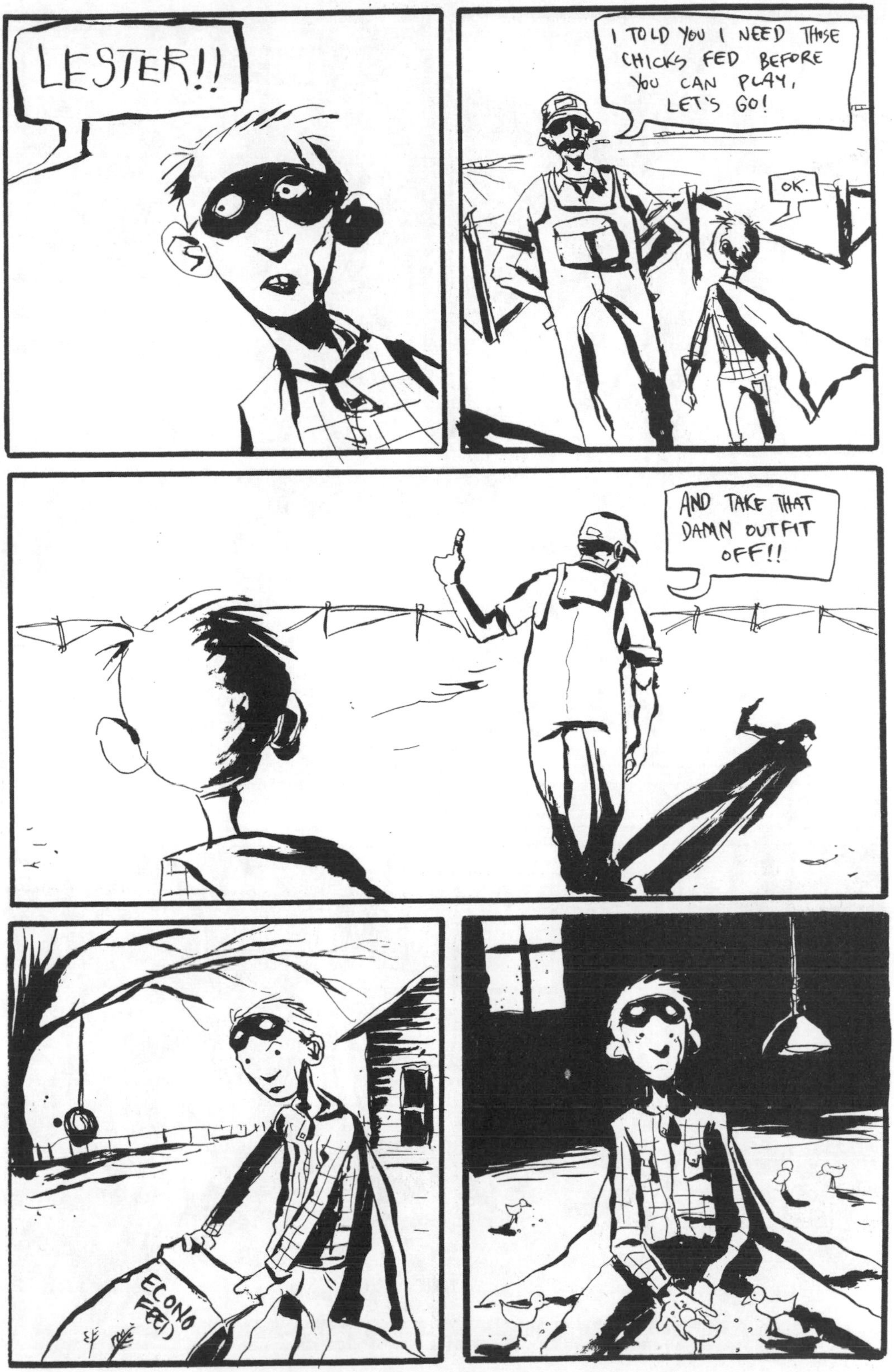
LESTER!!
I TOLD YOU I NEED THOSE CHICKS FED BEFORE YOU CAN PLAY, LET'S GO!
OK.
AND TAKE THAT DAMN OUTFIT OFF!!
ECONO FEED

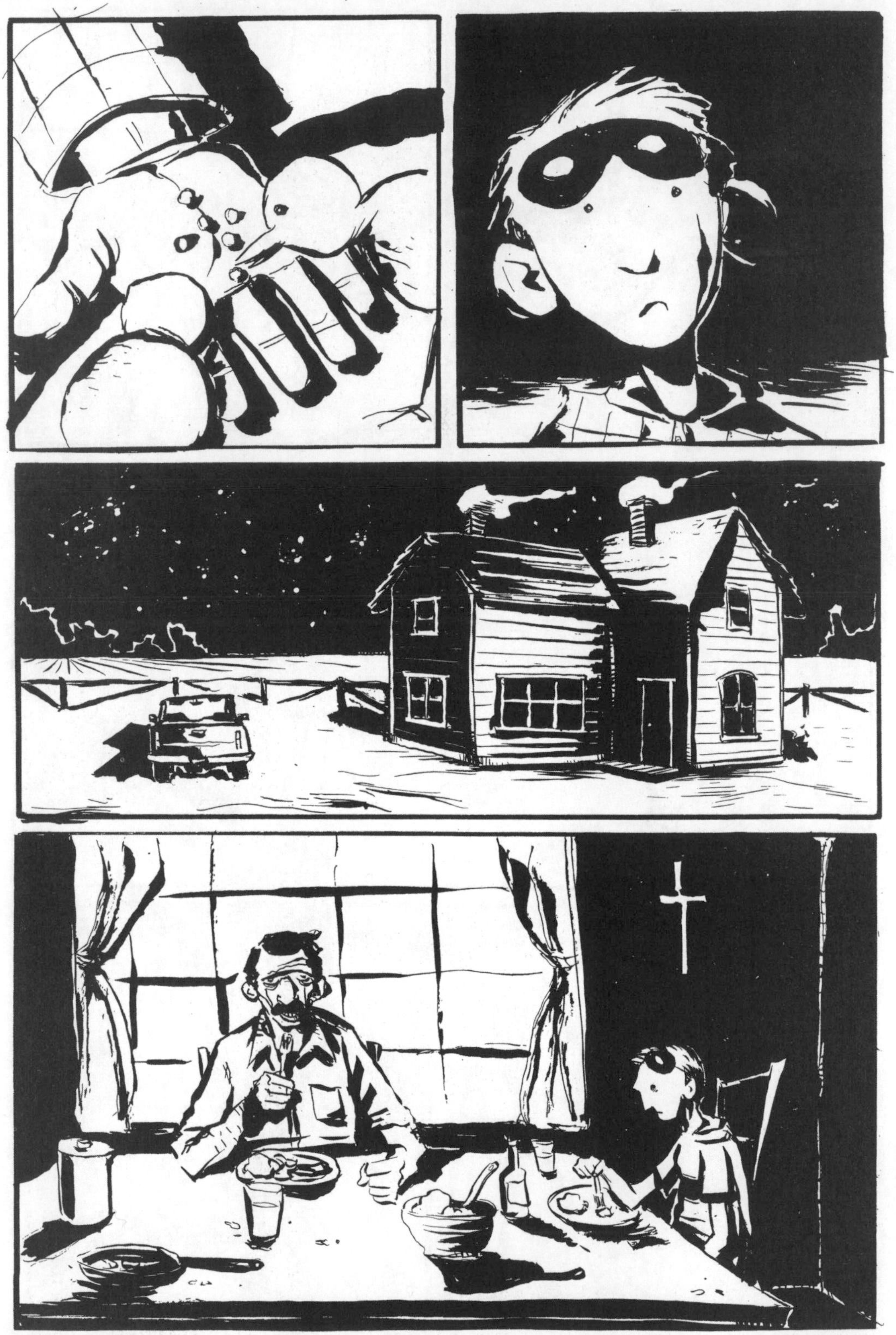

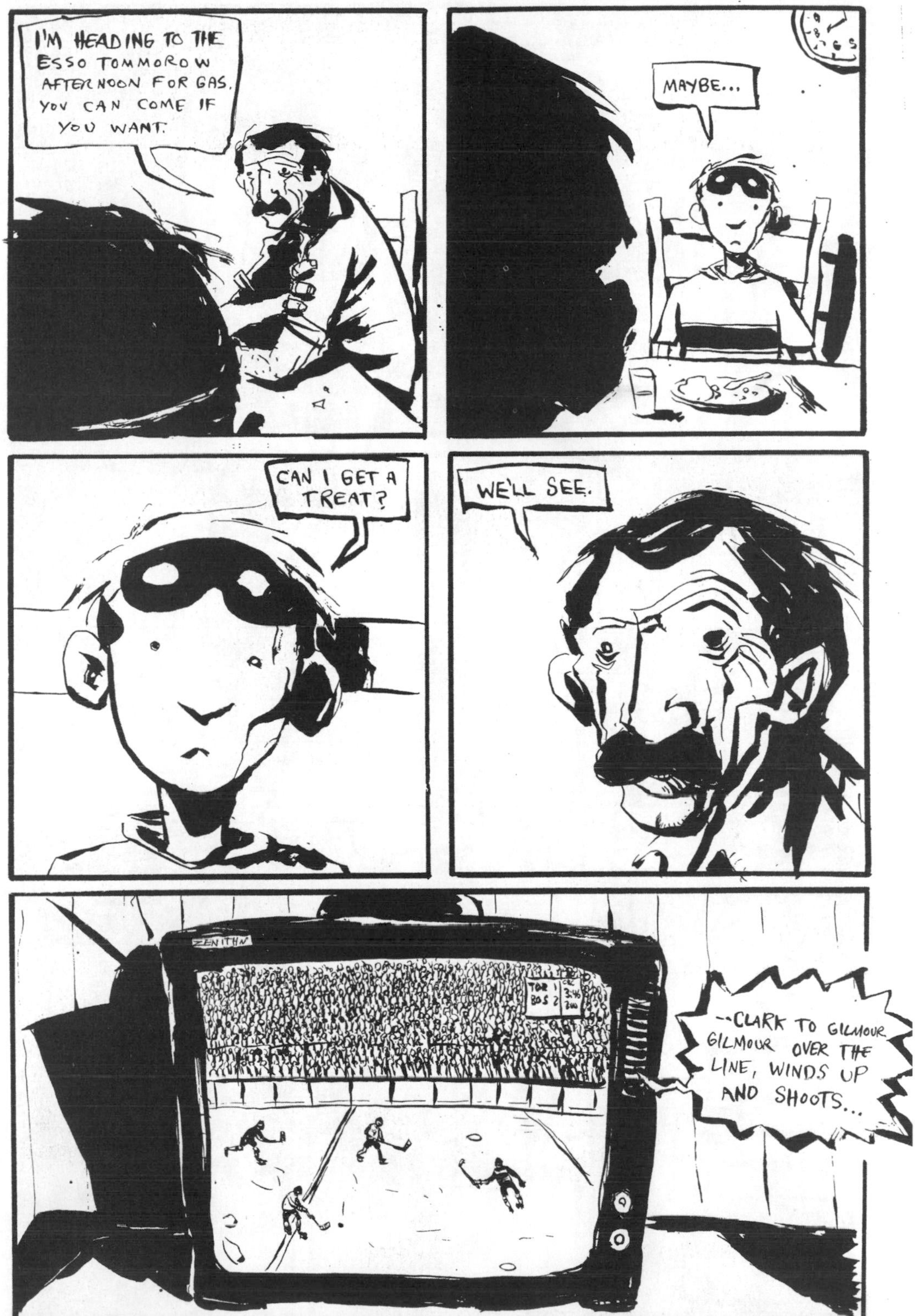
I'M HEADING TO THE ESSO TOMMOROW AFTERNOON FOR GAS. YOU CAN COME IF YOU WANT.
MAYBE...
CAN I GET A TREAT?
WE'LL SEE.
ZENITH
TOR 1
BOS 2
--CLARK TO GILMOUR GILMOUR OVER THE LINE, WINDS UP AND SHOOTS...

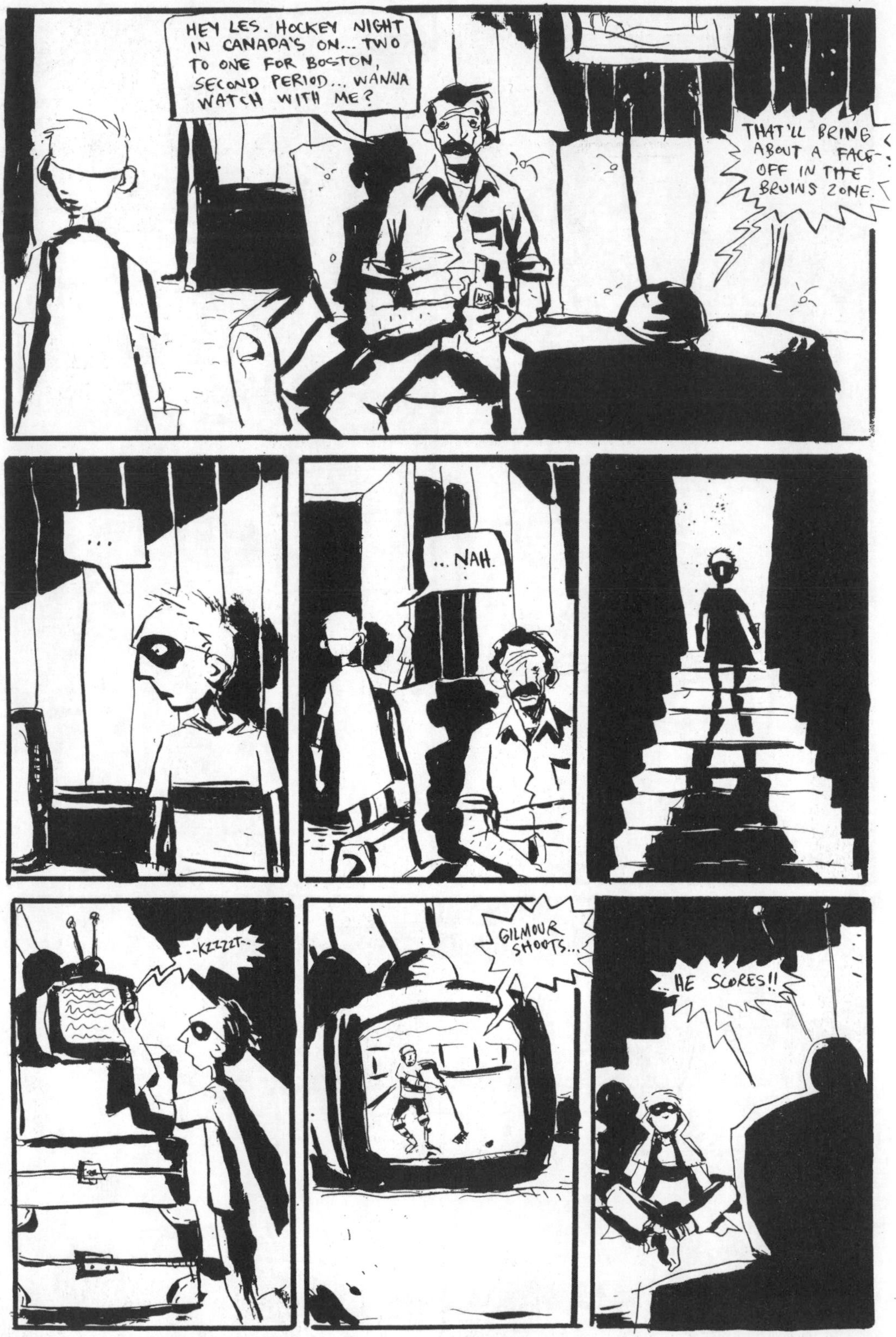
HEY LES. HOCKEY NIGHT IN CANADA'S ON... TWO TO ONE FOR BOSTON, SECOND PERIOD... WANNA WATCH WITH ME?
THAT'LL BRING ABOUT A FACE-OFF IN THE BRUINS ZONE.
...
... NAH.
--KZZZZT--
GILMOUR SHOOTS...
..HE SCORES!!

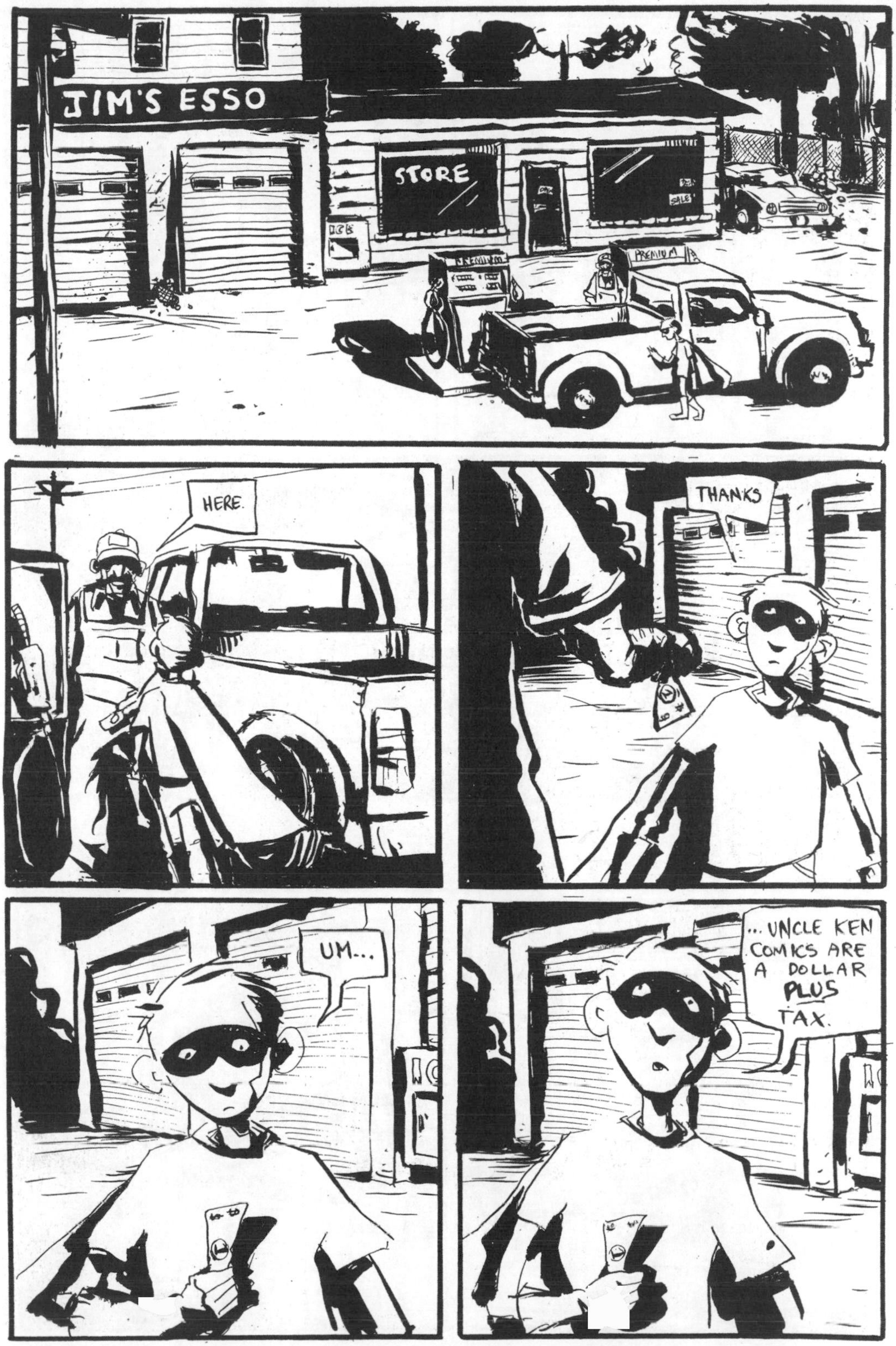

JIM'S ESSO
STORE
PREMIUM
HERE.
THANKS
UM...
...UNCLE KEN COMICS ARE A DOLLAR PLUS TAX.

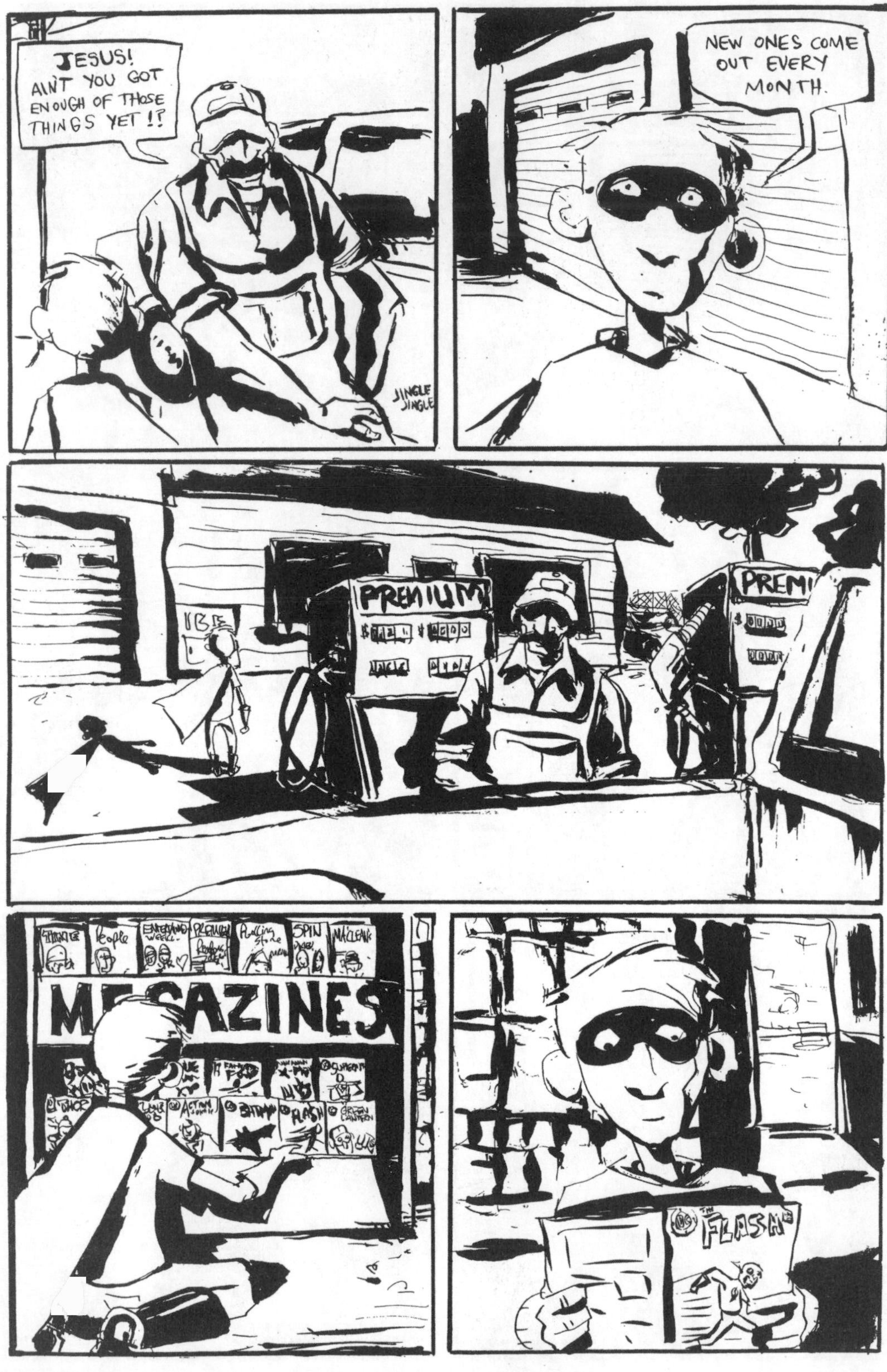
JESUS! AIN'T YOU GOT ENOUGH OF THOSE THINGS YET!?
JINGLE JINGLE
NEW ONES COME OUT EVERY MONTH.
PREMIUM
PREMI
People
SPIN
FLASH
GREEN LANTERN
THE FLASH

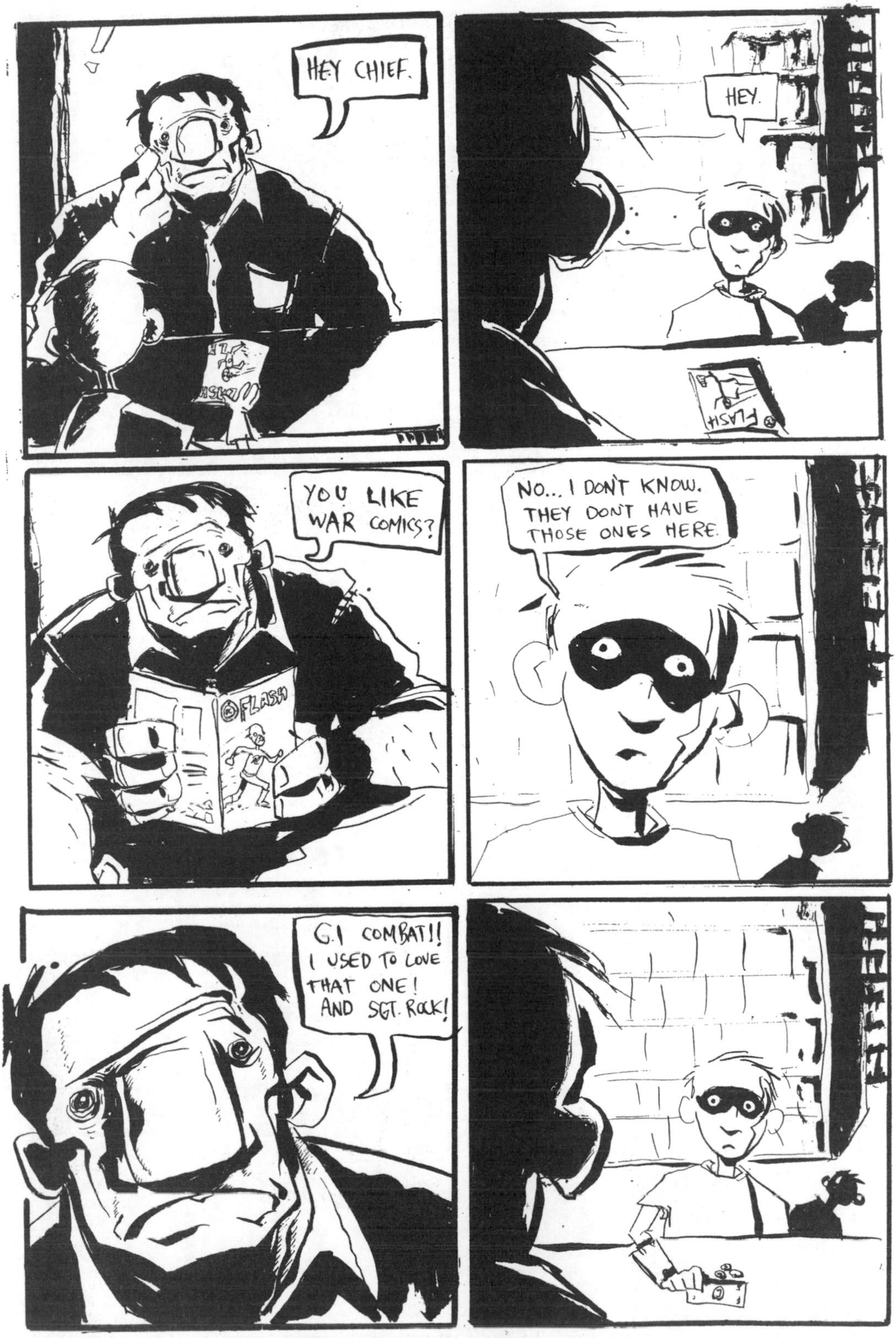
HEY CHIEF.
HEY.
YOU LIKE WAR COMICS?
FLASH
NO... I DON'T KNOW. THEY DON'T HAVE THOSE ONES HERE.
G.I COMBAT!! I USED TO LOVE THAT ONE! AND SGT. ROCK!

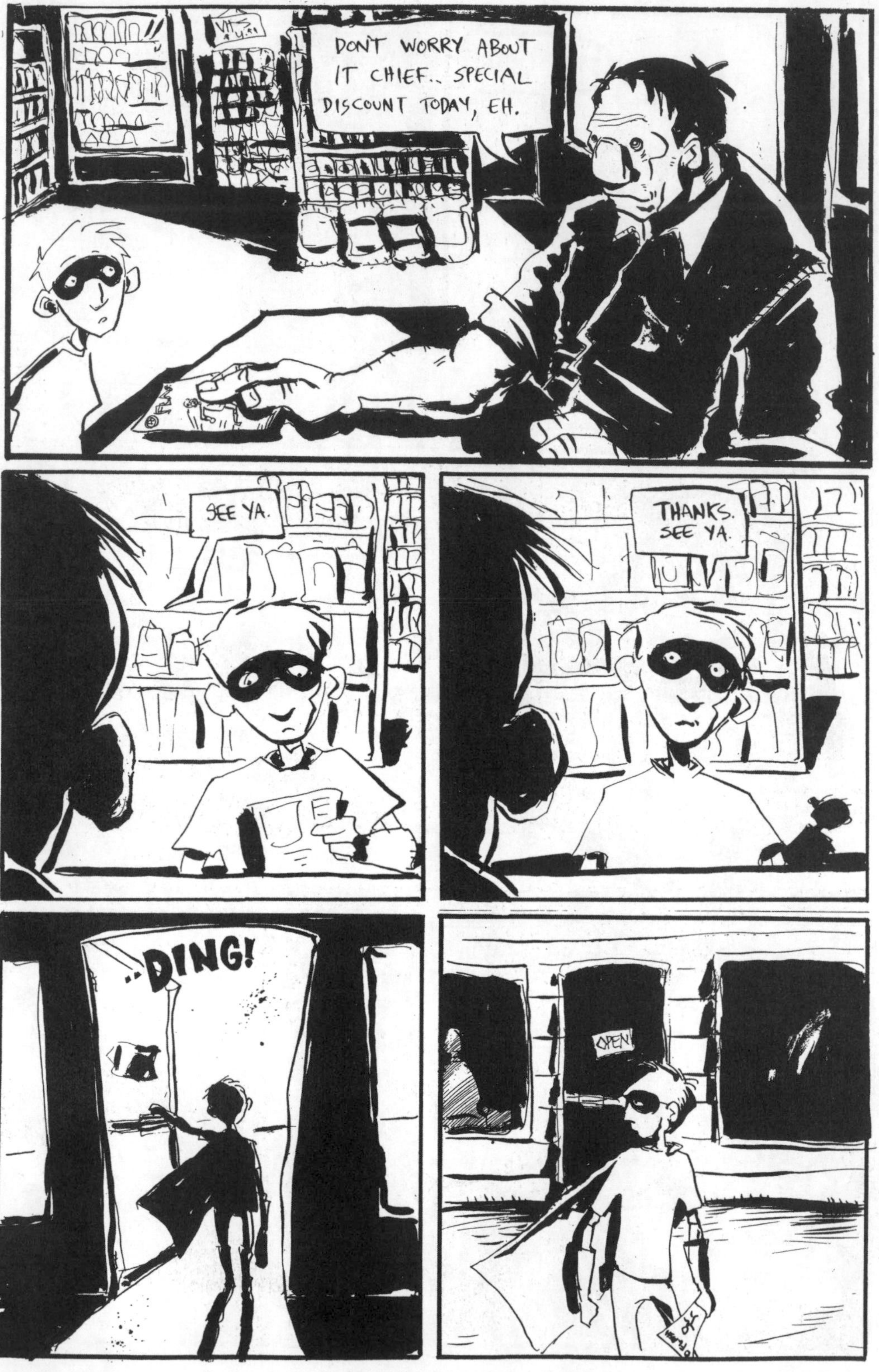
DON'T WORRY ABOUT IT CHIEF.. SPECIAL DISCOUNT TODAY, EH.
SEE YA.
THANKS. SEE YA.
..DING!
OPEN

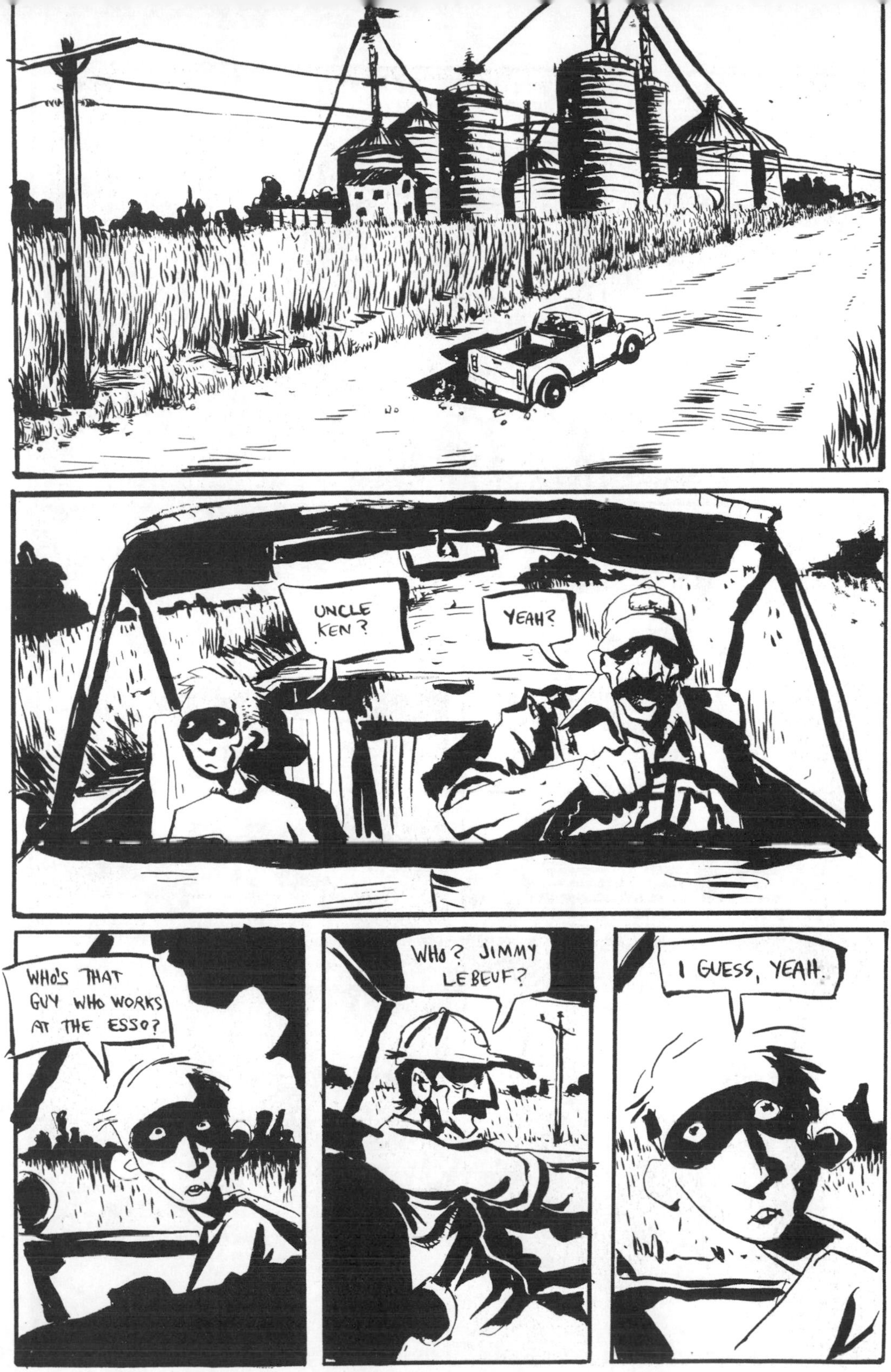
UNCLE KEN?
YEAH?
WHO'S THAT GUY WHO WORKS AT THE ESSO?
WHO? JIMMY LEBEUF?
I GUESS, YEAH.

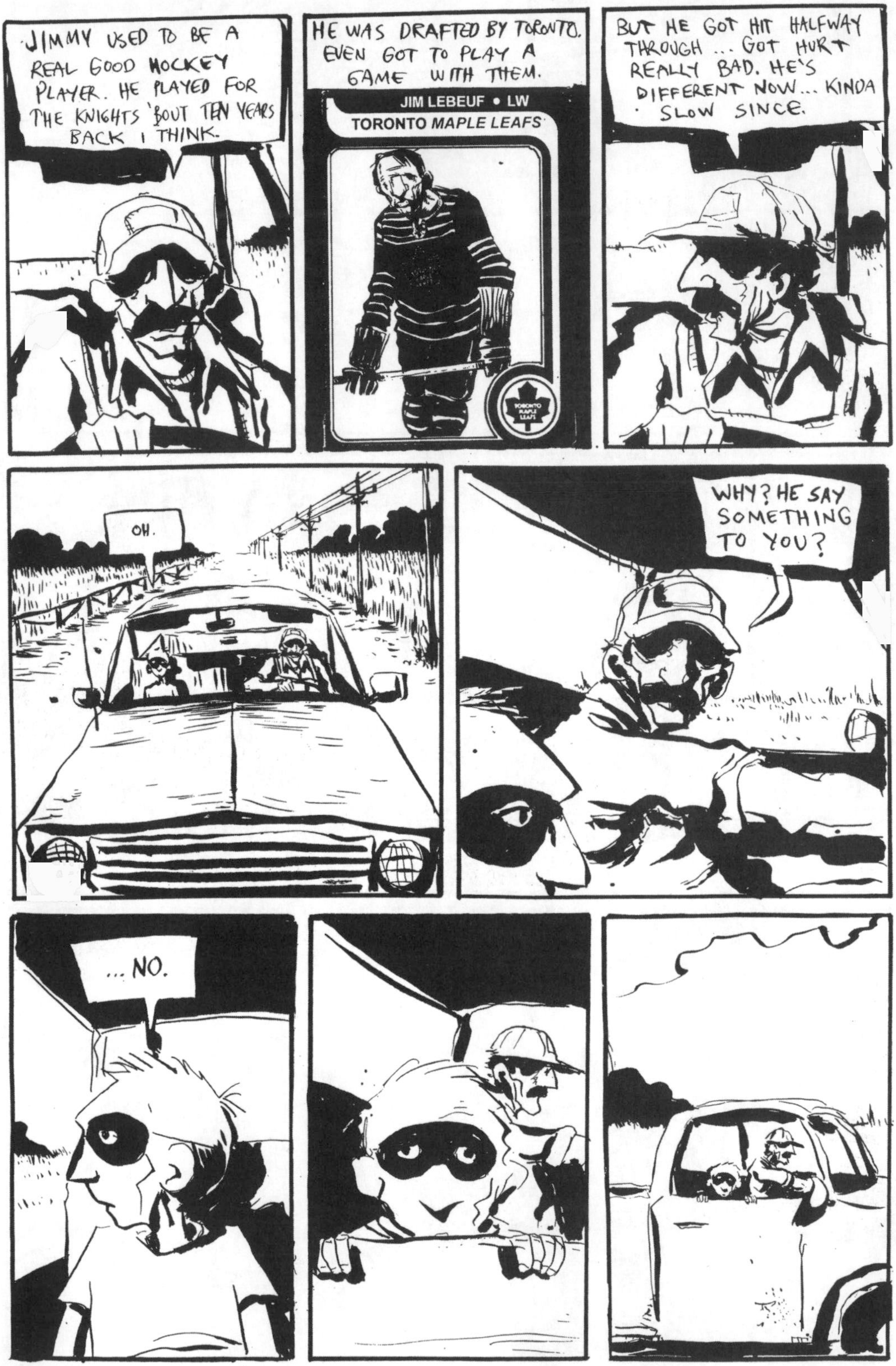
JIMMY USED TO BE A REAL GOOD HOCKEY PLAYER. HE PLAYED FOR THE KNIGHTS 'BOUT TEN YEARS BACK I THINK.
HE WAS DRAFTED BY TORONTO. EVEN GOT TO PLAY A GAME WITH THEM.
JIM LEBEUF • LW
TORONTO MAPLE LEAFS
TORONTO MAPLE LEAFS
BUT HE GOT HIT HALFWAY THROUGH ... GOT HURT REALLY BAD. HE'S DIFFERENT NOW... KINDA SLOW SINCE.
OH.
WHY? HE SAY SOMETHING TO YOU?
...NO.

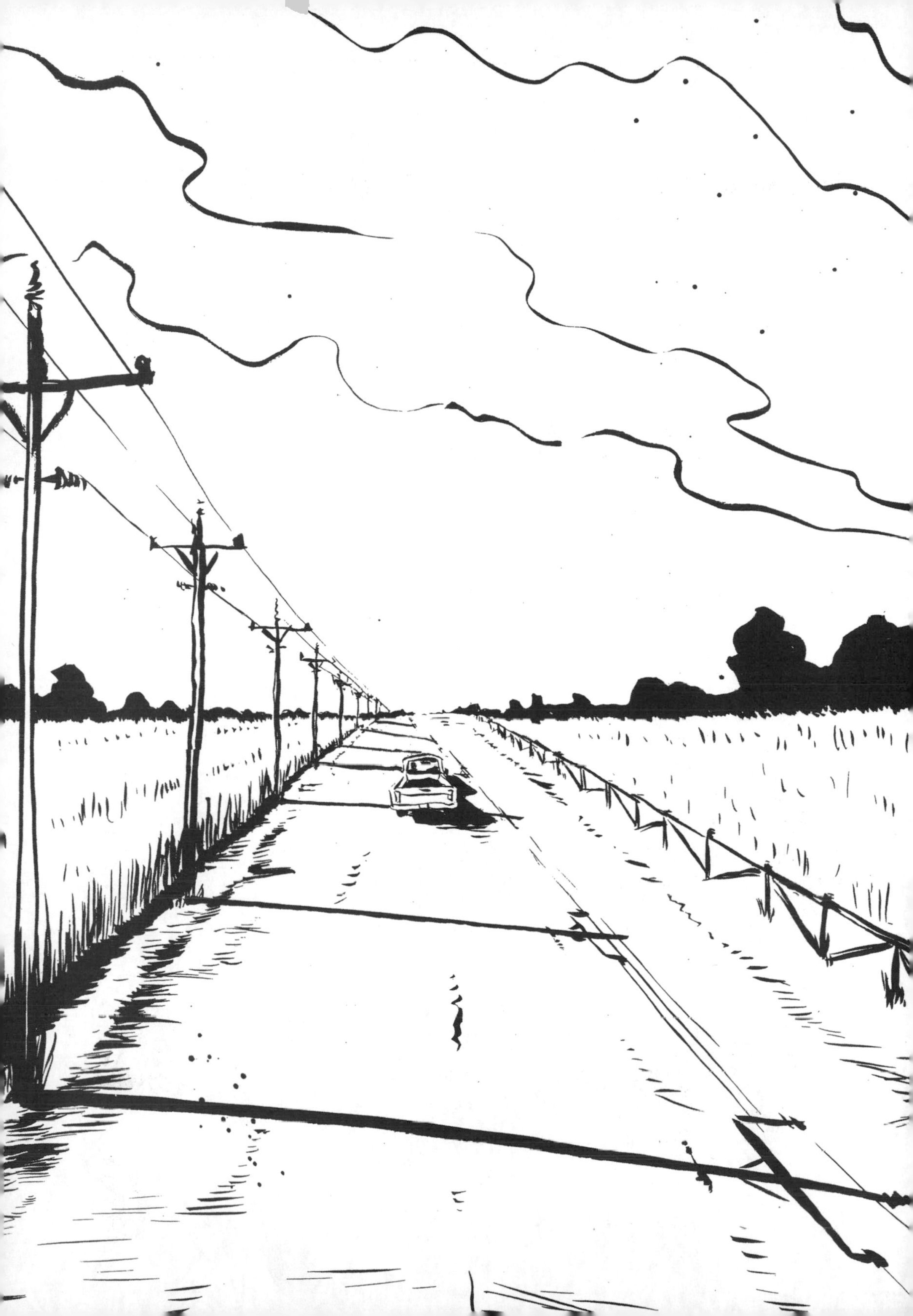

FALL

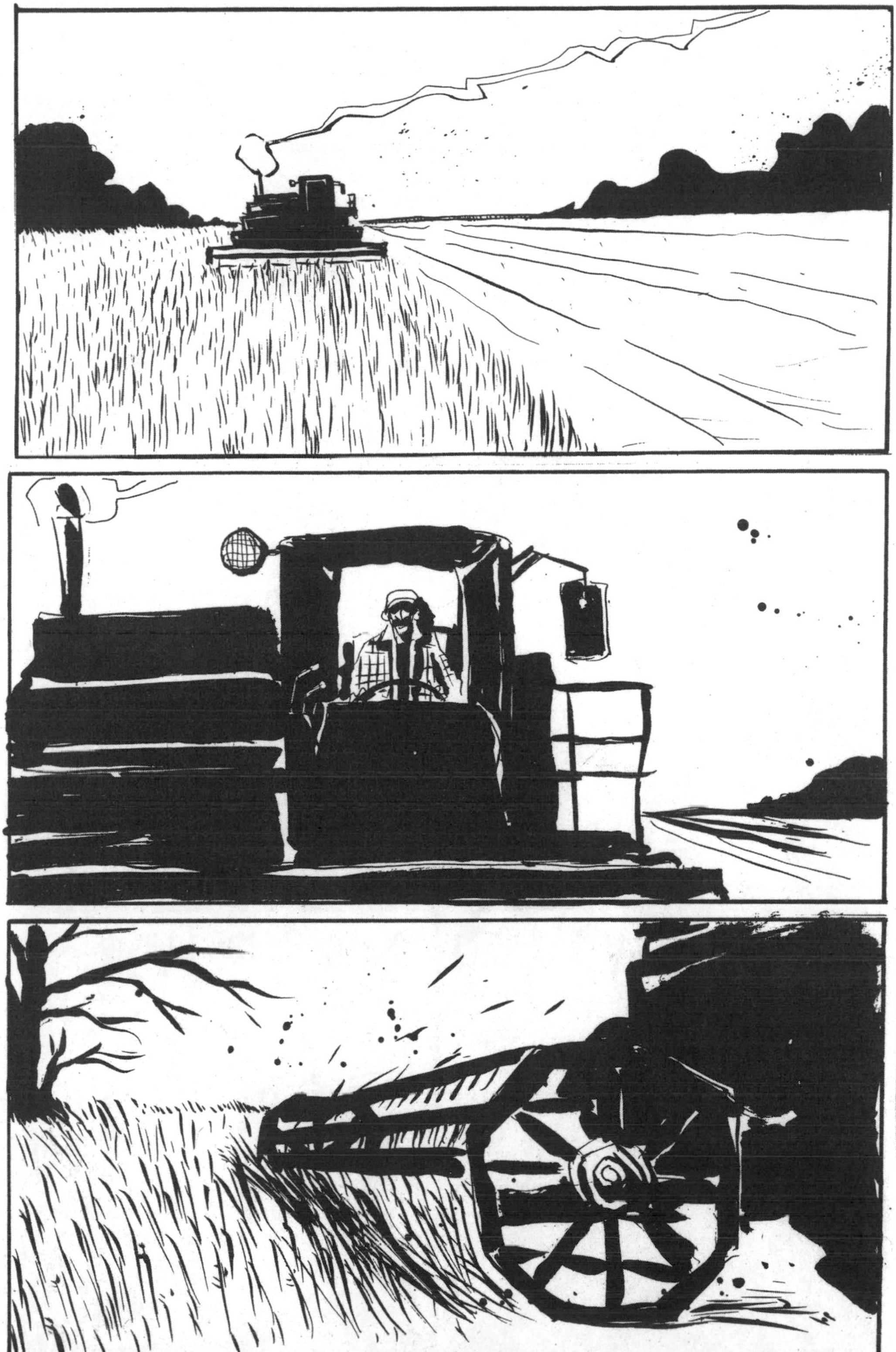

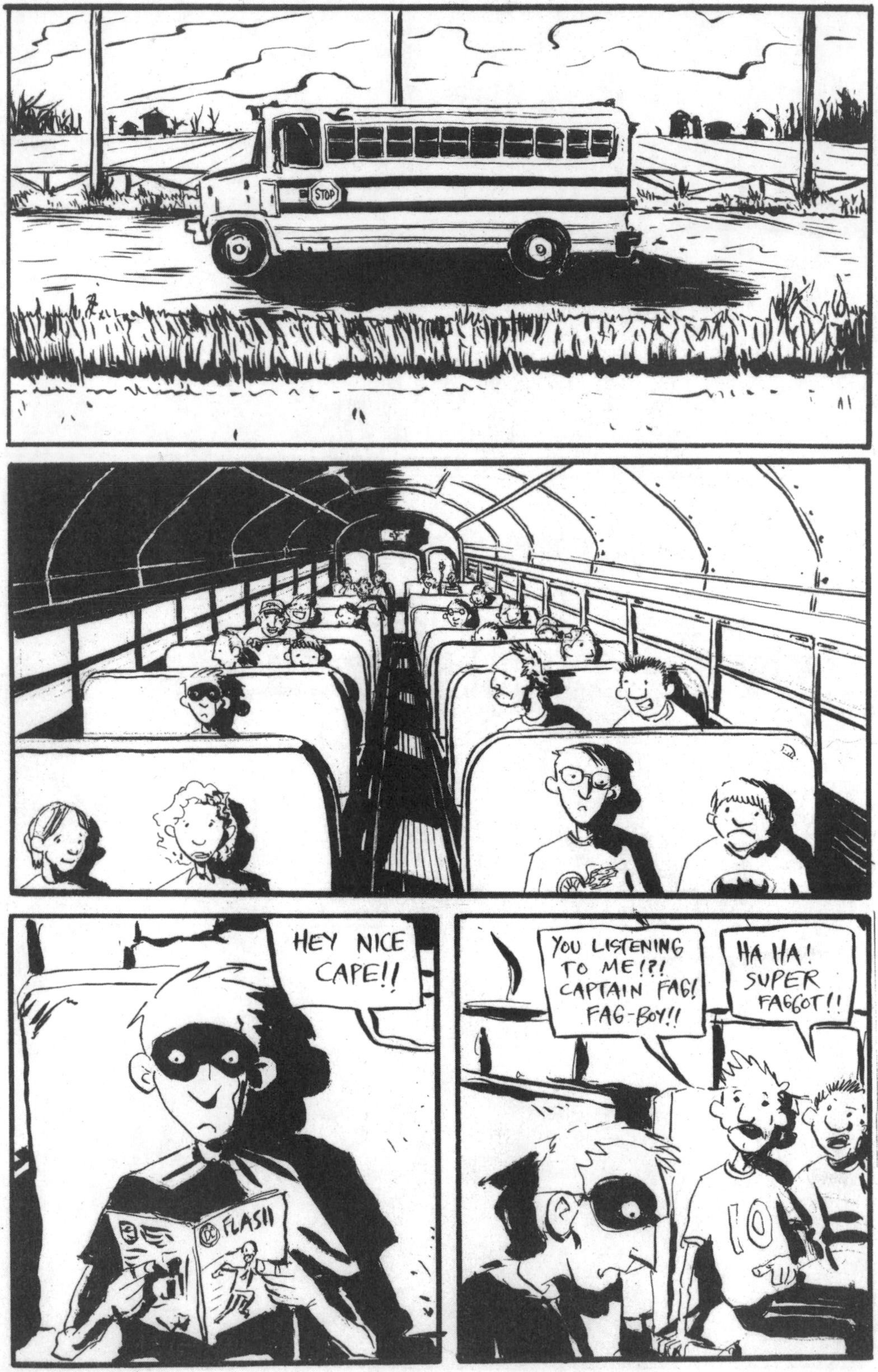
STOP
HEY NICE CAPE!!
FLASH
YOU LISTENING TO ME!?! CAPTAIN FAG! FAG-BOY!!
HA HA! SUPER FAGGOT!!

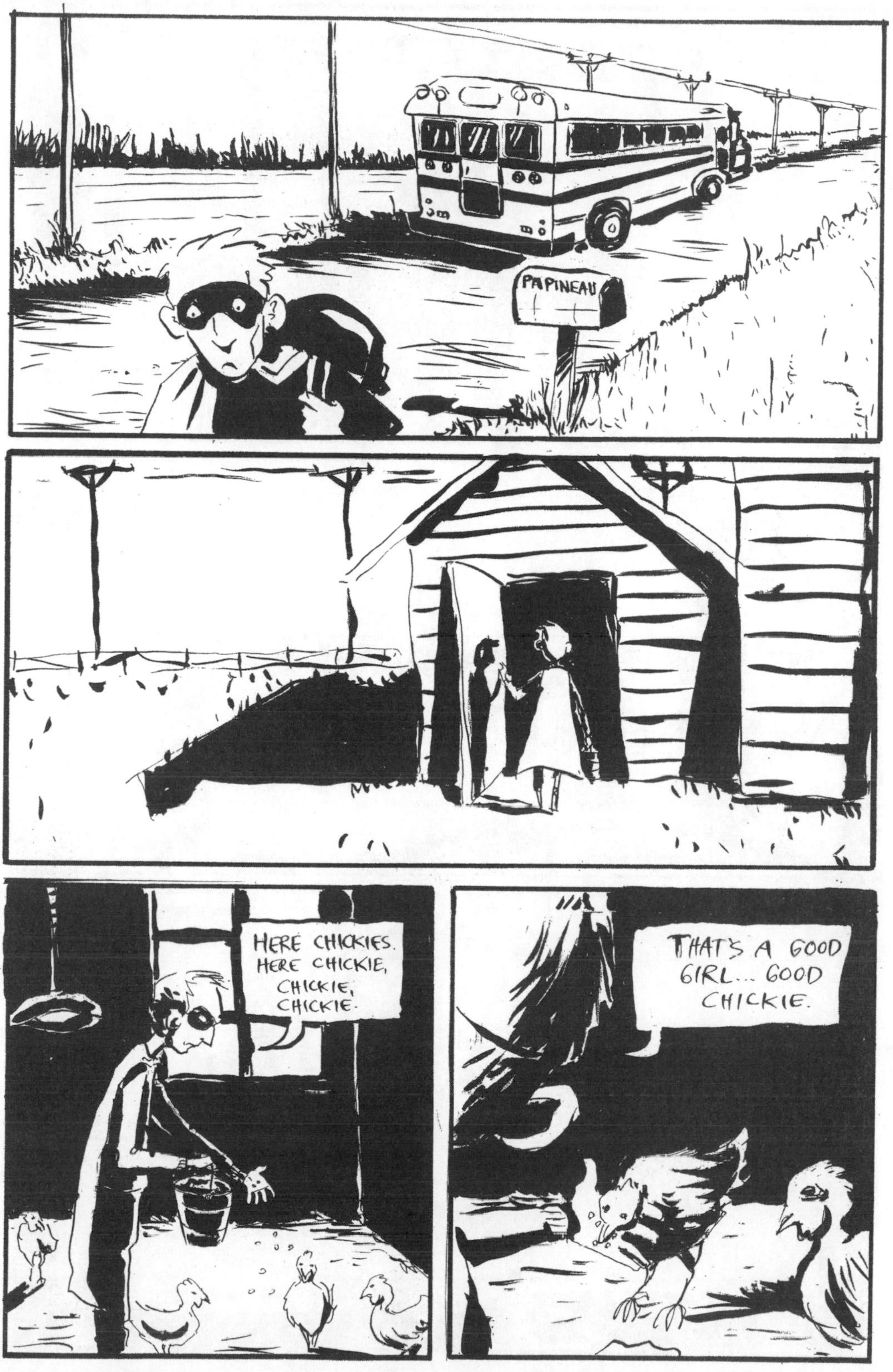
PAPINEAU
HERE CHICKIES. HERE CHICKIE, CHICKIE, CHICKIE.
THAT'S A GOOD GIRL... GOOD CHICKIE.

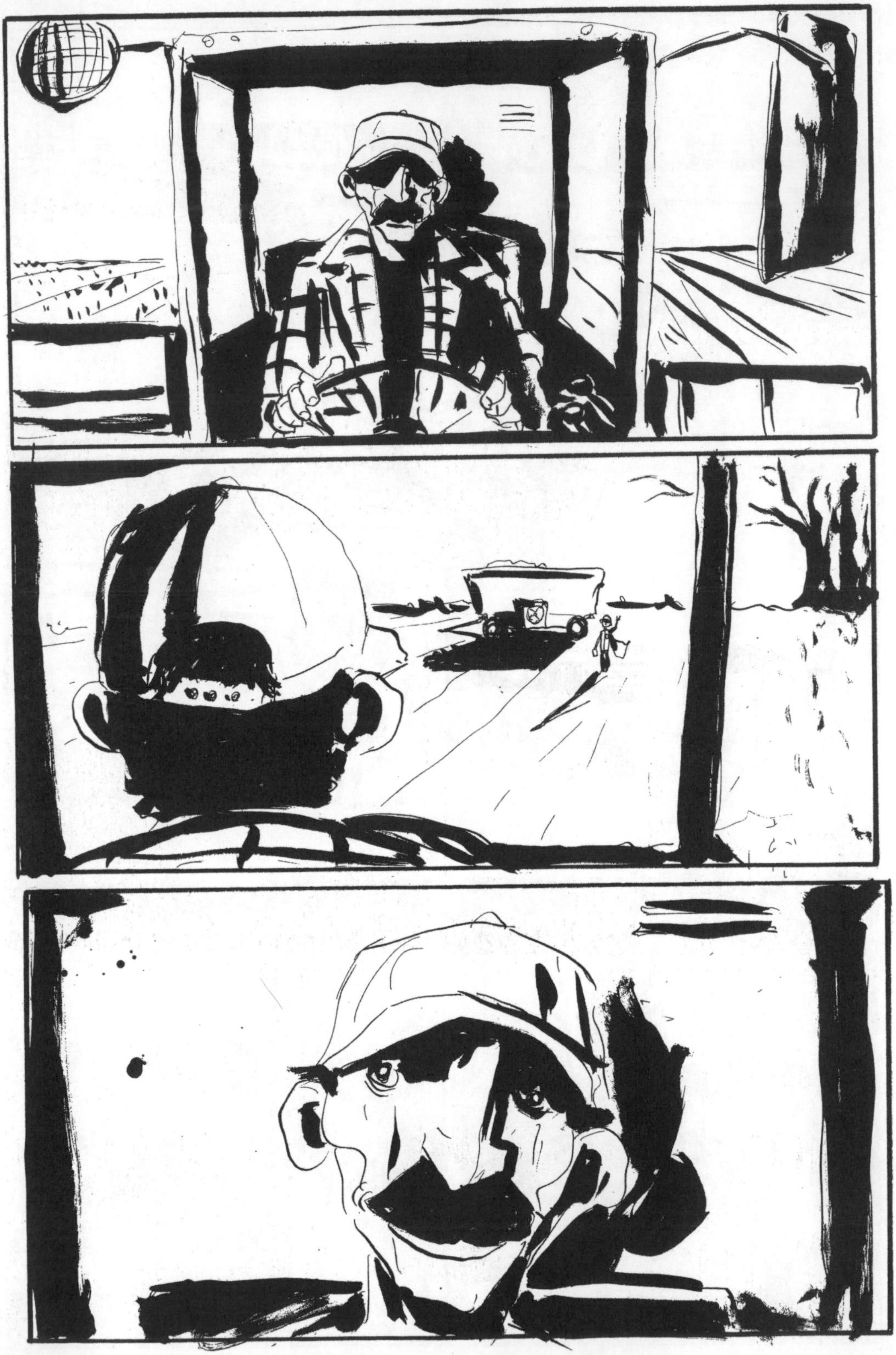

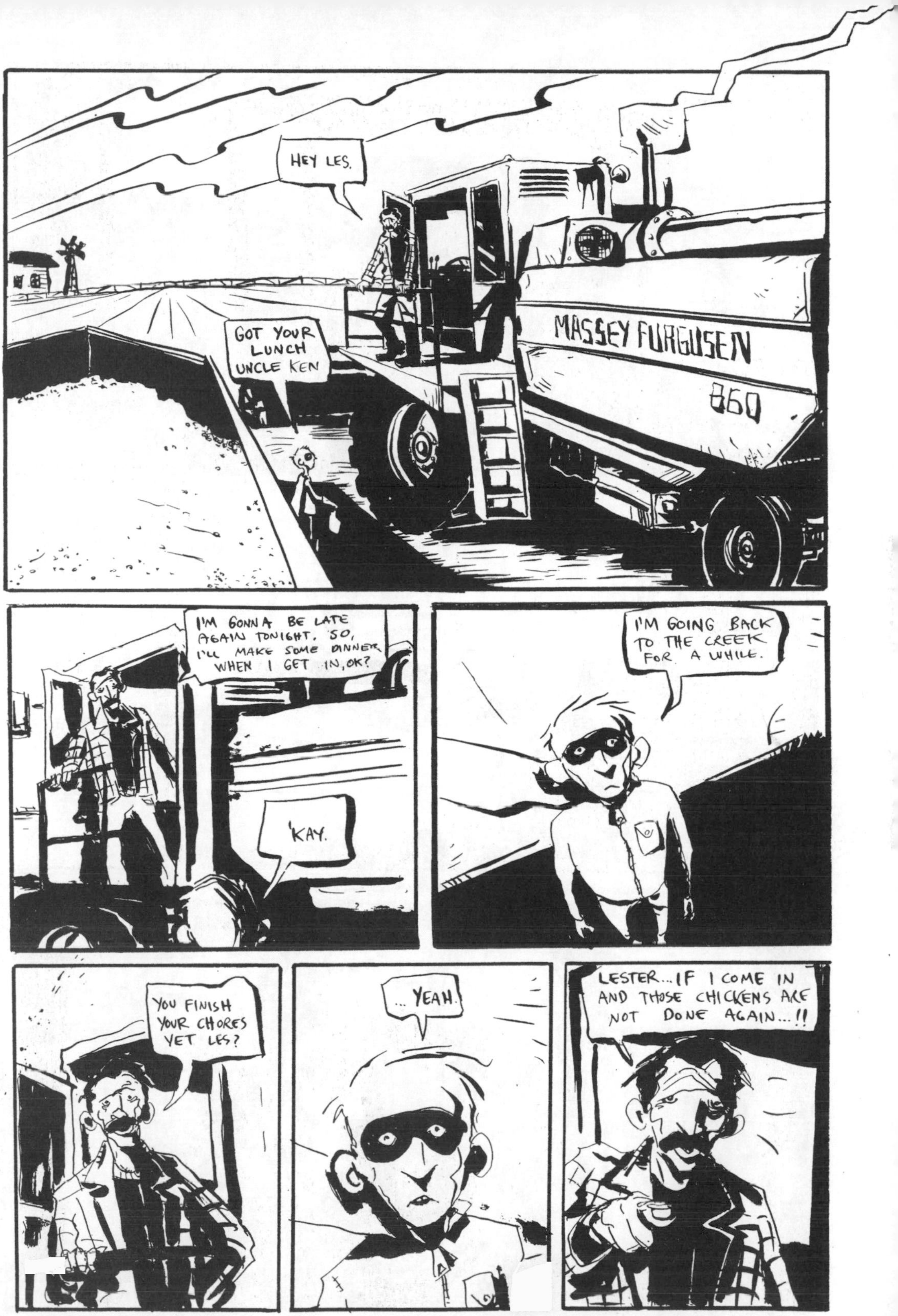
HEY LES.
GOT YOUR LUNCH UNCLE KEN
MASSEY FURGUSEN
860
I'M GONNA BE LATE AGAIN TONIGHT. SO, I'LL MAKE SOME DINNER WHEN I GET IN, OK?
'KAY.
I'M GOING BACK TO THE CREEK FOR A WHILE.
YOU FINISH YOUR CHORES YET LES?
...YEAH.
LESTER... IF I COME IN AND THOSE CHICKENS ARE NOT DONE AGAIN...!!

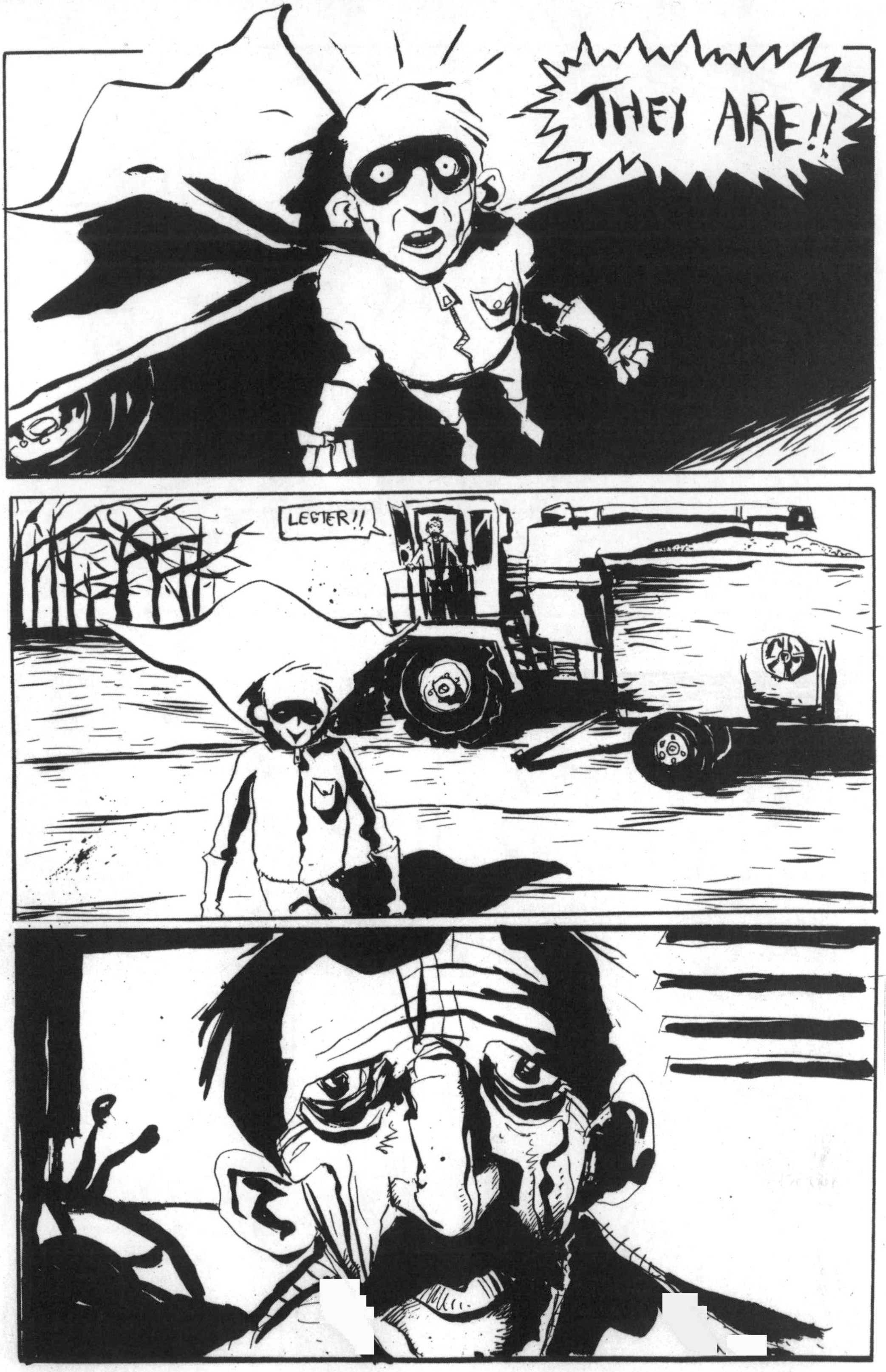
THEY ARE!!
LESTER!!

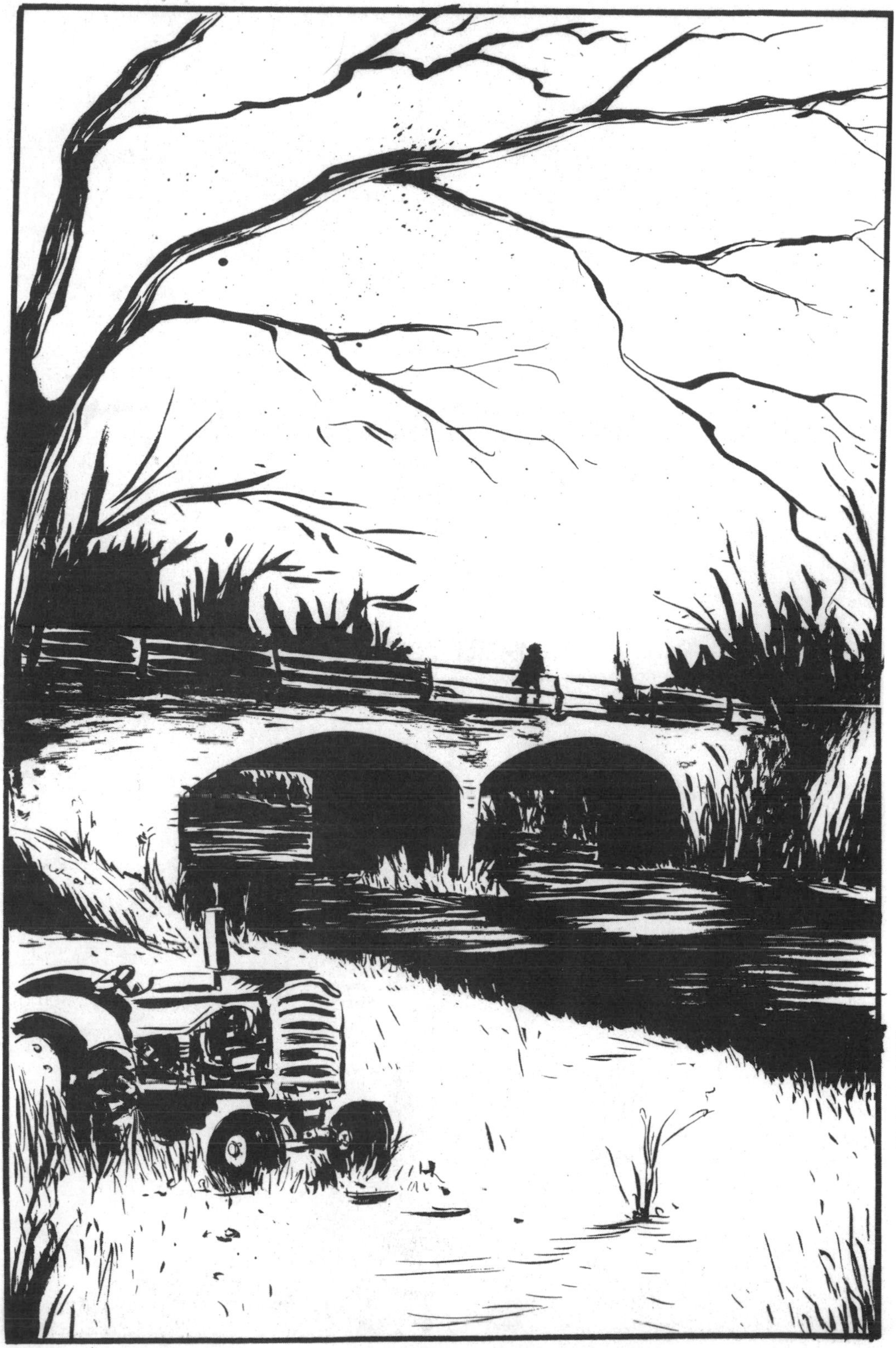

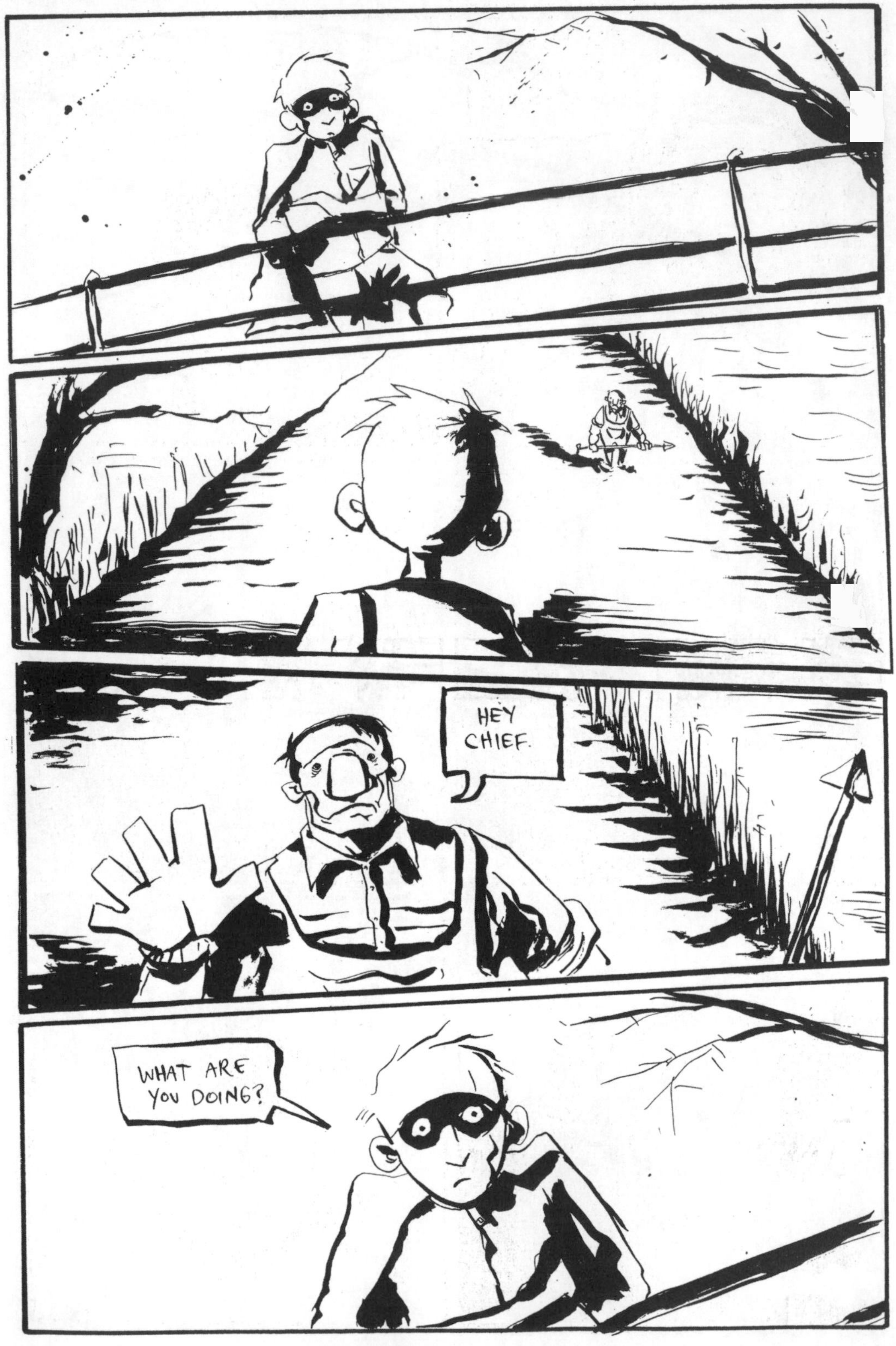
HEY CHIEF.
WHAT ARE YOU DOING?

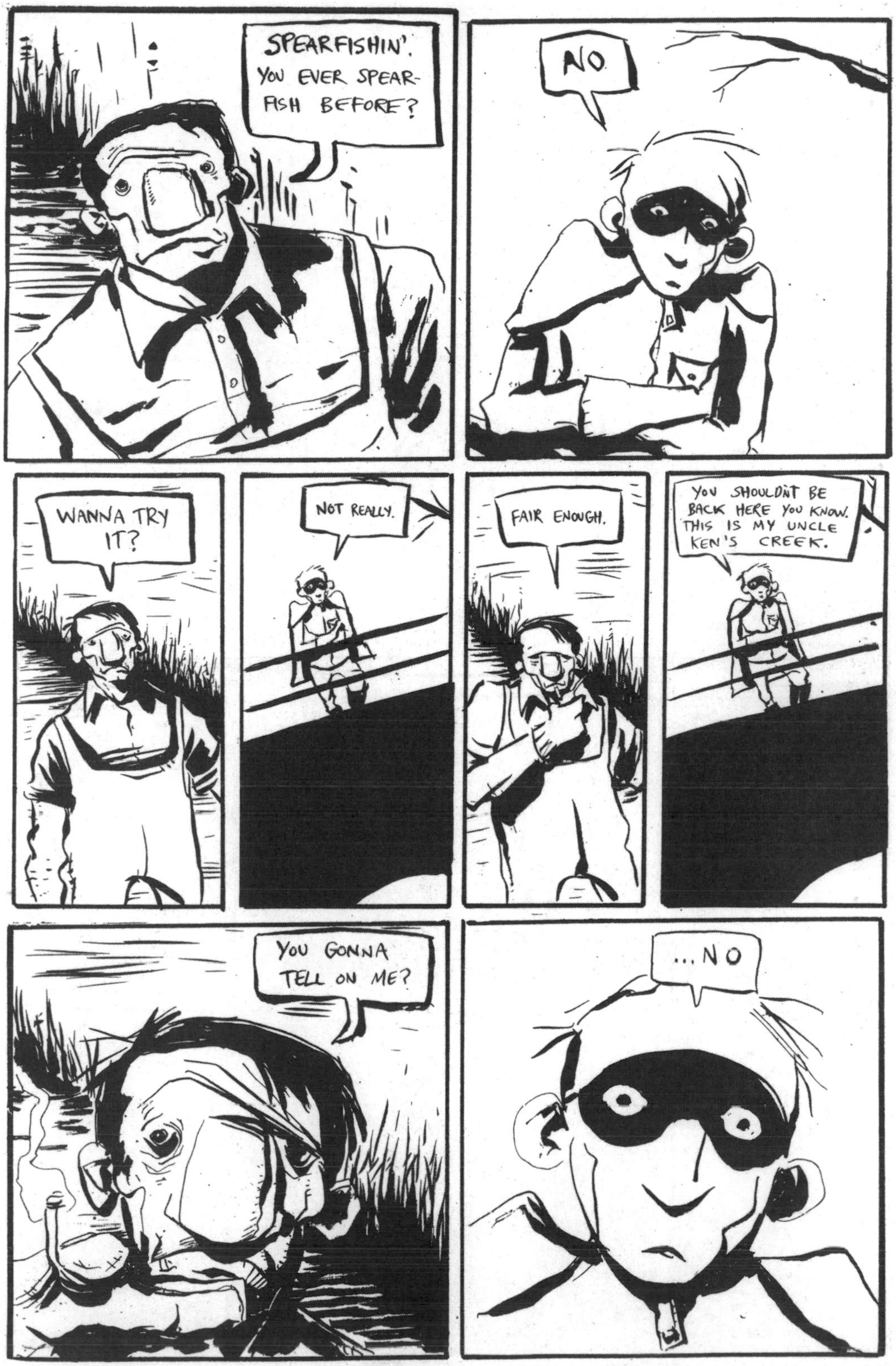
SPEARFISHIN'. YOU EVER SPEAR-FISH BEFORE?
NO.
WANNA TRY IT?
NOT REALLY.
FAIR ENOUGH.
YOU SHOULDN'T BE BACK HERE YOU KNOW. THIS IS MY UNCLE KEN'S CREEK.
YOU GONNA TELL ON ME?
...NO

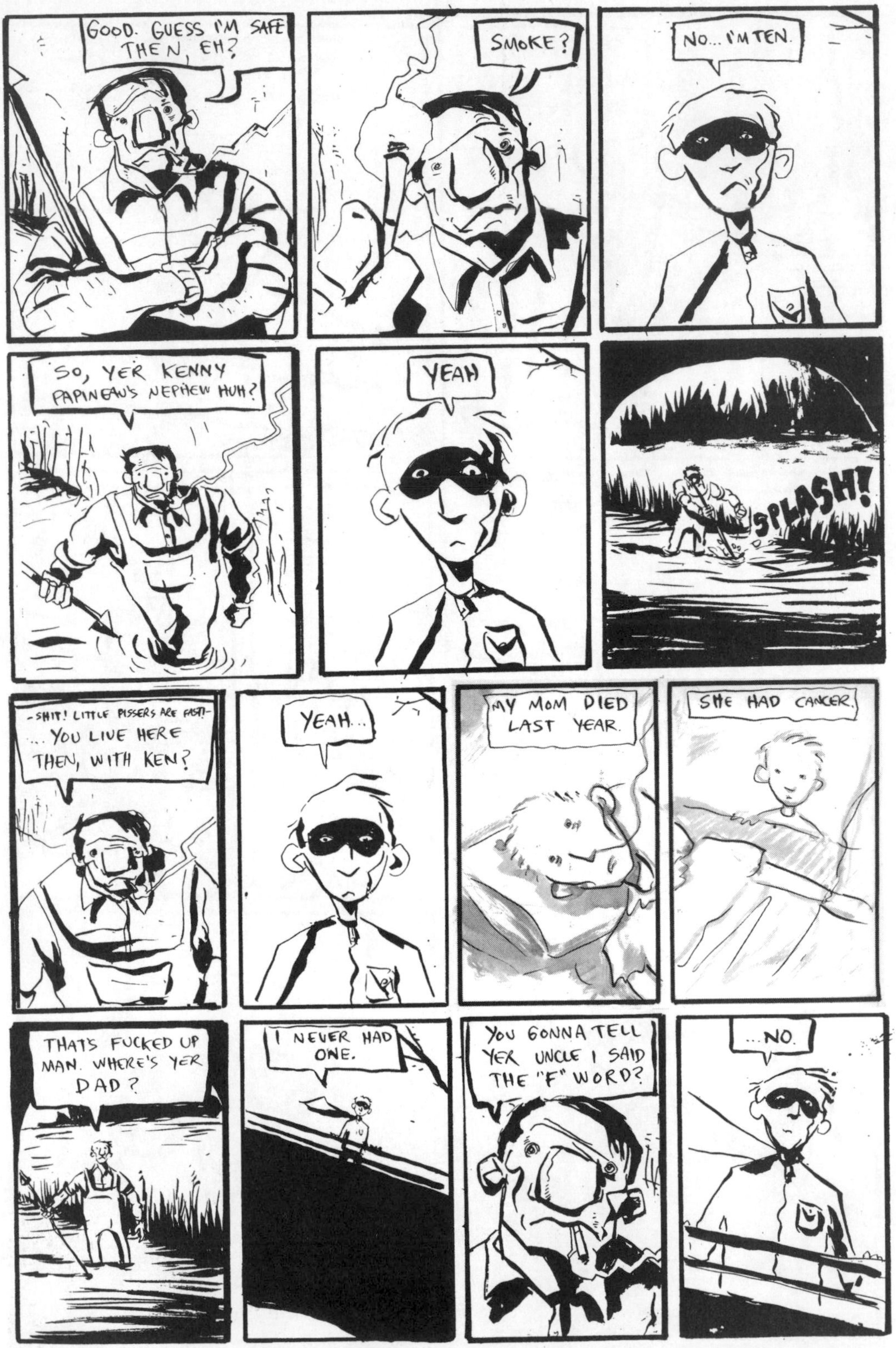
GOOD. GUESS I'M SAFE THEN, EH?
SMOKE?
NO... I'M TEN.
SO, YER KENNY PAPINEAU'S NEPHEW HUH?
YEAH
SPLASH!
-SHIT! LITTLE PISSERS ARE FAST!- ... YOU LIVE HERE THEN, WITH KEN?
YEAH...
MY MOM DIED LAST YEAR.
SHE HAD CANCER.
THAT'S FUCKED UP MAN. WHERE'S YER DAD?
I NEVER HAD ONE.
YOU GONNA TELL YER UNCLE I SAID THE "F" WORD?
...NO.

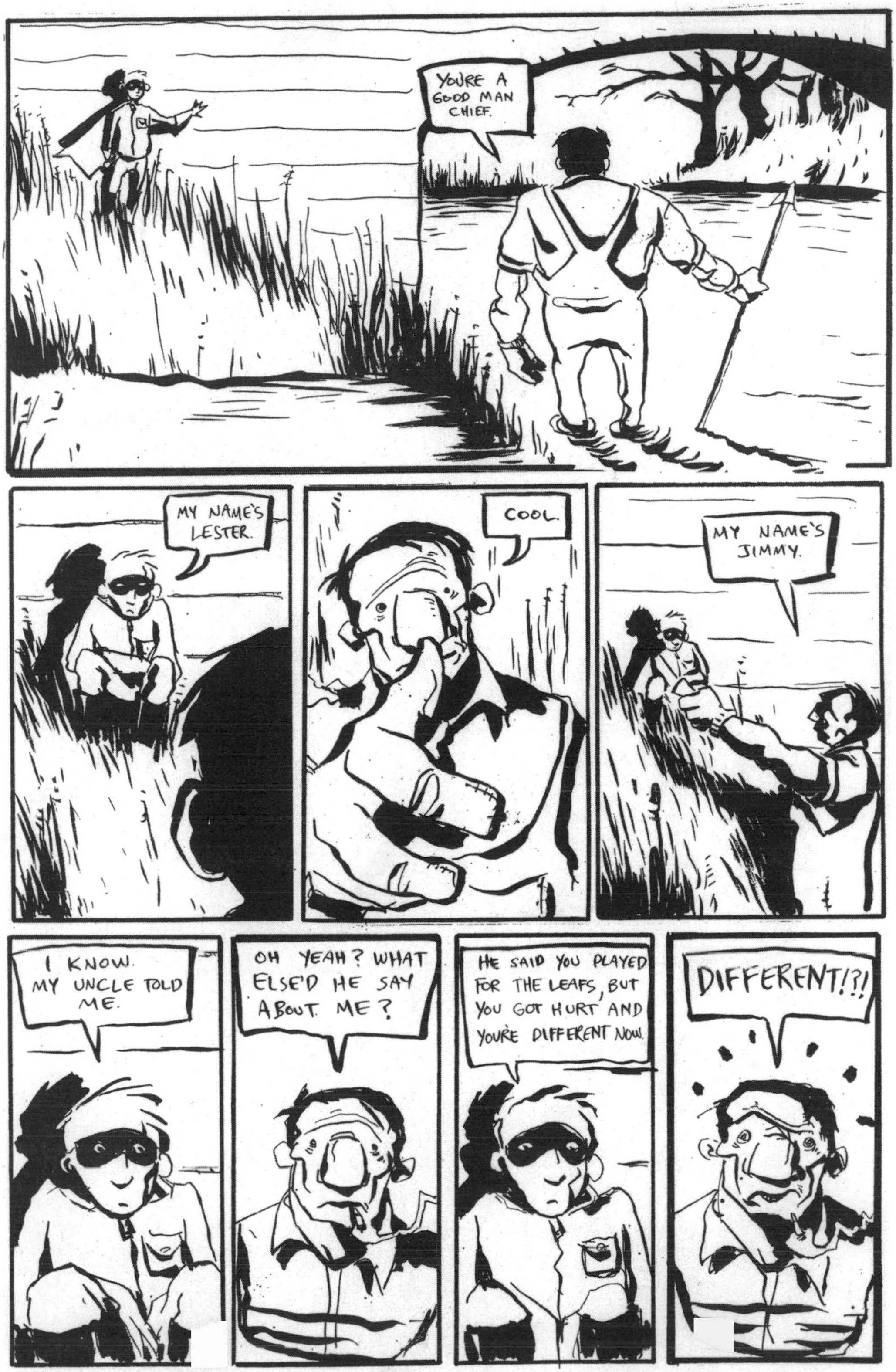
YOU'RE A GOOD MAN CHIEF.
MY NAME'S LESTER.
COOL.
MY NAME'S JIMMY.
I KNOW. MY UNCLE TOLD ME.
OH YEAH? WHAT ELSE'D HE SAY ABOUT ME?
HE SAID YOU PLAYED FOR THE LEAFS, BUT YOU GOT HURT AND YOU'RE DIFFERENT NOW.
DIFFERENT!?!

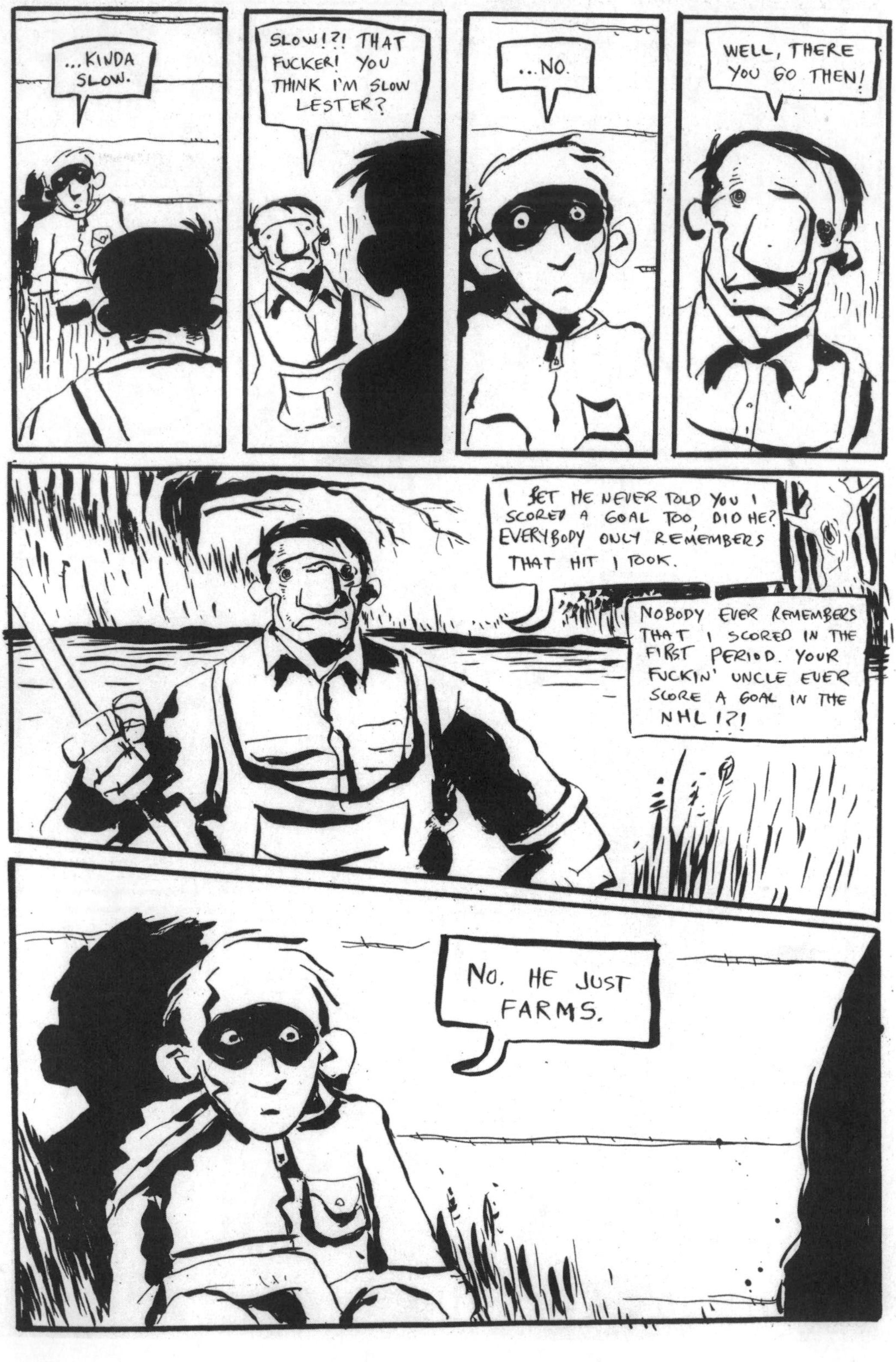
...KINDA SLOW.
SLOW!?! THAT FUCKER! YOU THINK I'M SLOW LESTER?
...NO.
WELL, THERE YOU GO THEN!
I BET HE NEVER TOLD YOU I SCORED A GOAL TOO, DID HE? EVERYBODY ONLY REMEMBERS THAT HIT I TOOK.
NOBODY EVER REMEMBERS THAT I SCORED IN THE FIRST PERIOD. YOUR FUCKIN' UNCLE EVER SCORE A GOAL IN THE NHL!?!
NO. HE JUST FARMS.

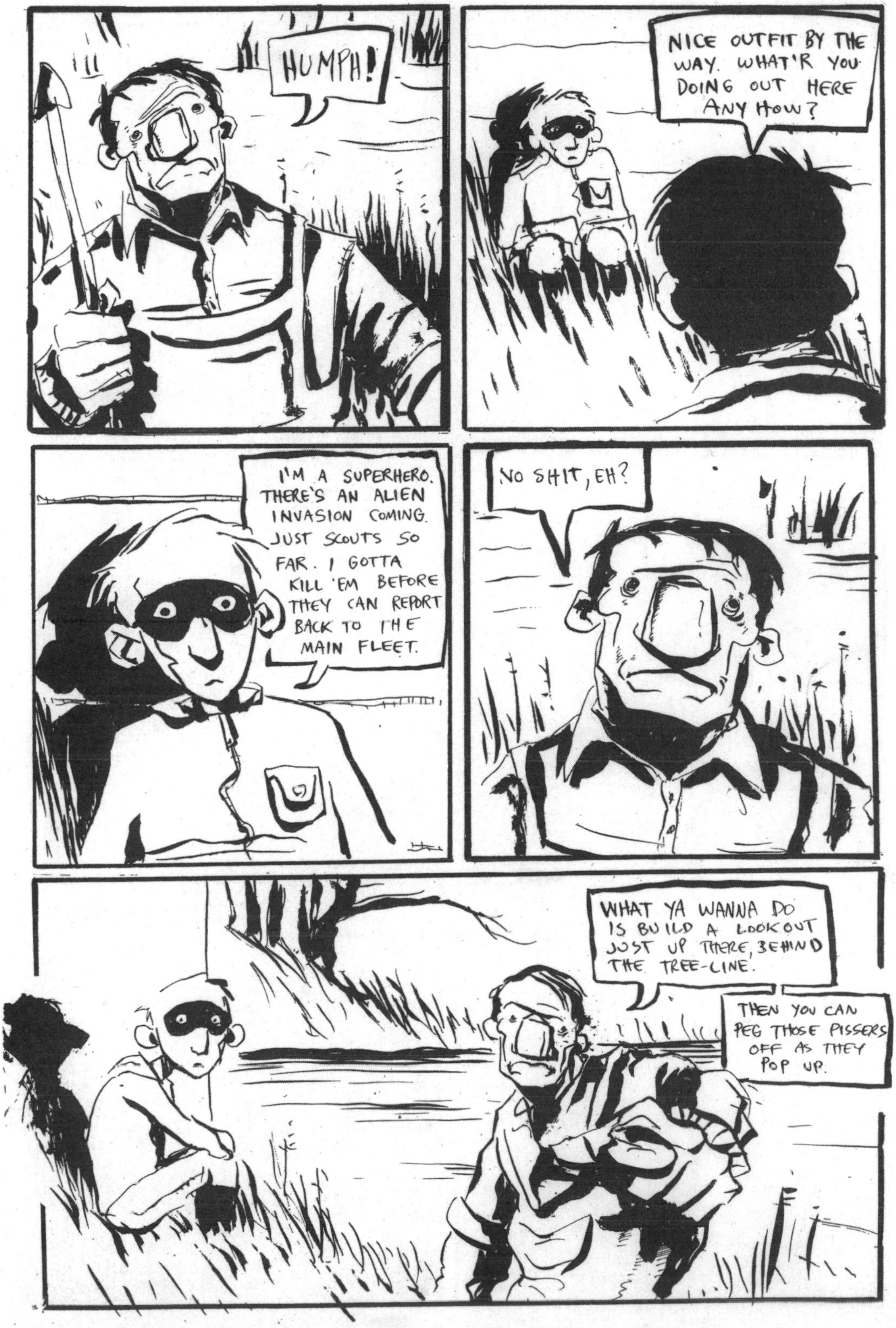
HUMPH!
NICE OUTFIT BY THE WAY. WHAT'R YOU DOING OUT HERE ANY HOW?
I'M A SUPERHERO. THERE'S AN ALIEN INVASION COMING. JUST SCOUTS SO FAR. I GOTTA KILL 'EM BEFORE THEY CAN REPORT BACK TO THE MAIN FLEET.
NO SHIT, EH?
WHAT YA WANNA DO IS BUILD A LOOKOUT JUST UP THERE, BEHIND THE TREE-LINE.
THEN YOU CAN PEG THOSE PISSERS OFF AS THEY POP UP.

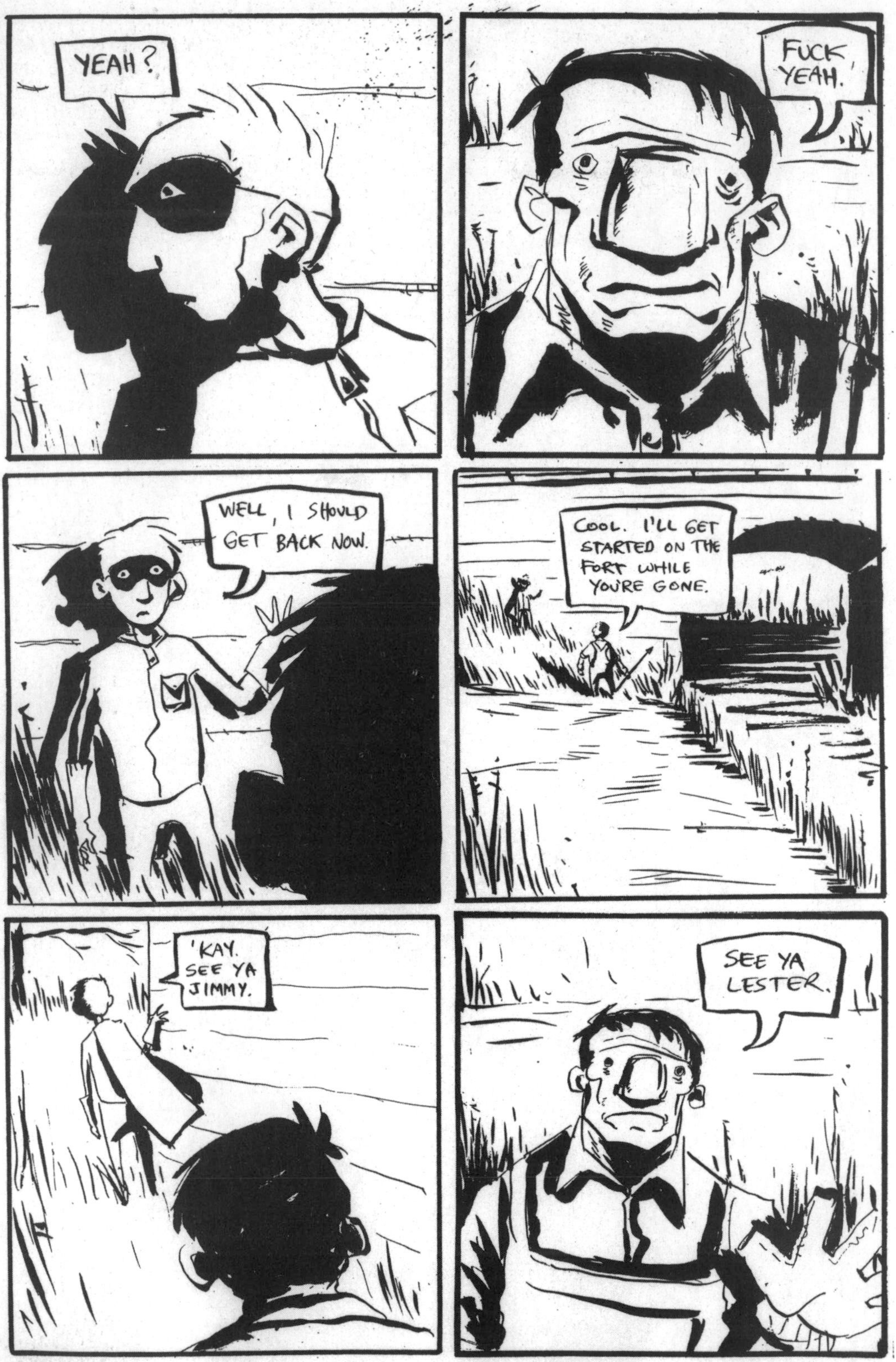
YEAH?
FUCK YEAH.
WELL, I SHOULD GET BACK NOW.
COOL. I'LL GET STARTED ON THE FORT WHILE YOU'RE GONE.
'KAY. SEE YA JIMMY.
SEE YA LESTER.

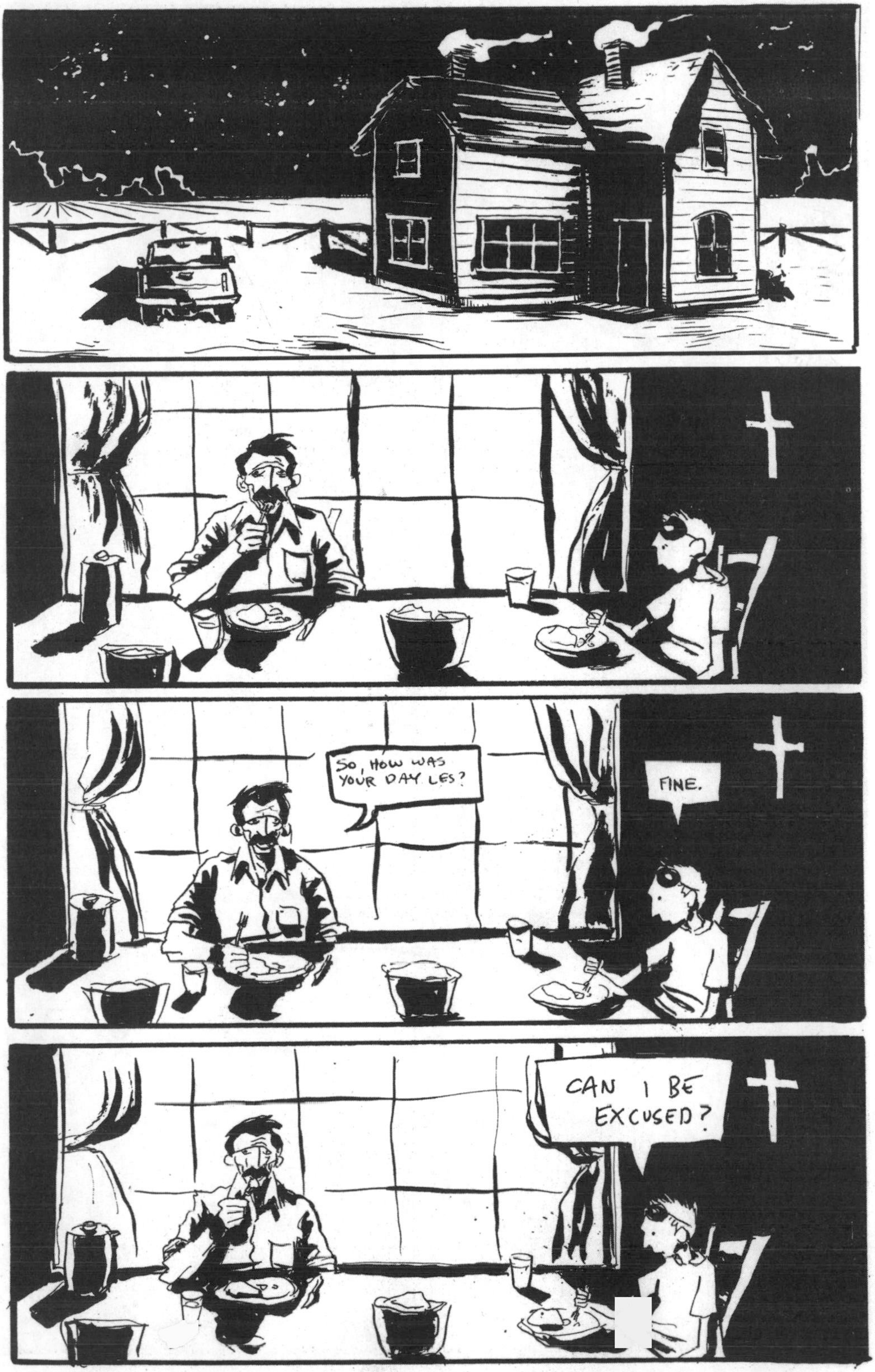
SO, HOW WAS YOUR DAY LES?
FINE.
CAN I BE EXCUSED?

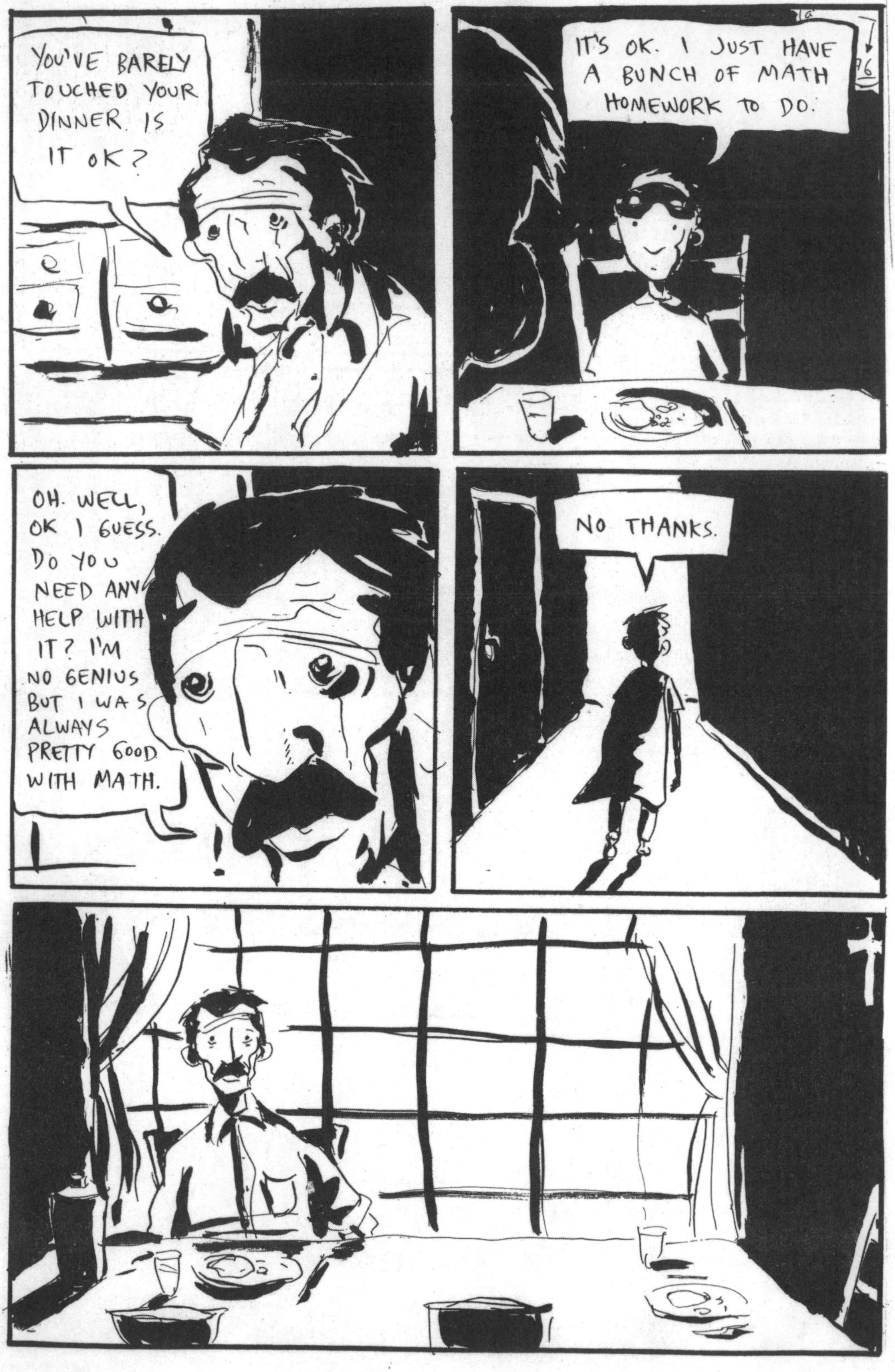
YOU'VE BARELY TOUCHED YOUR DINNER. IS IT OK?
IT'S OK. I JUST HAVE A BUNCH OF MATH HOMEWORK TO DO.
OH. WELL, OK I GUESS. DO YOU NEED ANY HELP WITH IT? I'M NO GENIUS BUT I WAS ALWAYS PRETTY GOOD WITH MATH.
NO THANKS.

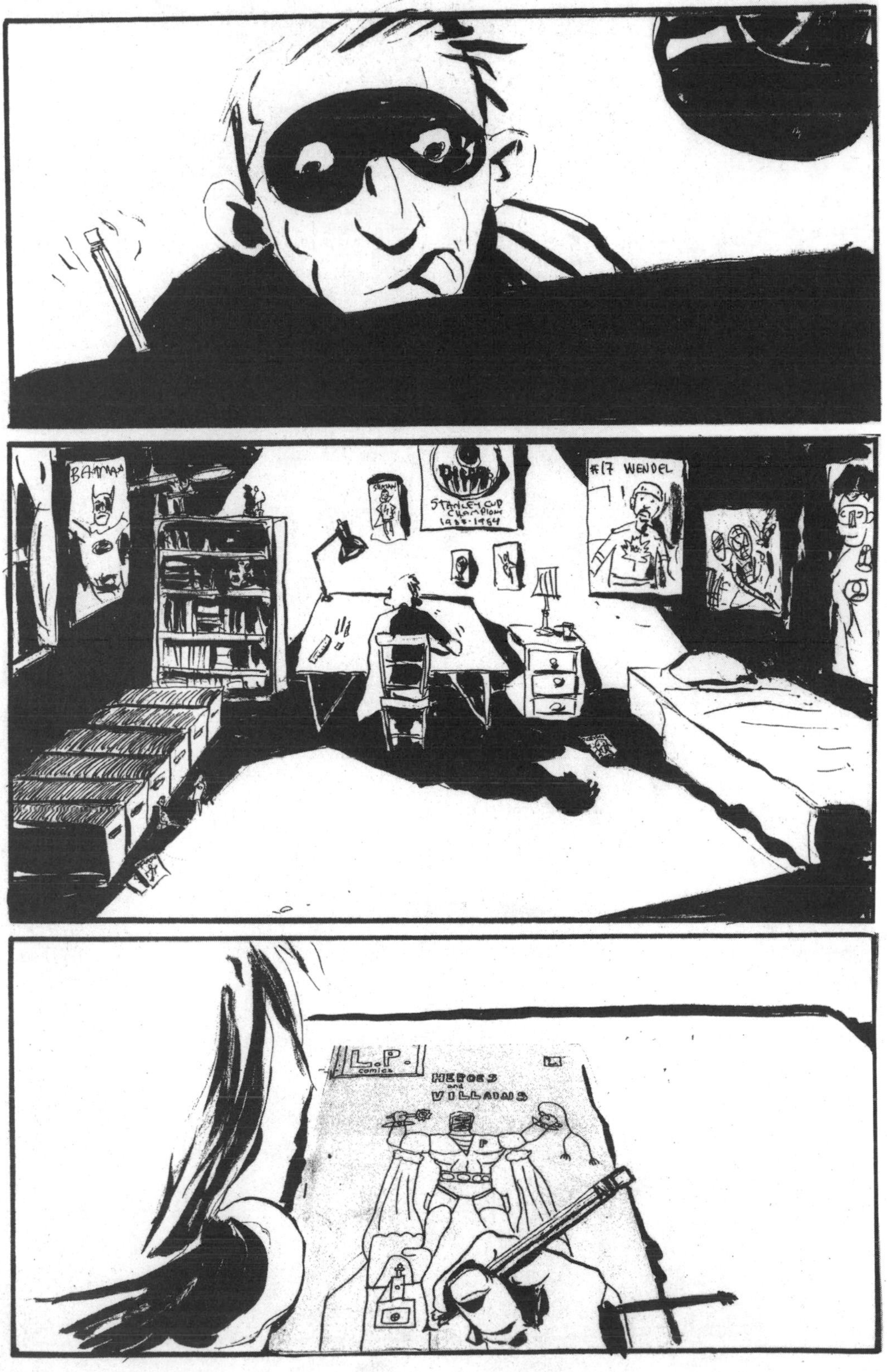
BATMAN
STANLEY CUP
#17 WENDEL
L.P.
comics
HEROES and VILLAINS

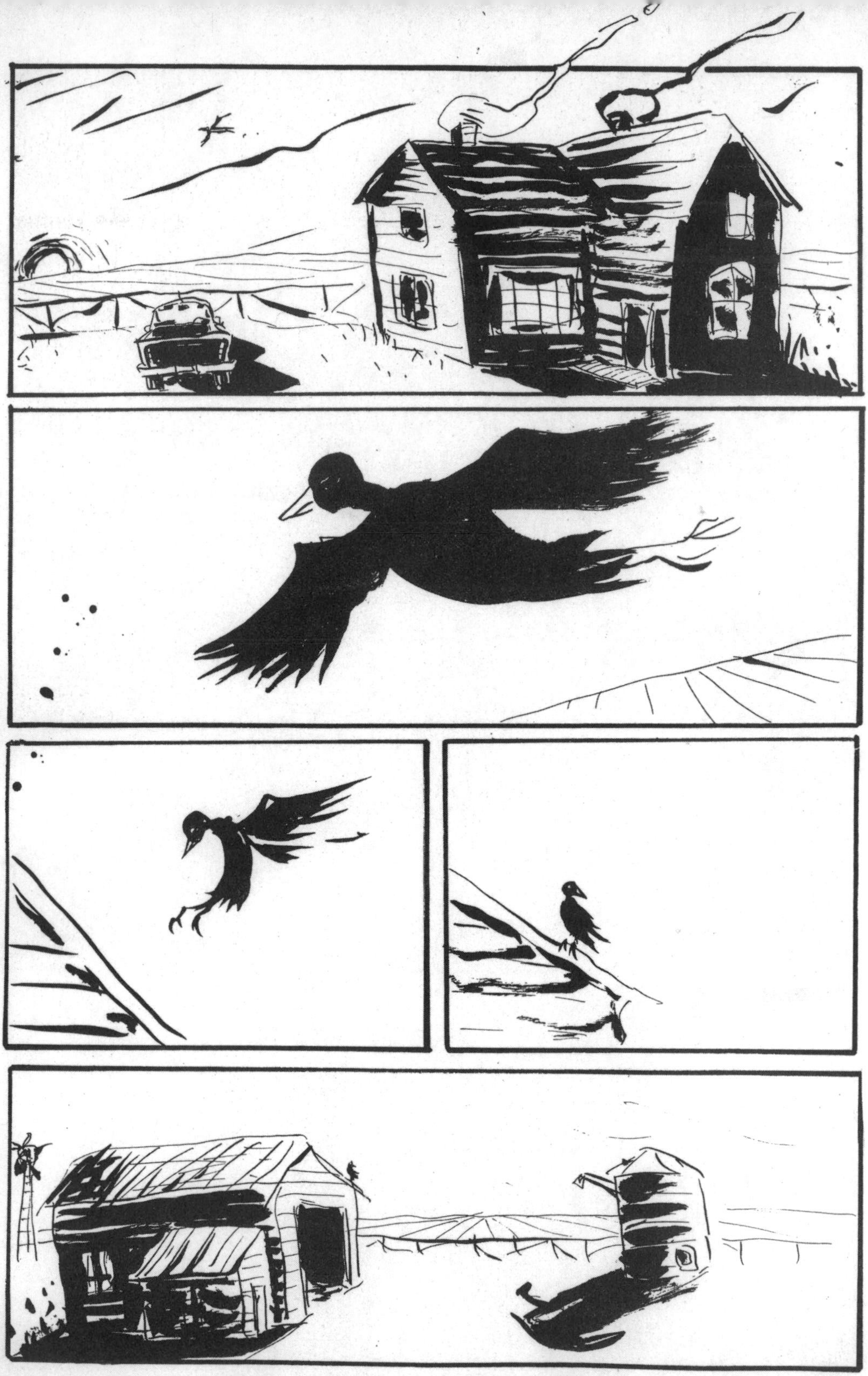

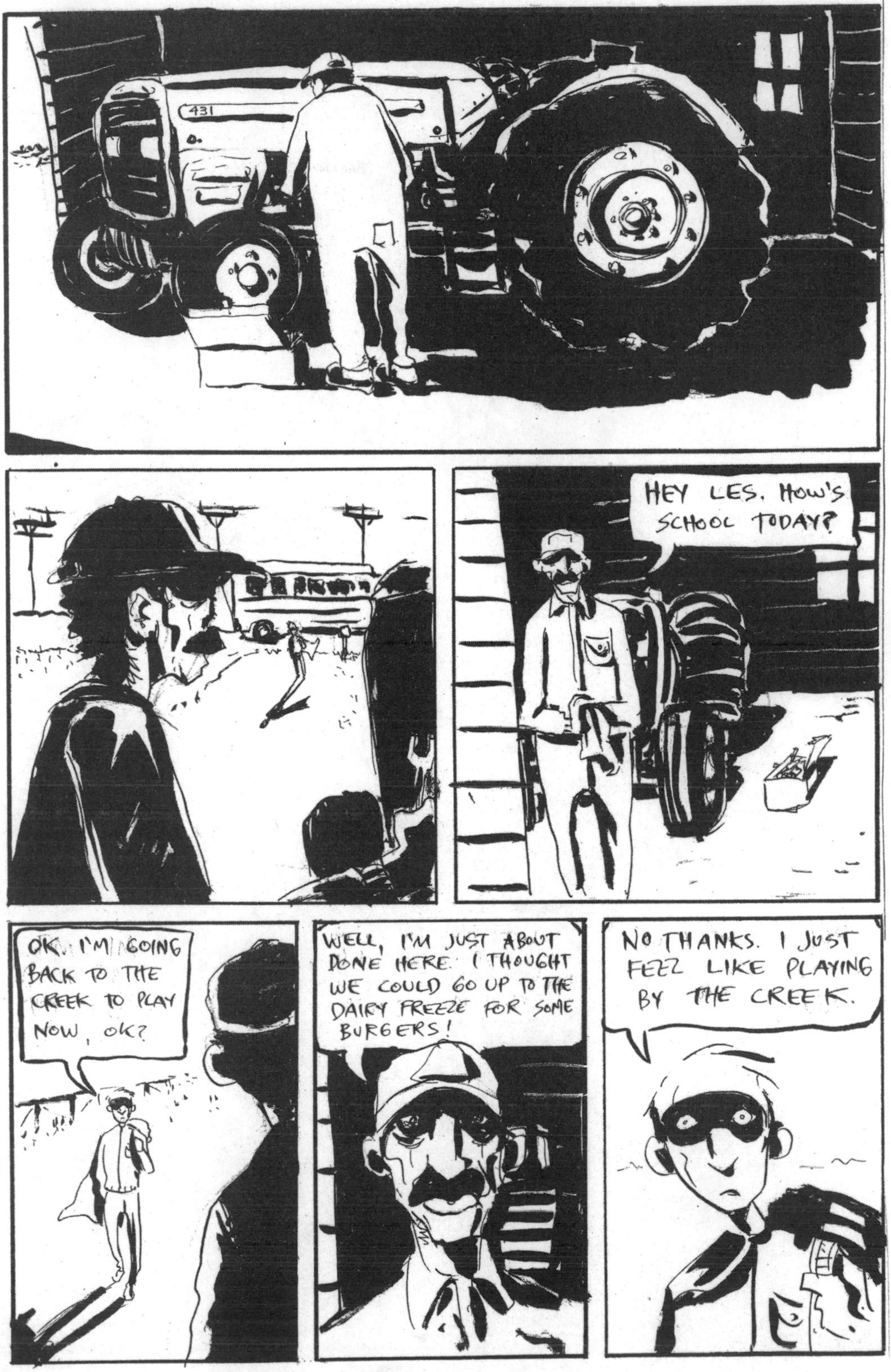
431
HEY LES. HOW'S SCHOOL TODAY?
OK. I'M GOING BACK TO THE CREEK TO PLAY NOW, OK?
WELL, I'M JUST ABOUT DONE HERE. I THOUGHT WE COULD GO UP TO THE DAIRY FREEZE FOR SOME BURGERS!
NO THANKS. I JUST FEEL LIKE PLAYING BY THE CREEK.

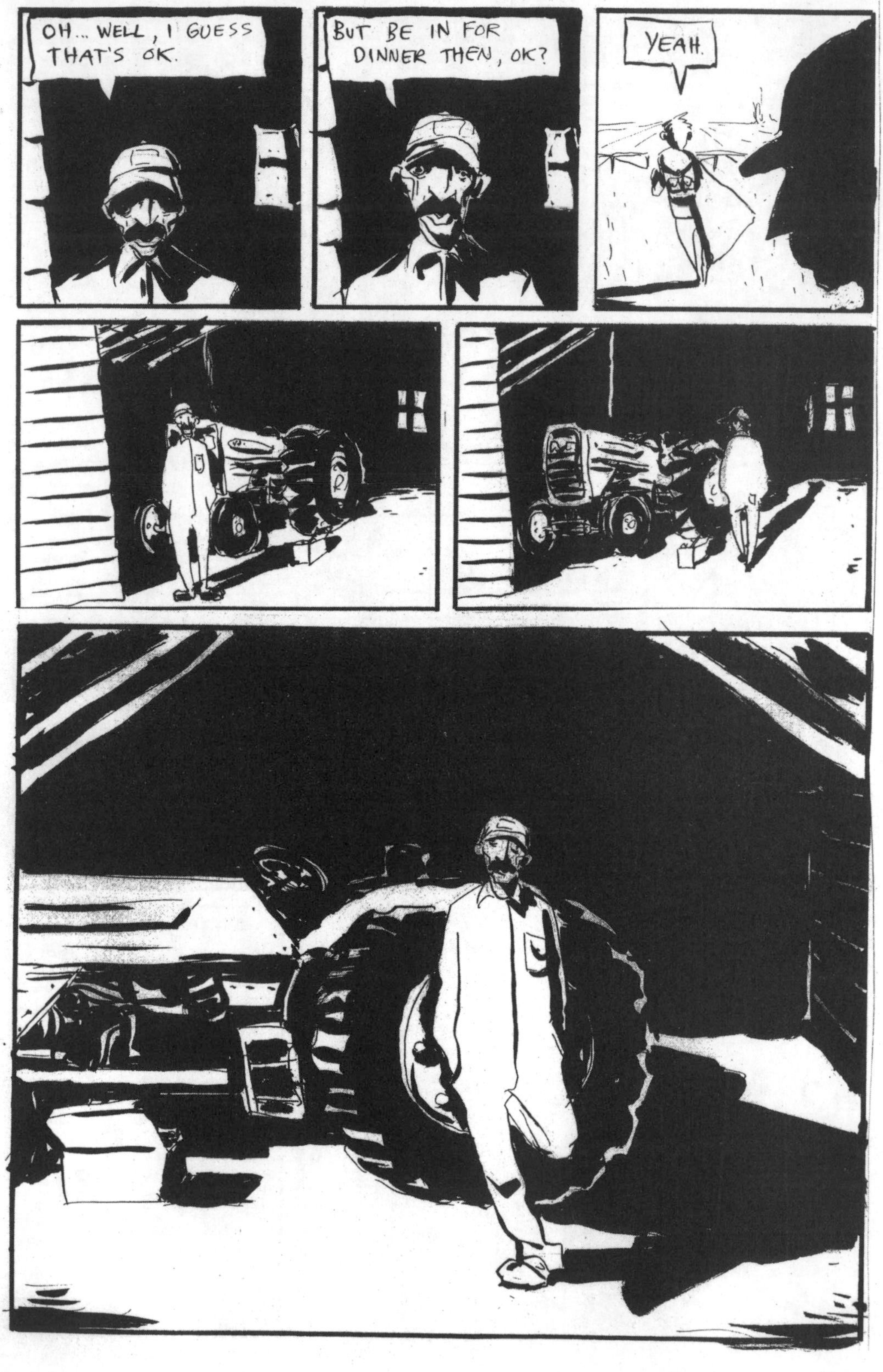
OH... WELL, I GUESS THAT'S OK.
BUT BE IN FOR DINNER THEN, OK?
YEAH.

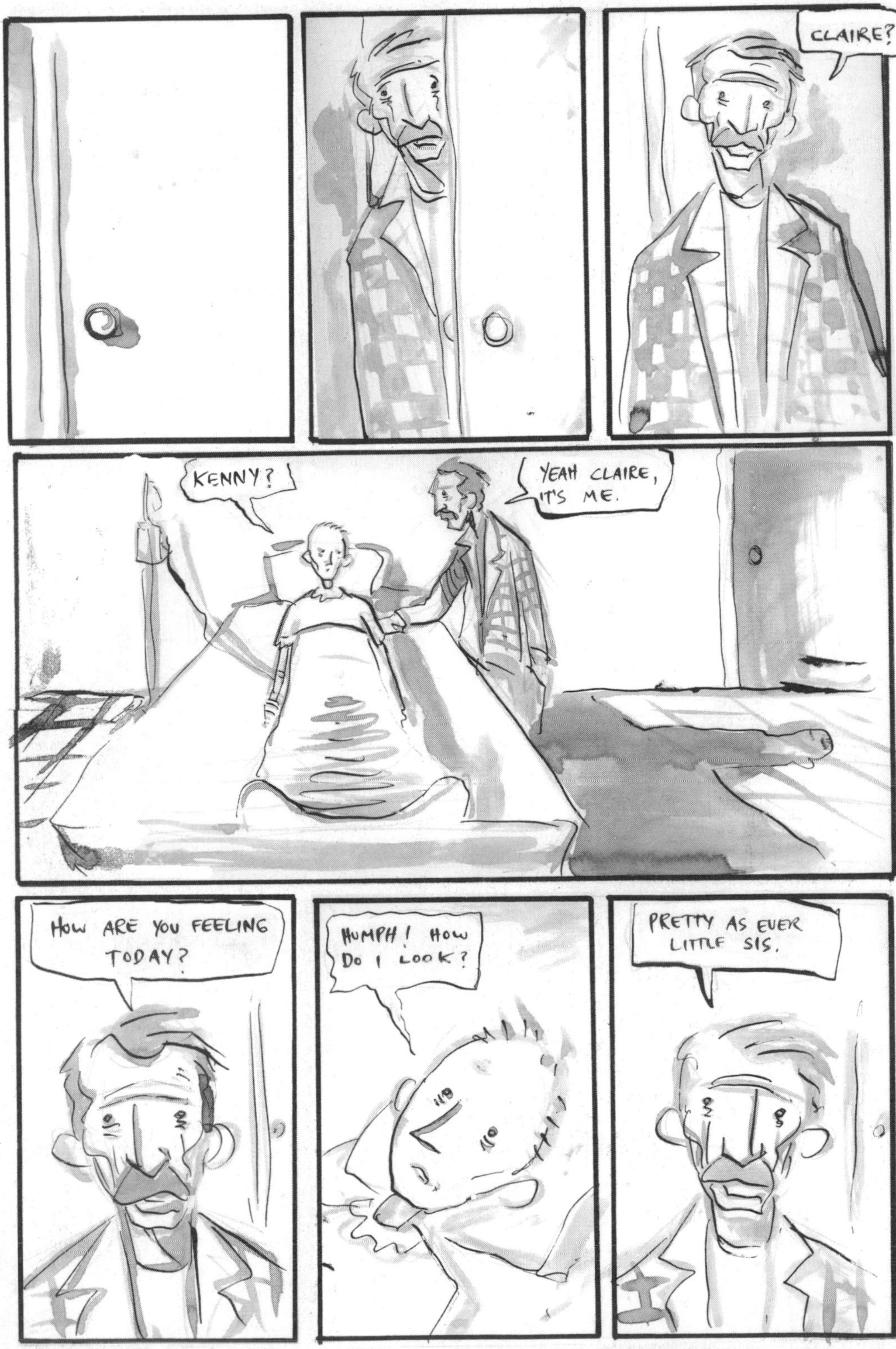
CLAIRE?
KENNY?
YEAH CLAIRE, IT'S ME.
HOW ARE YOU FEELING TODAY?
HUMPH! HOW DO I LOOK?
PRETTY AS EVER LITTLE SIS.

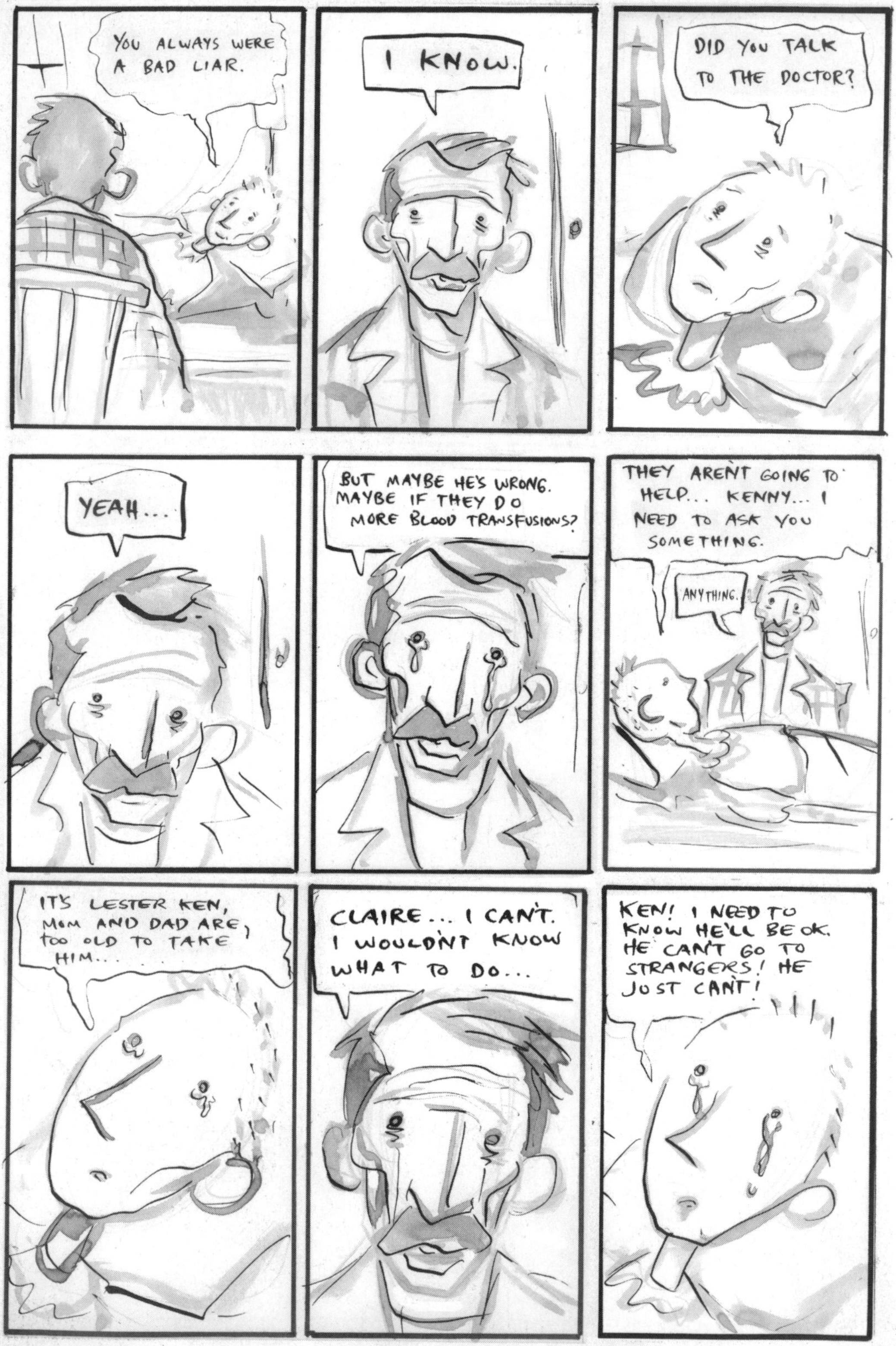
YOU ALWAYS WERE A BAD LIAR.
I KNOW.
DID YOU TALK TO THE DOCTOR?
YEAH...
BUT MAYBE HE'S WRONG. MAYBE IF THEY DO MORE BLOOD TRANSFUSIONS?
THEY AREN'T GOING TO HELP... KENNY... I NEED TO ASK YOU SOMETHING.
ANYTHING.
IT'S LESTER KEN, MOM AND DAD ARE, TOO OLD TO TAKE HIM...
CLAIRE... I CAN'T. I WOULDN'T KNOW WHAT TO DO...
KEN! I NEED TO KNOW HE'LL BE OK. HE CAN'T GO TO STRANGERS! HE JUST CAN'T!

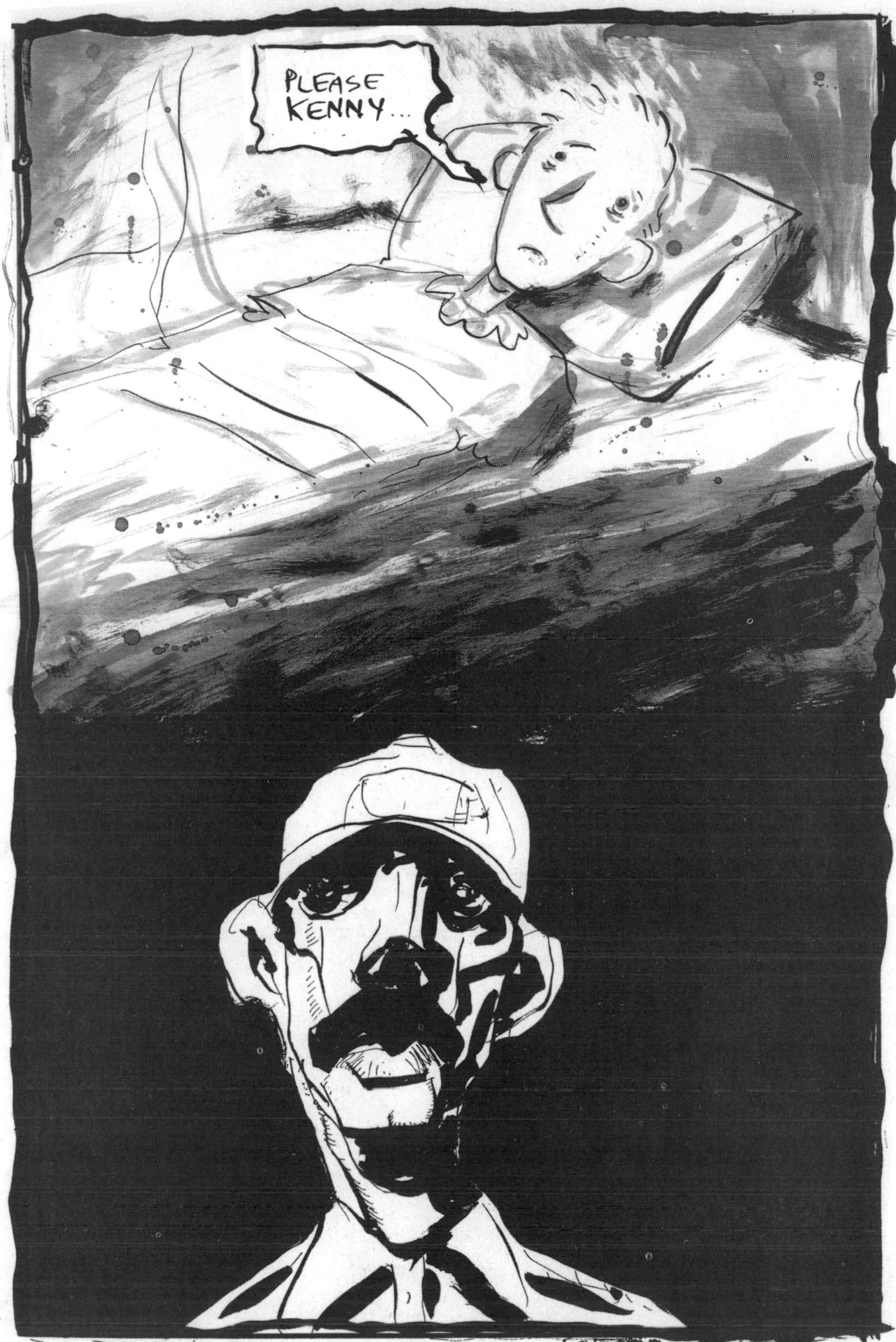
PLEASE KENNY...

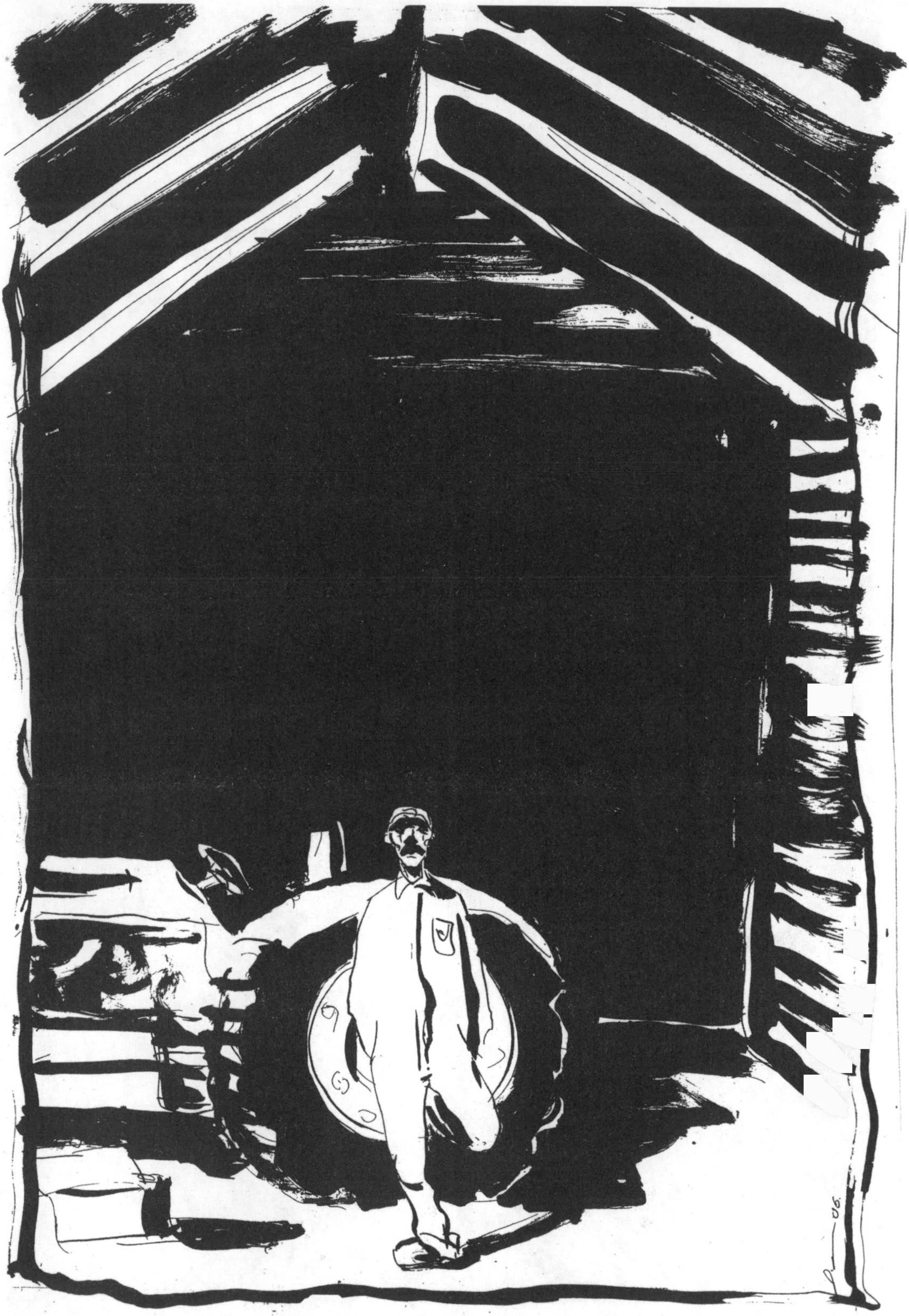

WINTER

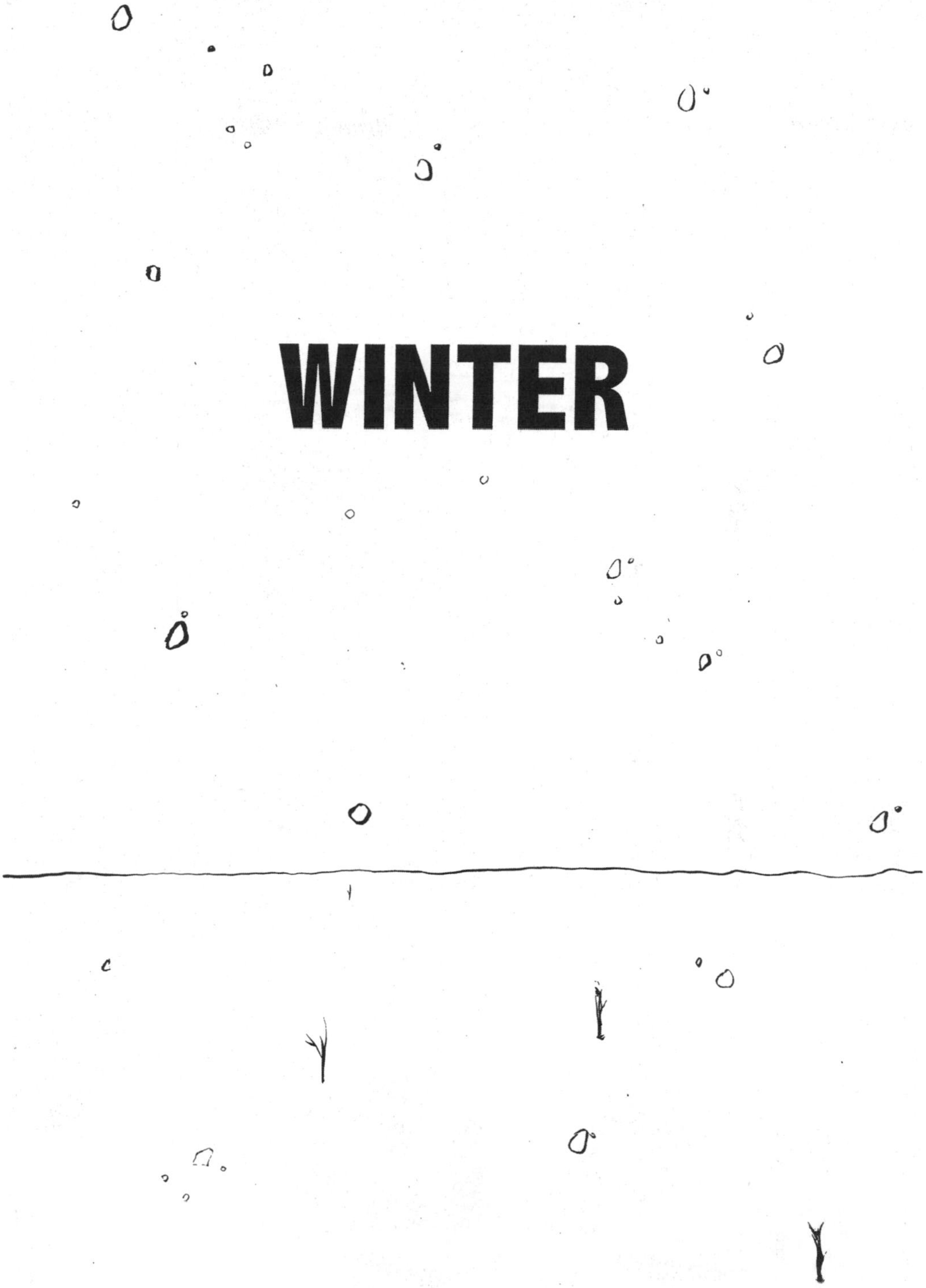

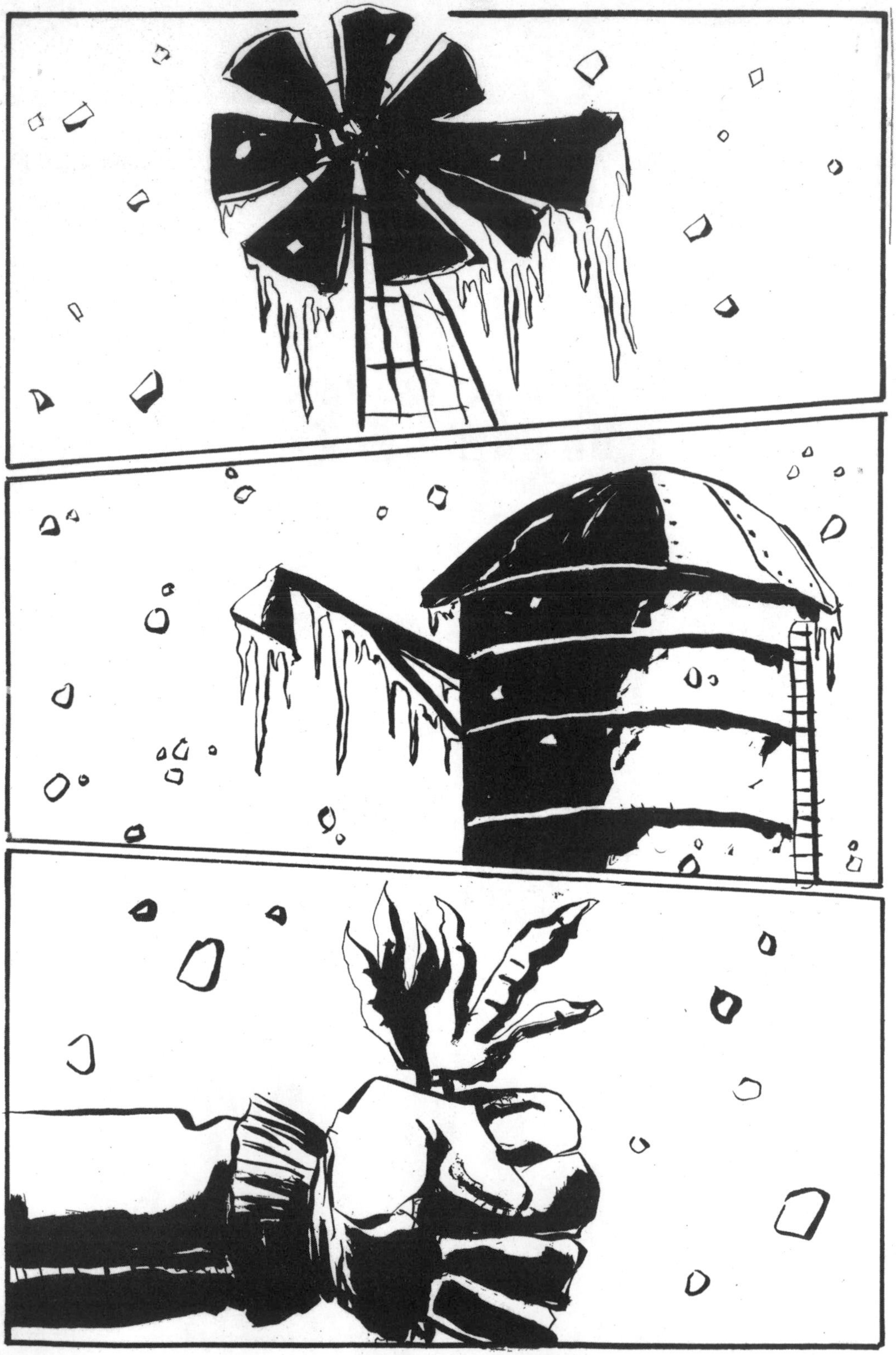

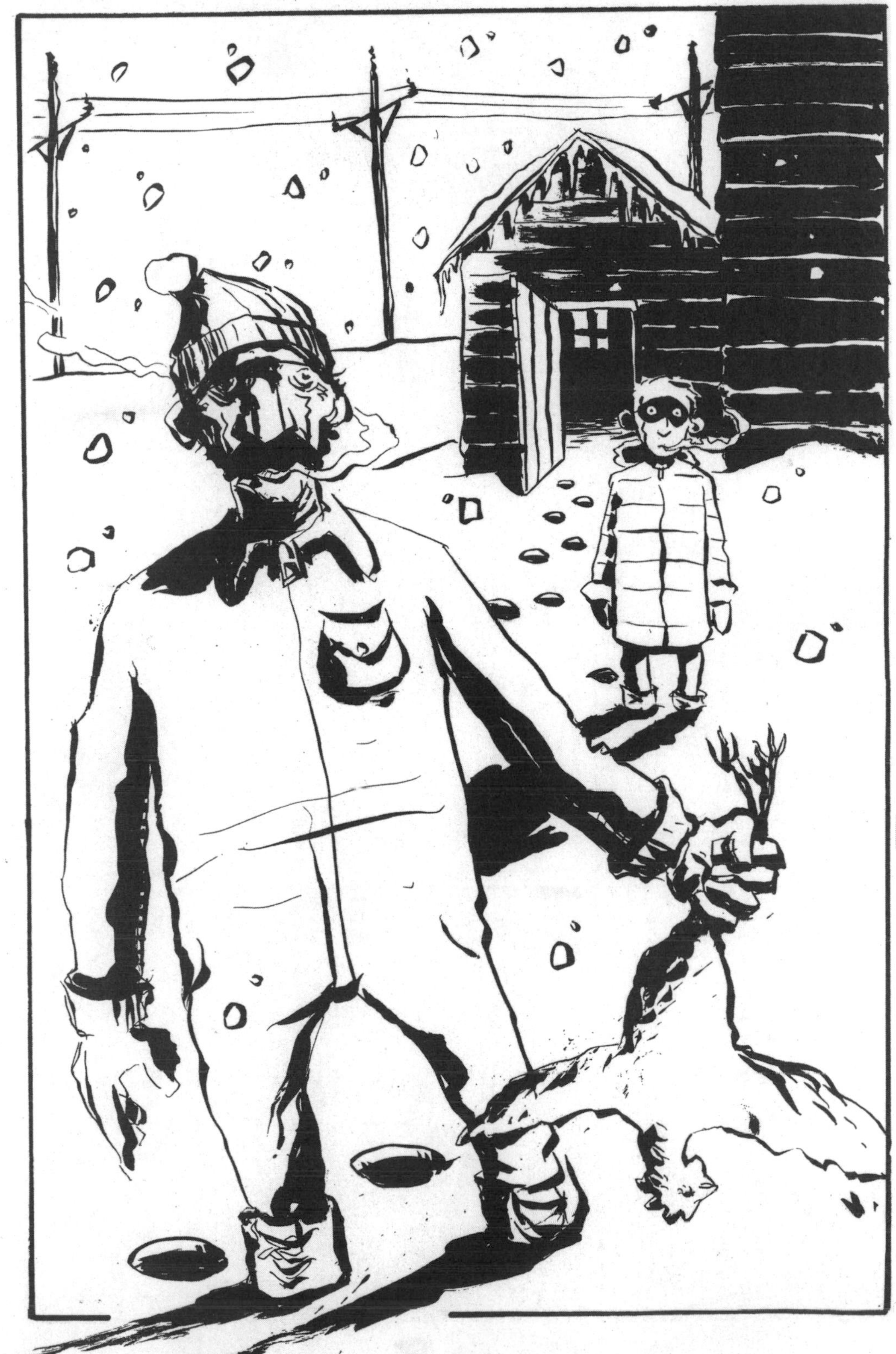

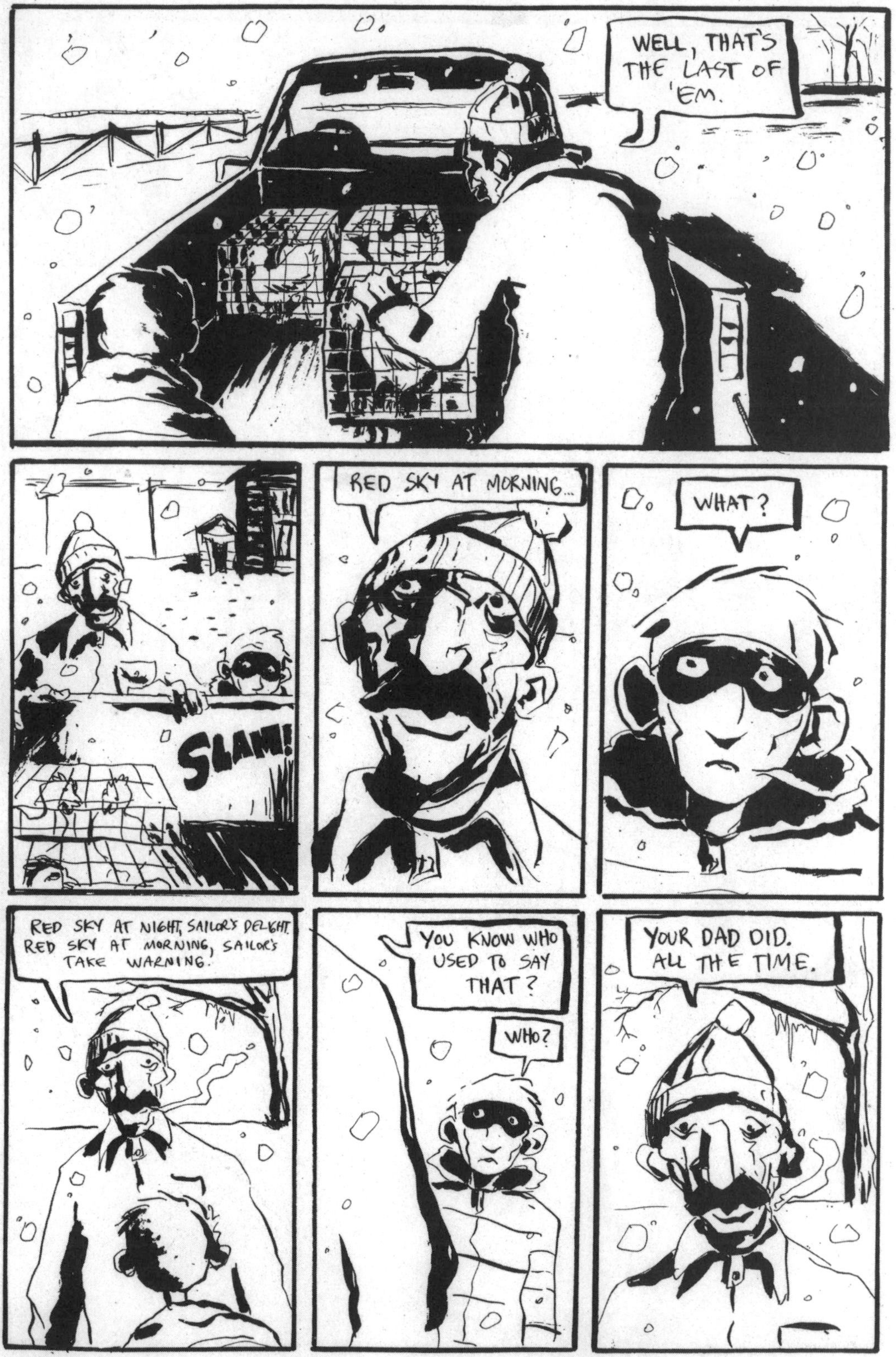
WELL, THAT'S THE LAST OF 'EM.
SLAM!
RED SKY AT MORNING...
WHAT?
RED SKY AT NIGHT, SAILOR'S DELIGHT. RED SKY AT MORNING, SAILOR'S TAKE WARNING.
YOU KNOW WHO USED TO SAY THAT?
WHO?
YOUR DAD DID. ALL THE TIME.

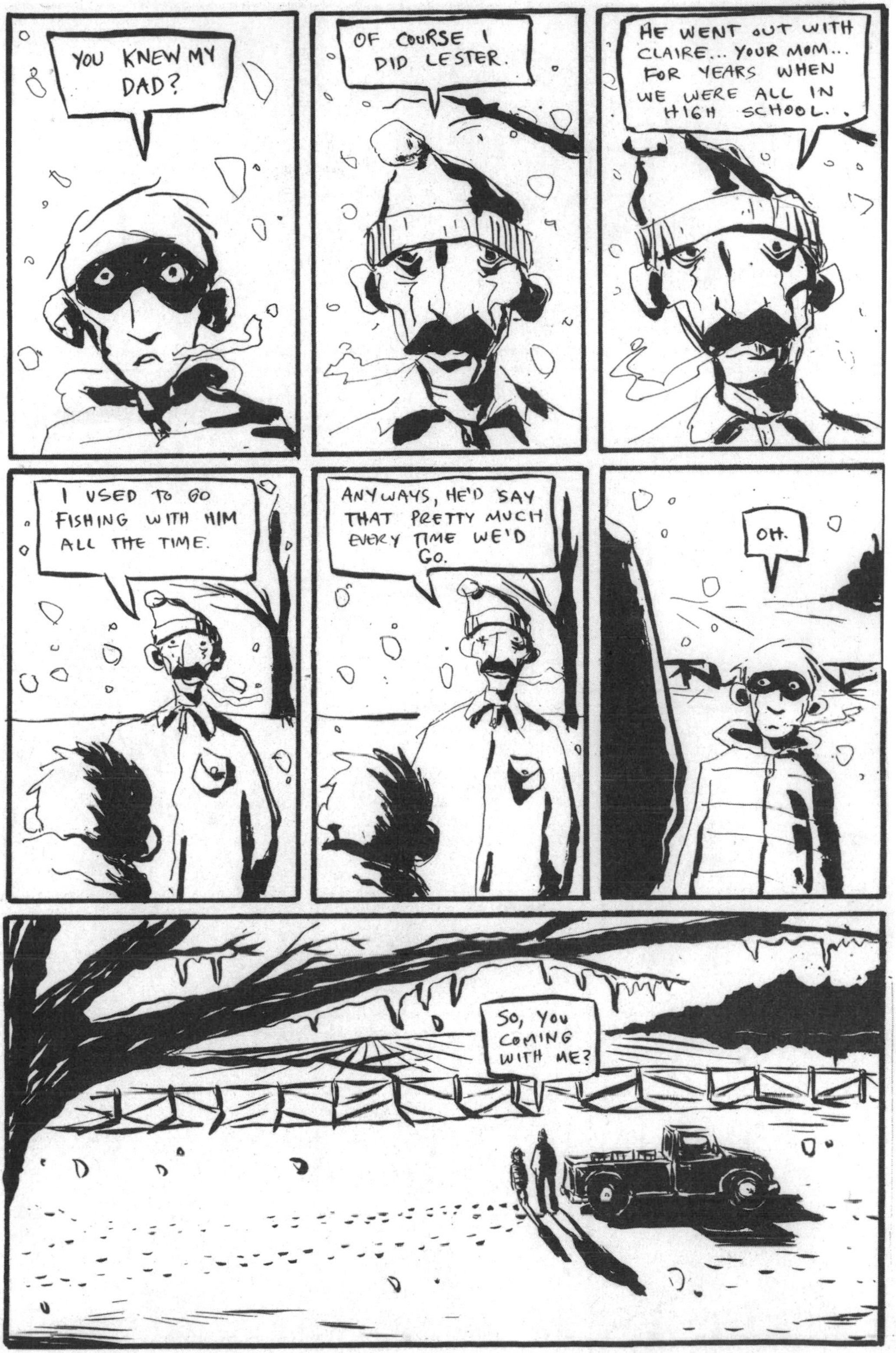
YOU KNEW MY DAD?
OF COURSE I DID LESTER.
HE WENT OUT WITH CLAIRE... YOUR MOM... FOR YEARS WHEN WE WERE ALL IN HIGH SCHOOL.
I USED TO GO FISHING WITH HIM ALL THE TIME.
ANYWAYS, HE'D SAY THAT PRETTY MUCH EVERY TIME WE'D GO.
OH.
So, YOU COMING WITH ME?

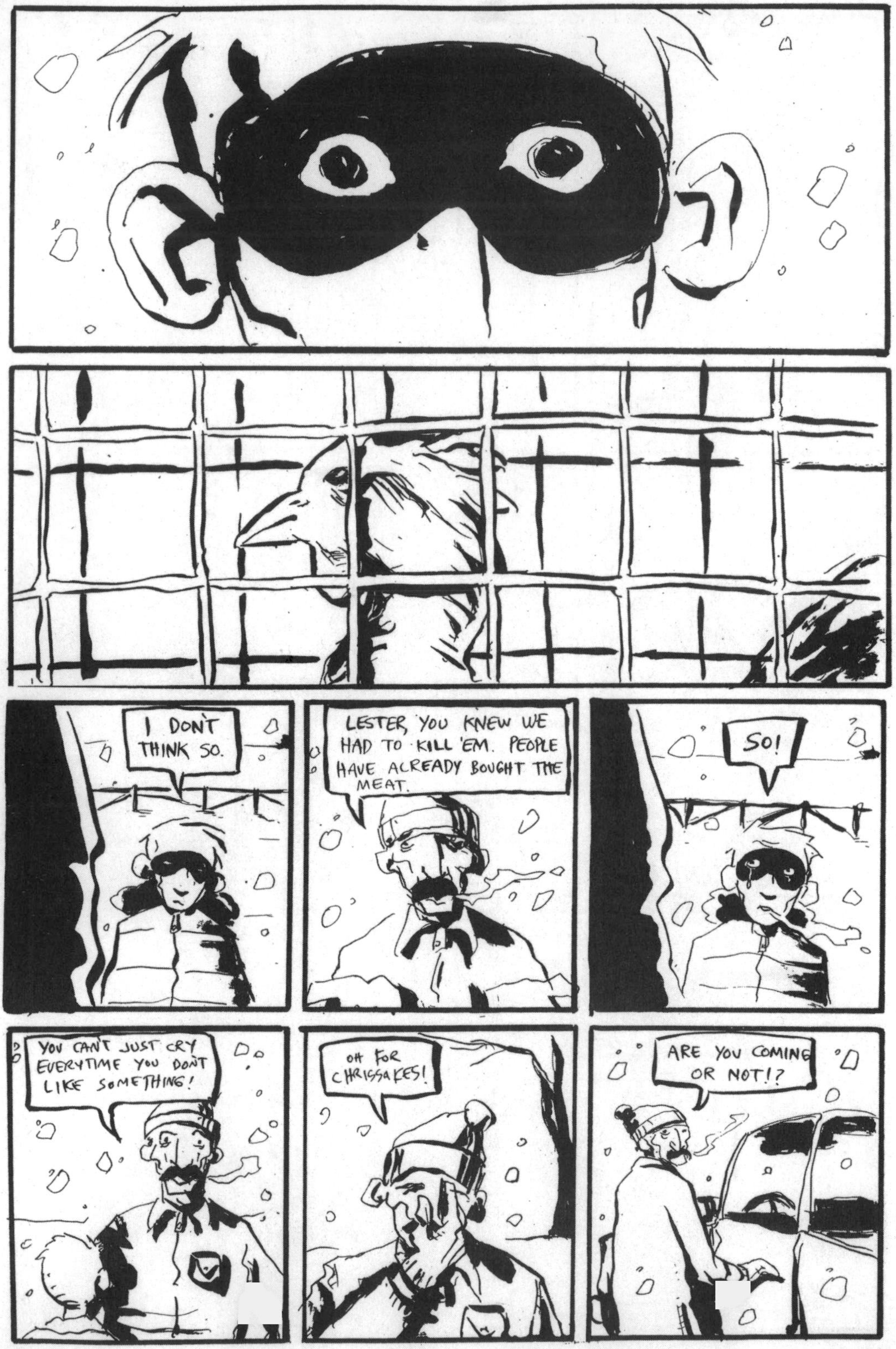

I DON'T THINK SO.
LESTER, YOU KNEW WE HAD TO KILL 'EM. PEOPLE HAVE ALREADY BOUGHT THE MEAT.
SO!
YOU CAN'T JUST CRY EVERYTIME YOU DON'T LIKE SOMETHING!
OH FOR CHRISSAKES!
ARE YOU COMING OR NOT!?

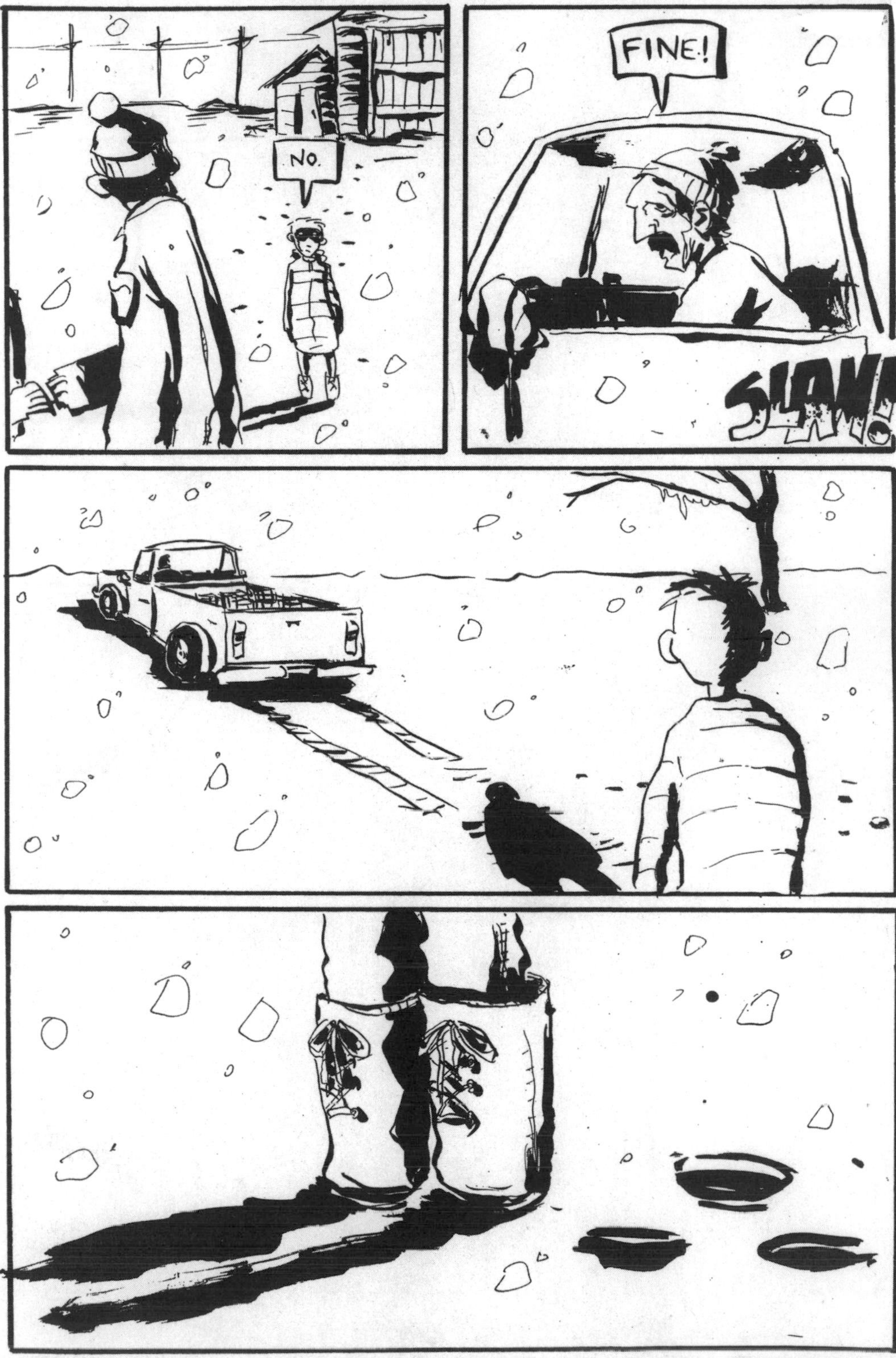
NO.
FINE!
SLAM!

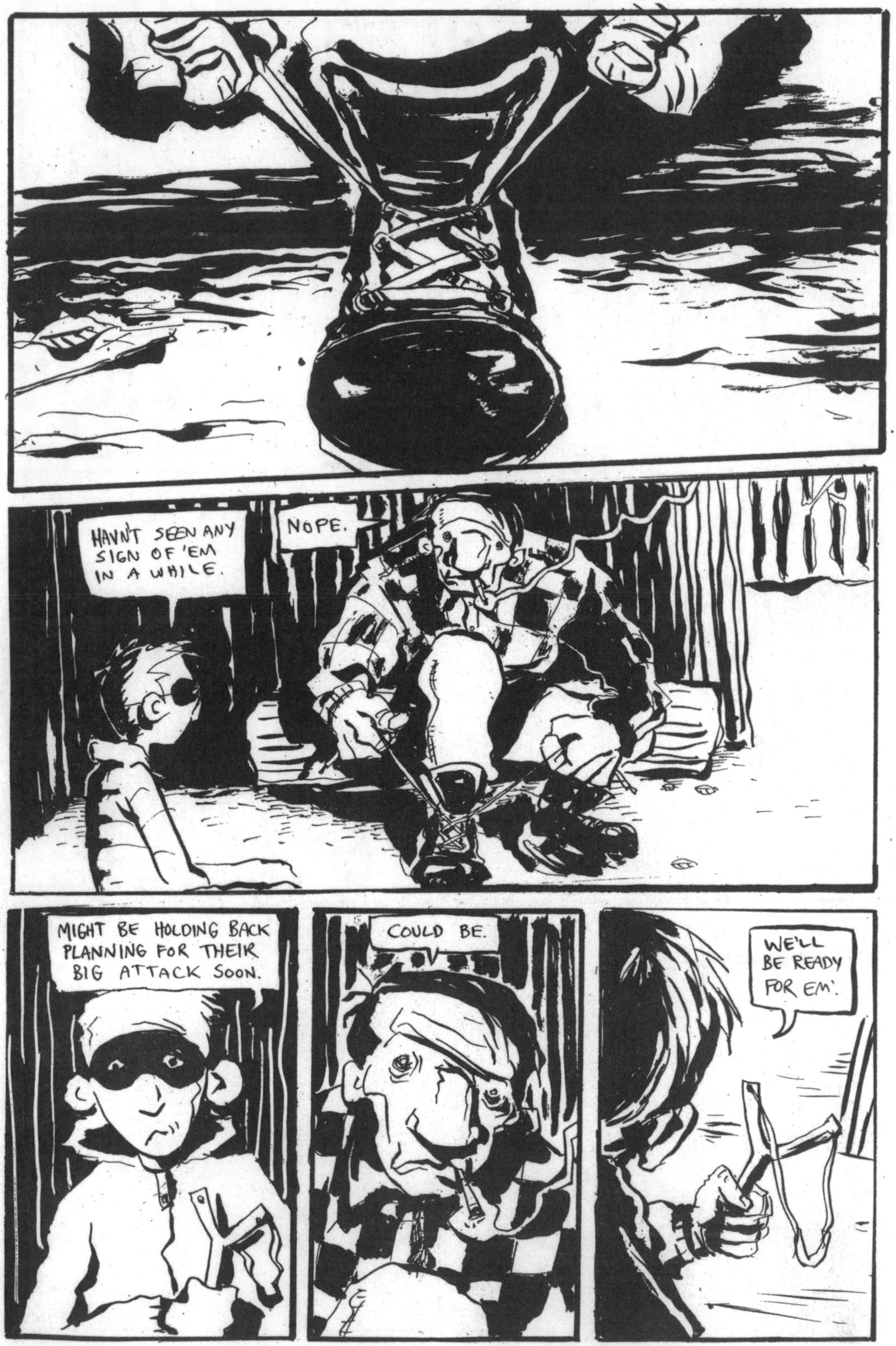
HAVN'T SEEN ANY SIGN OF 'EM IN A WHILE.
NOPE.
MIGHT BE HOLDING BACK PLANNING FOR THEIR BIG ATTACK SOON.
COULD BE.
WE'LL BE READY FOR EM'.

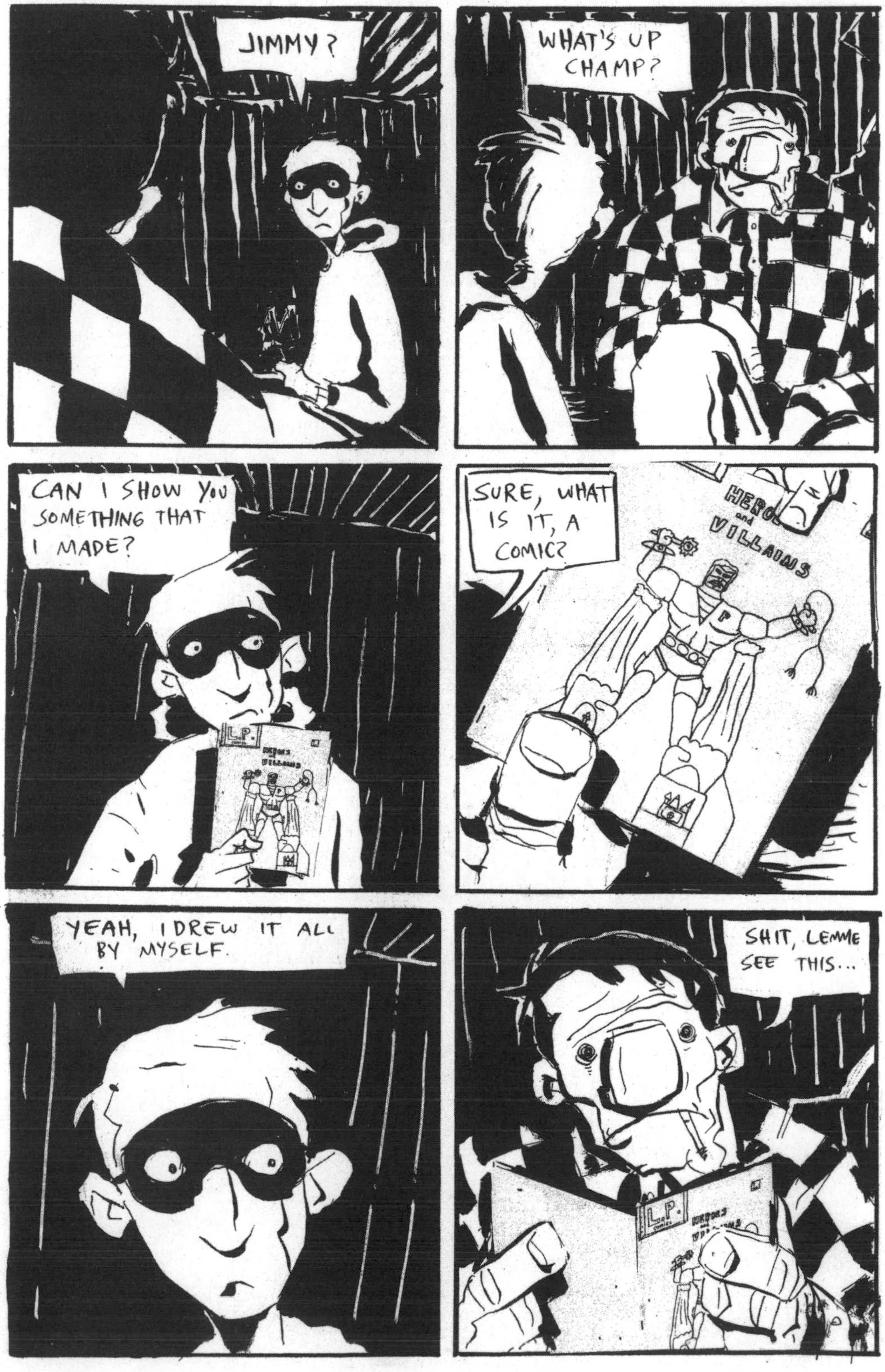
JIMMY?
WHAT'S UP CHAMP?
CAN I SHOW YOU SOMETHING THAT I MADE?
SURE, WHAT IS IT, A COMIC?
YEAH, I DREW IT ALL BY MYSELF.
SHIT, LEMME SEE THIS...

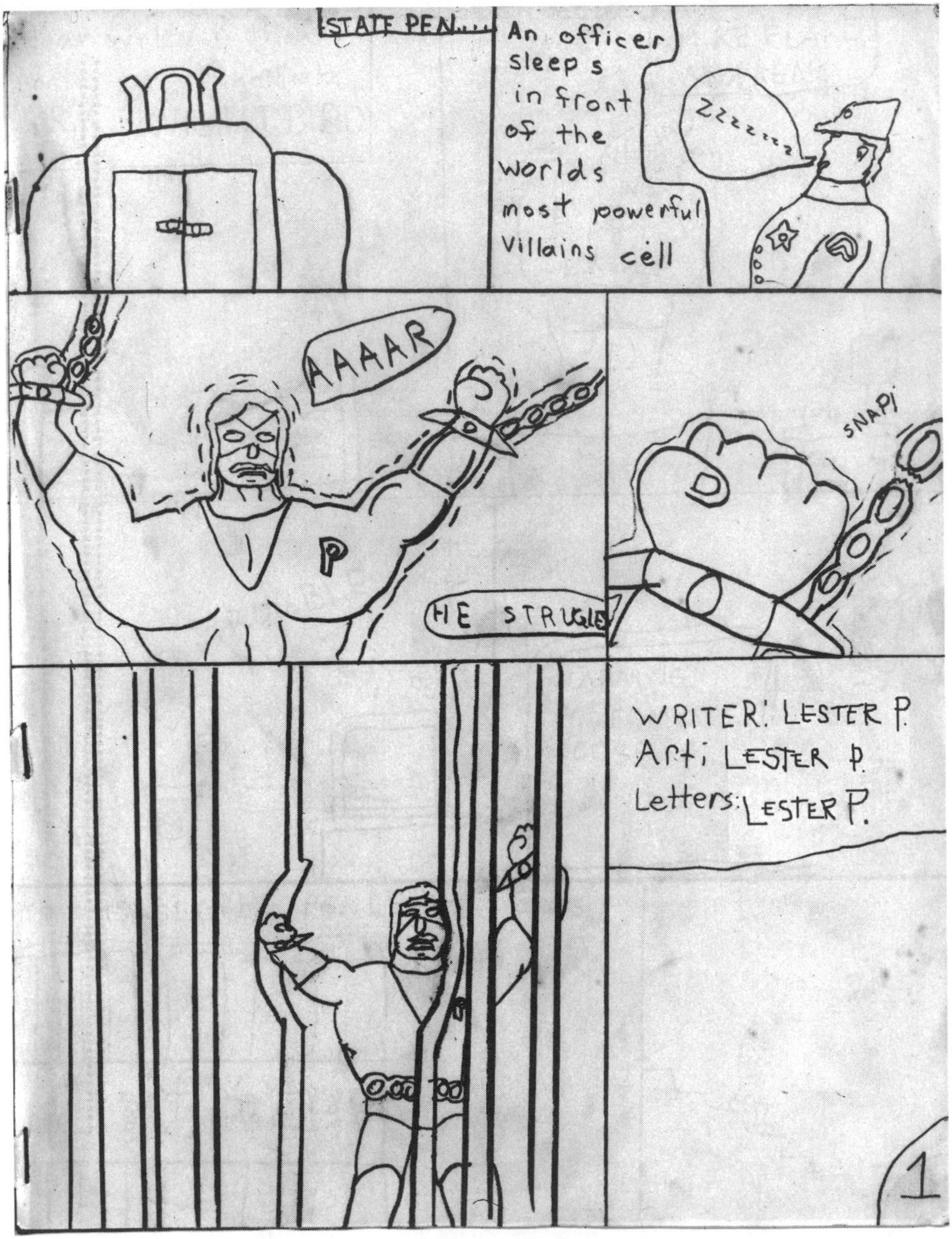
STATE PEN....
An officer sleep s in front of the worlds most powerful villains cell
Zzzzzzz
AAAAR
HE STRUGLE
SNAP!
WRITER: LESTER P.
Art: LESTER P.
Letters: LESTER P.
1

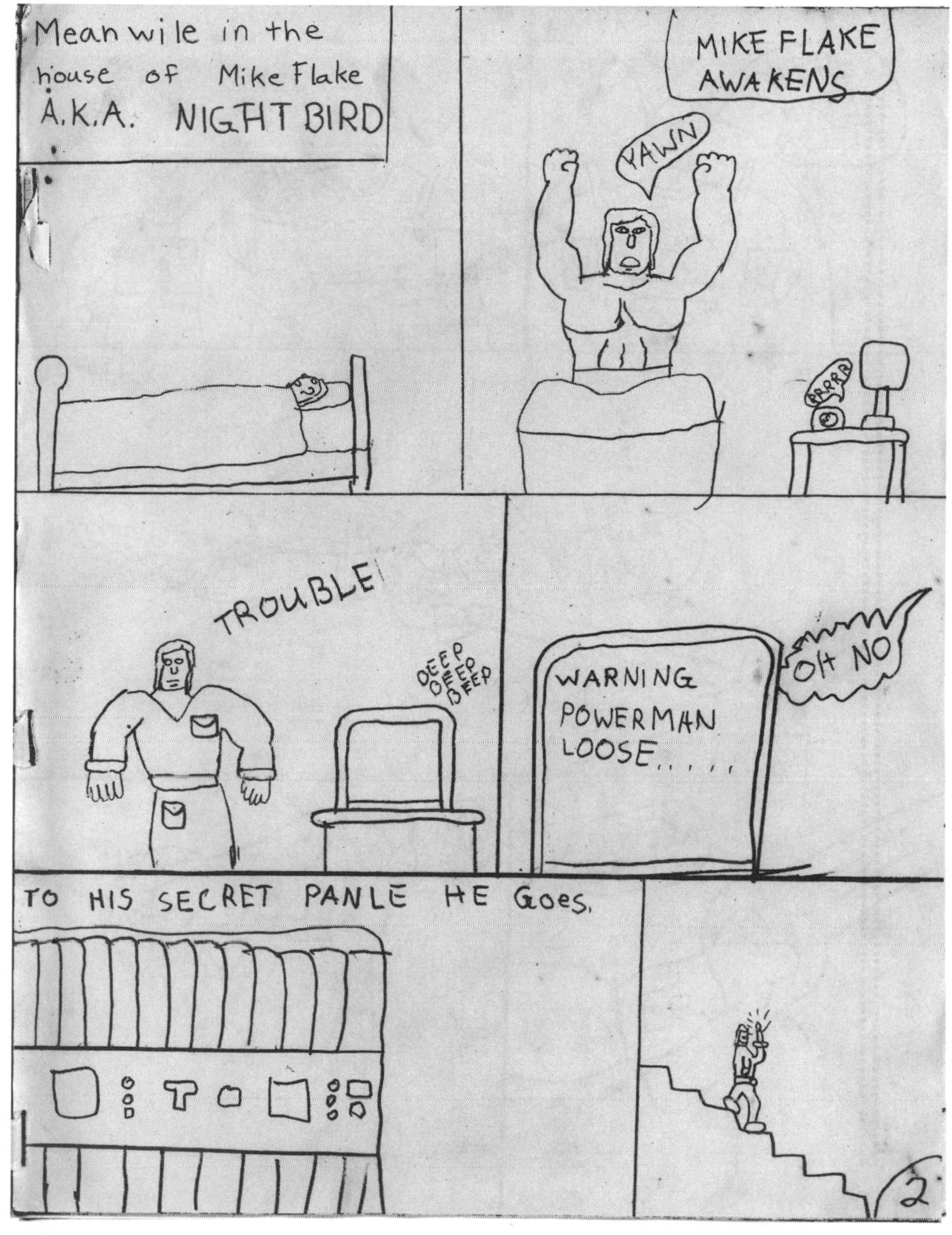
Mean wile in the house of Mike Flake A.K.A. NIGHT BIRD
MIKE FLAKE AWAKENS
YAWN
BRRRR
TROUBLE
DEEP DEEP BEEP
WARNING POWERMAN LOOSE......
OH NO
TO HIS SECRET PANLE HE Goes.
2

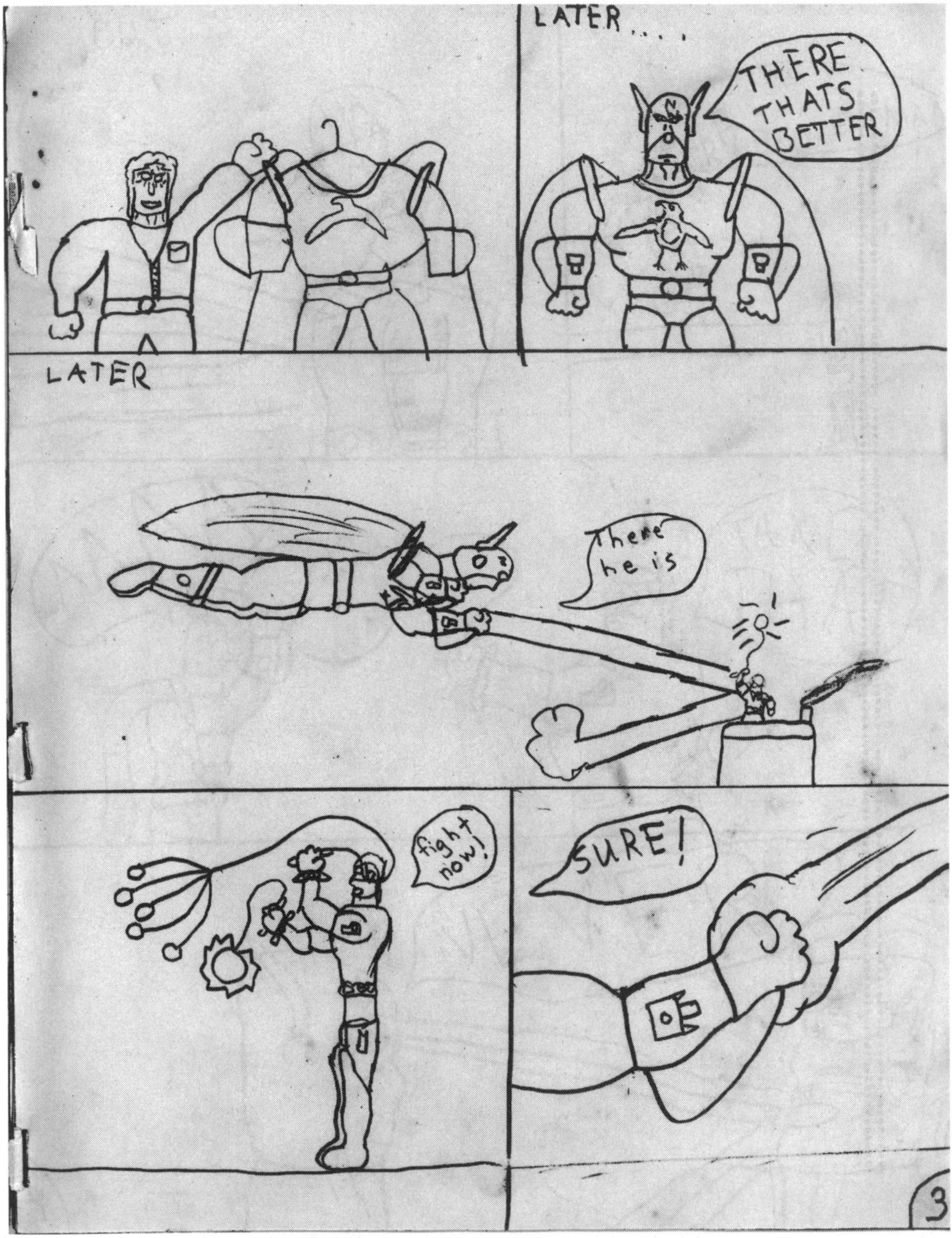
LATER....
THERE THATS BETTER
LATER
There he is
fight now!
SURE!
3

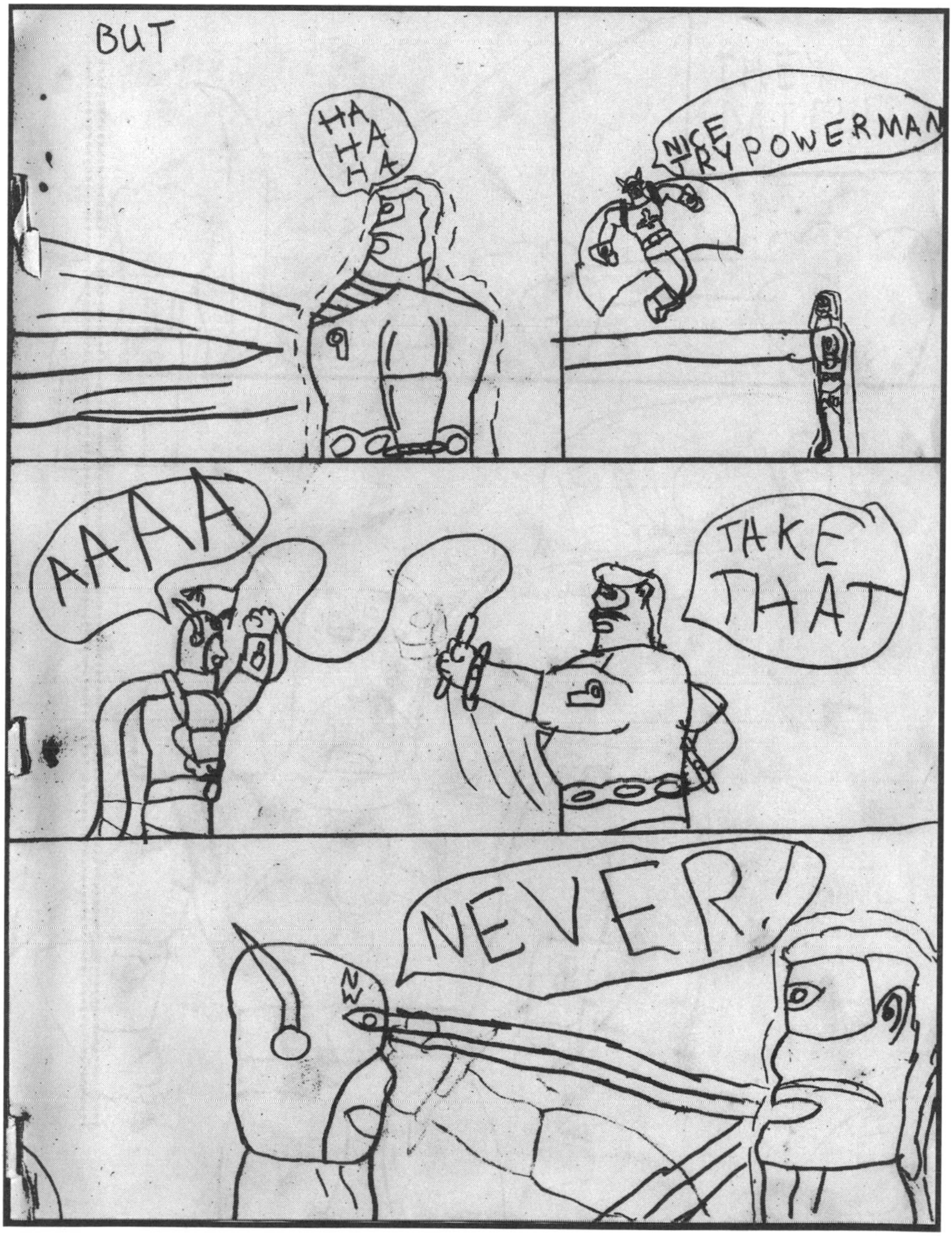
BUT
HA HA HA HA
NICE TRY POWERMAN
AAAA
TAKE THAT
NEVER!

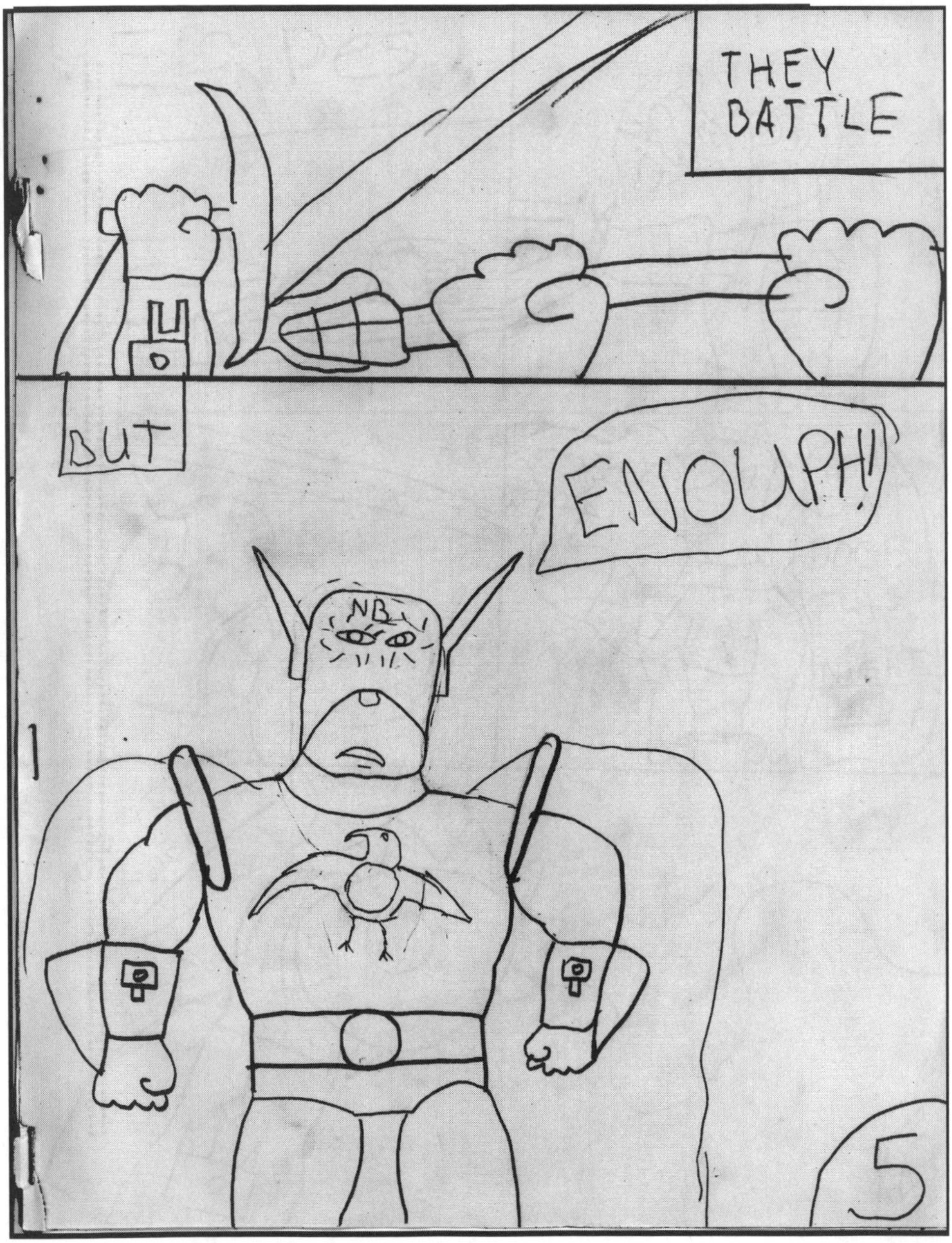
THEY BATTLE
BUT
ENOUPH!
5

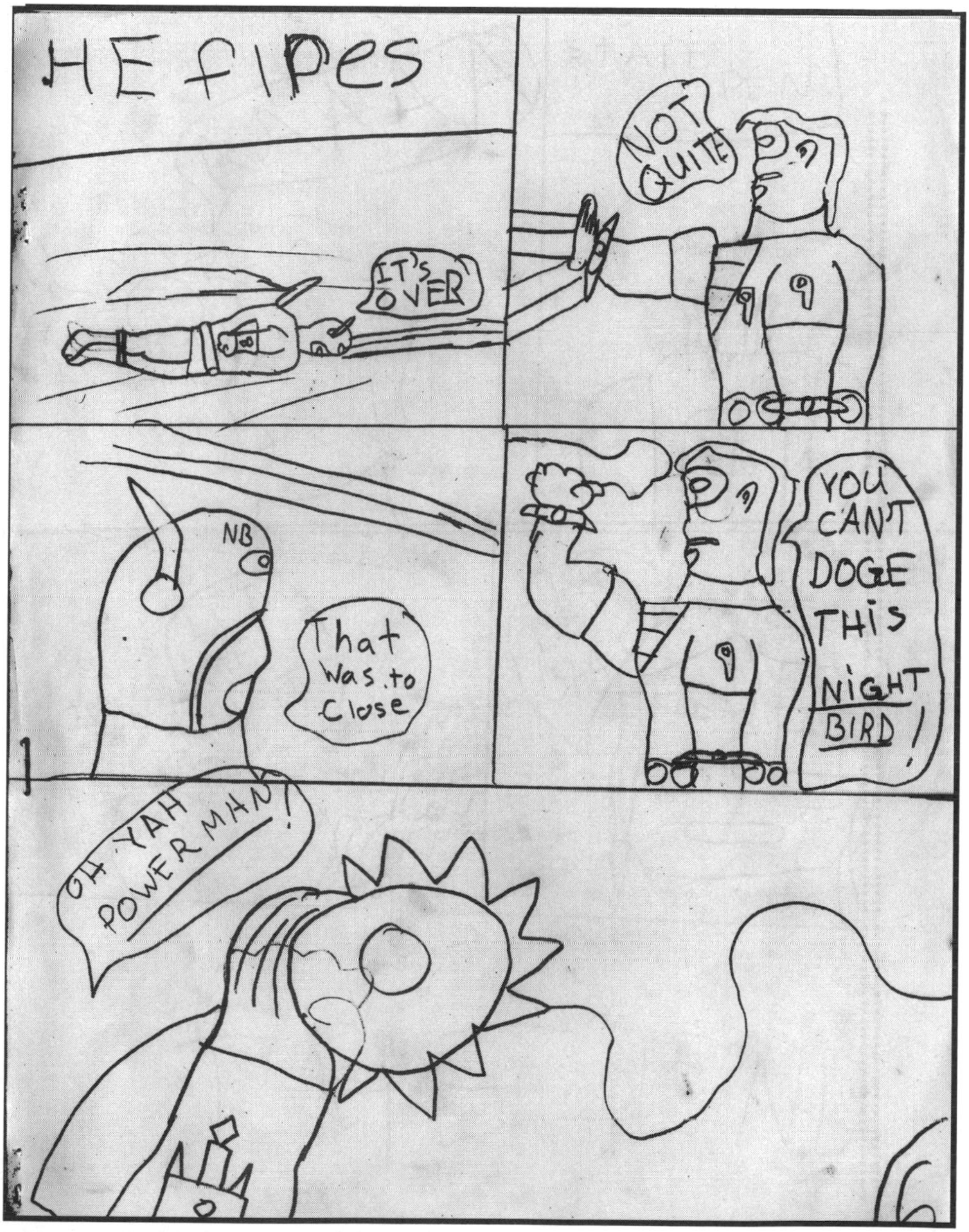
HE fIPes
IT's OVER
NOT QUITE
NB
That was to Close
YOU CAN'T DOGE THIS NIGHT BIRD!
OH YAH POWER MAN!
1

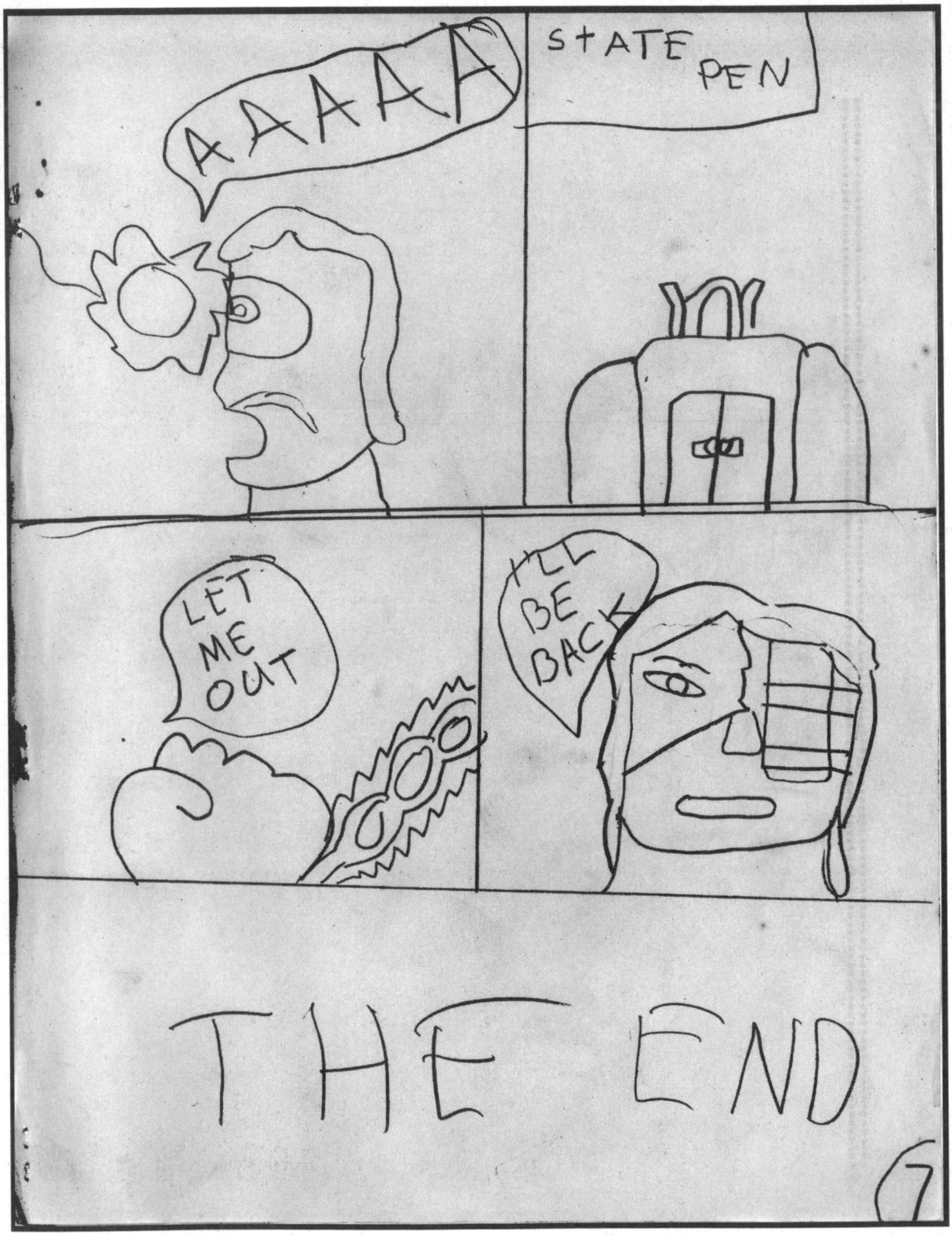
AAAAA
STATE PEN
LET ME OUT
I'LL BE BACK
THE END
7

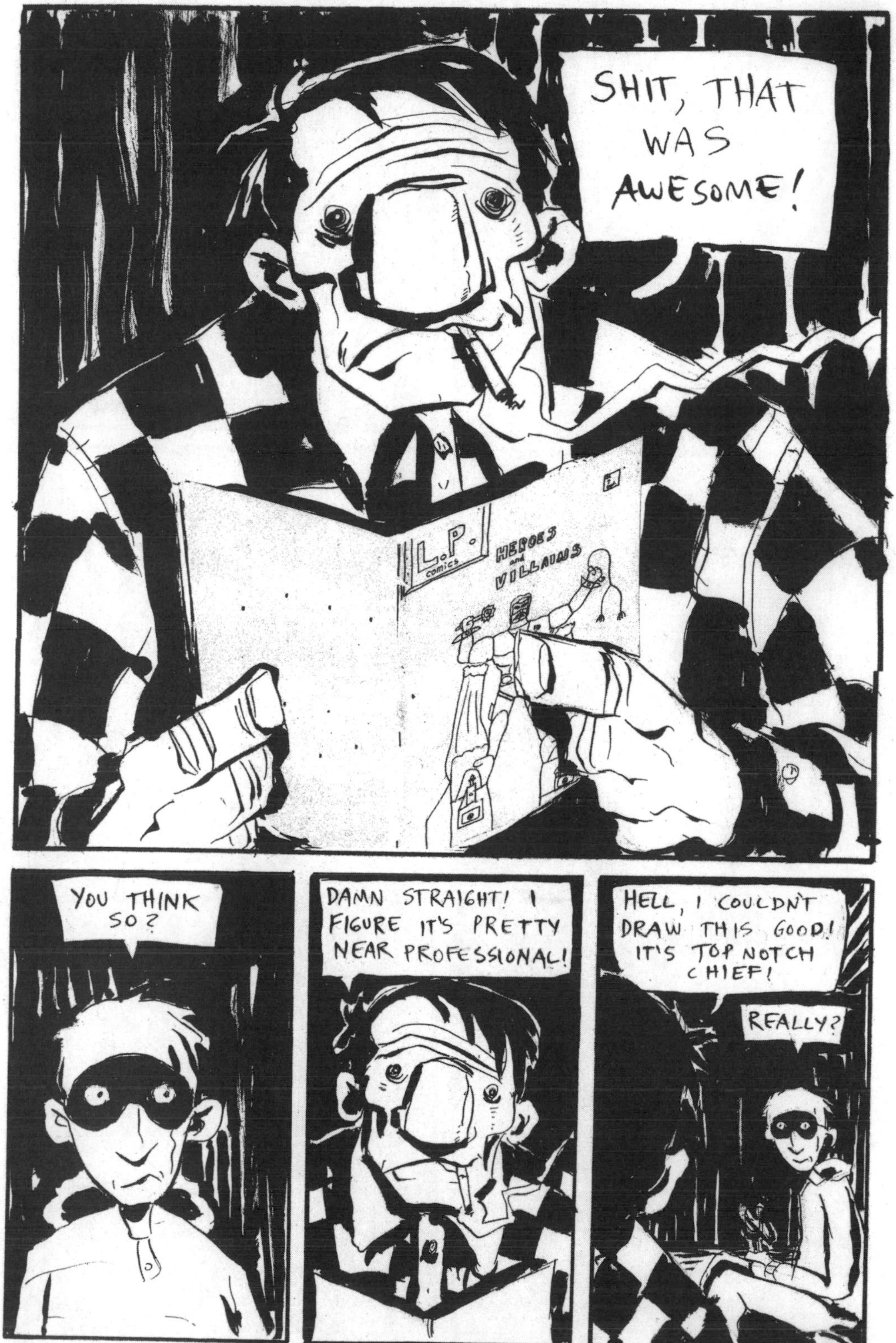
SHIT, THAT WAS AWESOME!
L.P. comics
HEROES and VILLAINS
YOU THINK SO?
DAMN STRAIGHT! I FIGURE IT'S PRETTY NEAR PROFESSIONAL!
HELL, I COULDN'T DRAW THIS GOOD! IT'S TOP NOTCH CHIEF!
REALLY?

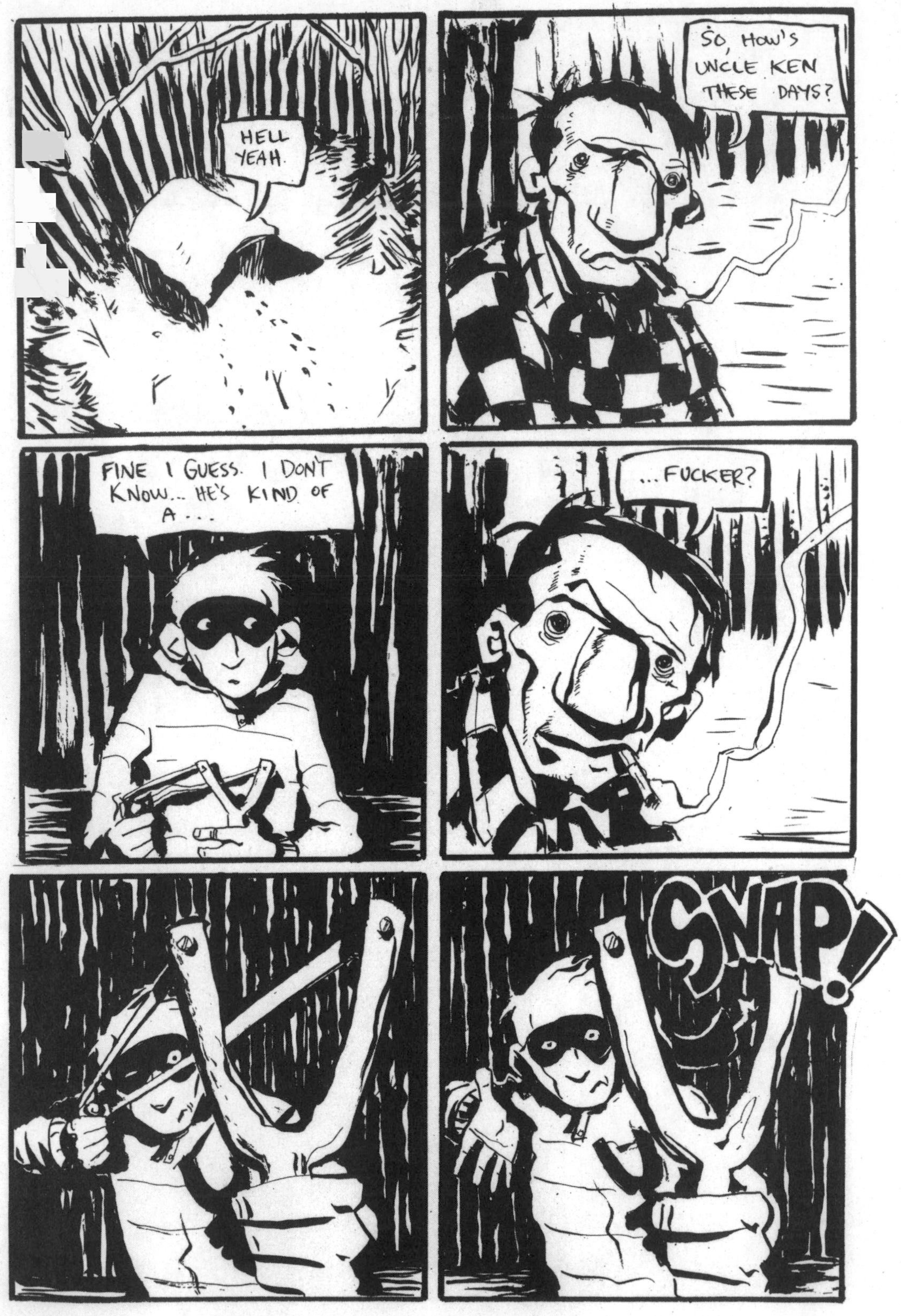
HELL YEAH.
SO, HOW'S UNCLE KEN THESE DAYS?
FINE I GUESS. I DON'T KNOW... HE'S KIND OF A...
...FUCKER?
SNAP!

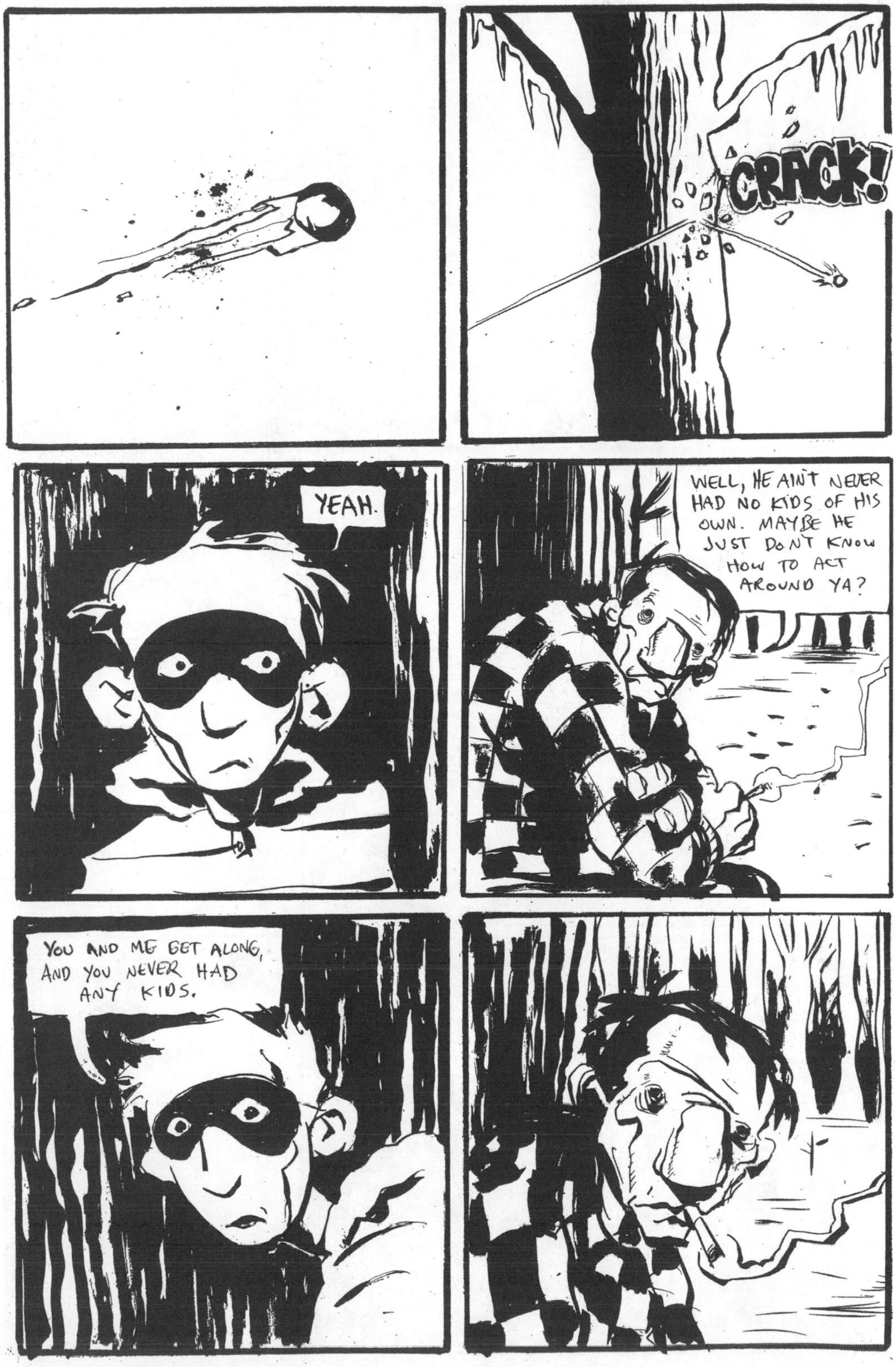
CRACK!
YEAH.
WELL, HE AIN'T NEVER HAD NO KIDS OF HIS OWN. MAYBE HE JUST DON'T KNOW HOW TO ACT AROUND YA?
YOU AND ME GET ALONG, AND YOU NEVER HAD ANY KIDS.

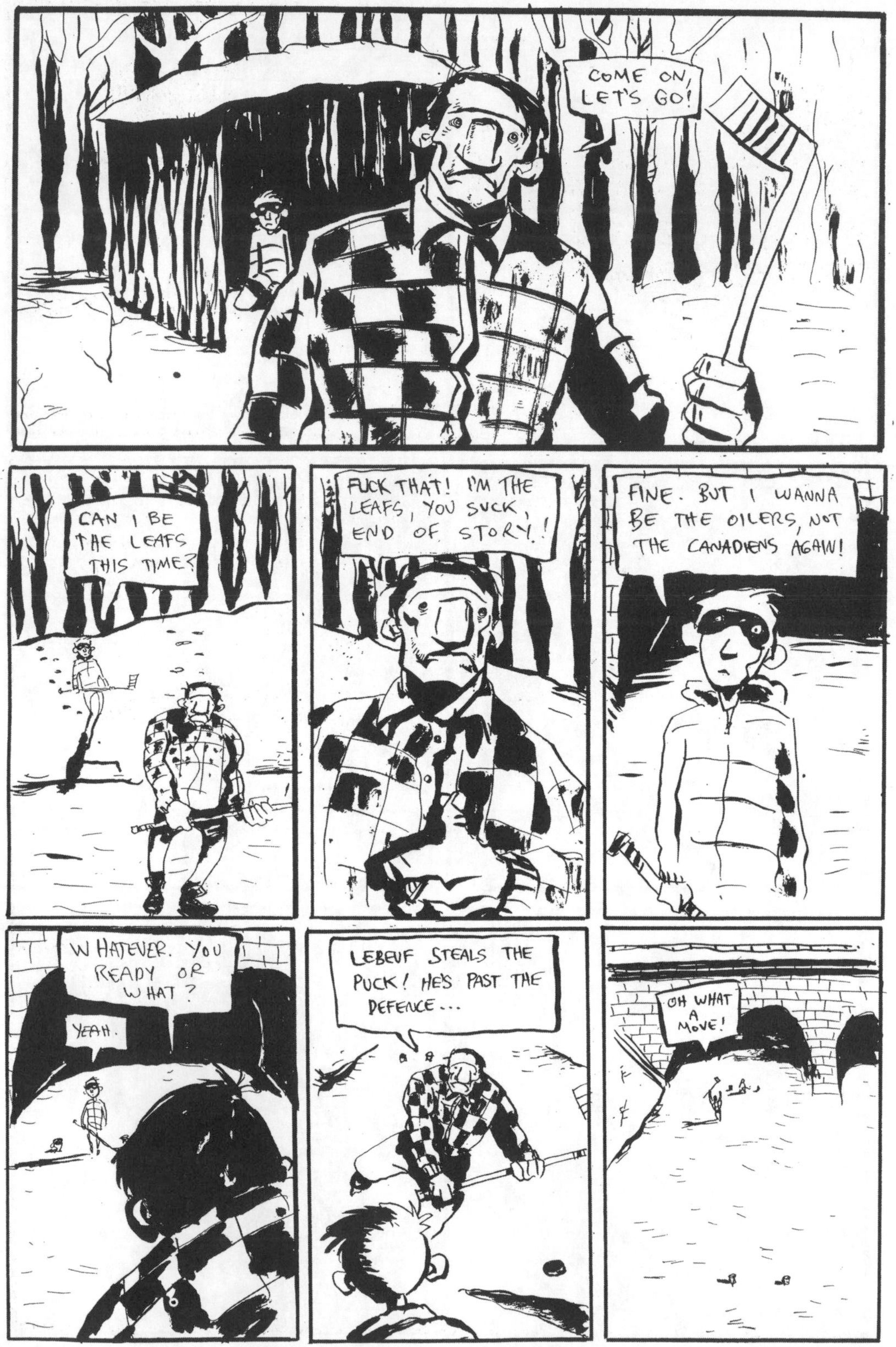
COME ON, LET'S GO!
CAN I BE THE LEAFS THIS TIME?
FUCK THAT! I'M THE LEAFS, YOU SUCK, END OF STORY!
FINE. BUT I WANNA BE THE OILERS, NOT THE CANADIENS AGAIN!
WHATEVER. YOU READY OR WHAT?
YEAH.
LEBEUF STEALS THE PUCK! HE'S PAST THE DEFENCE...
OH WHAT A MOVE!

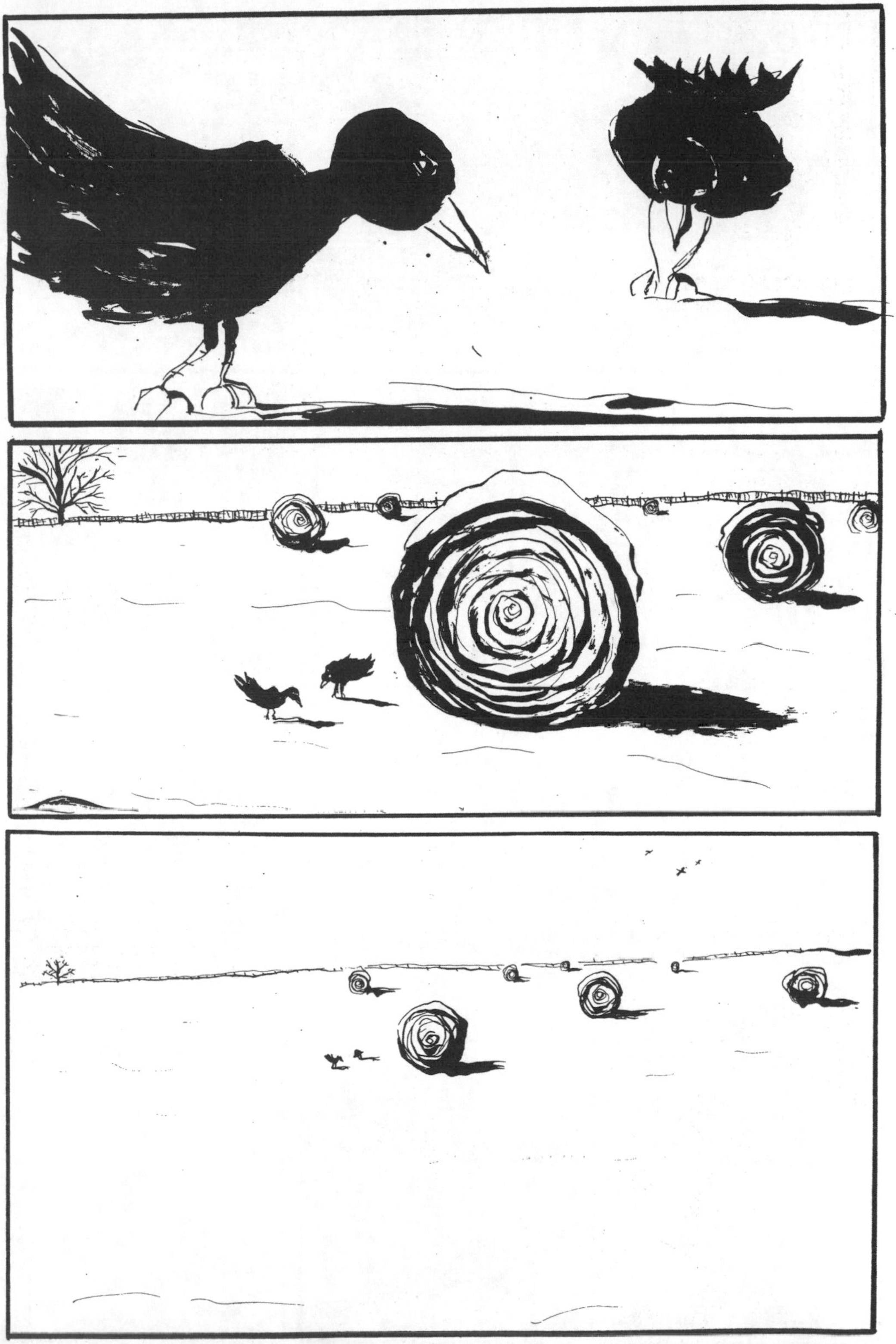

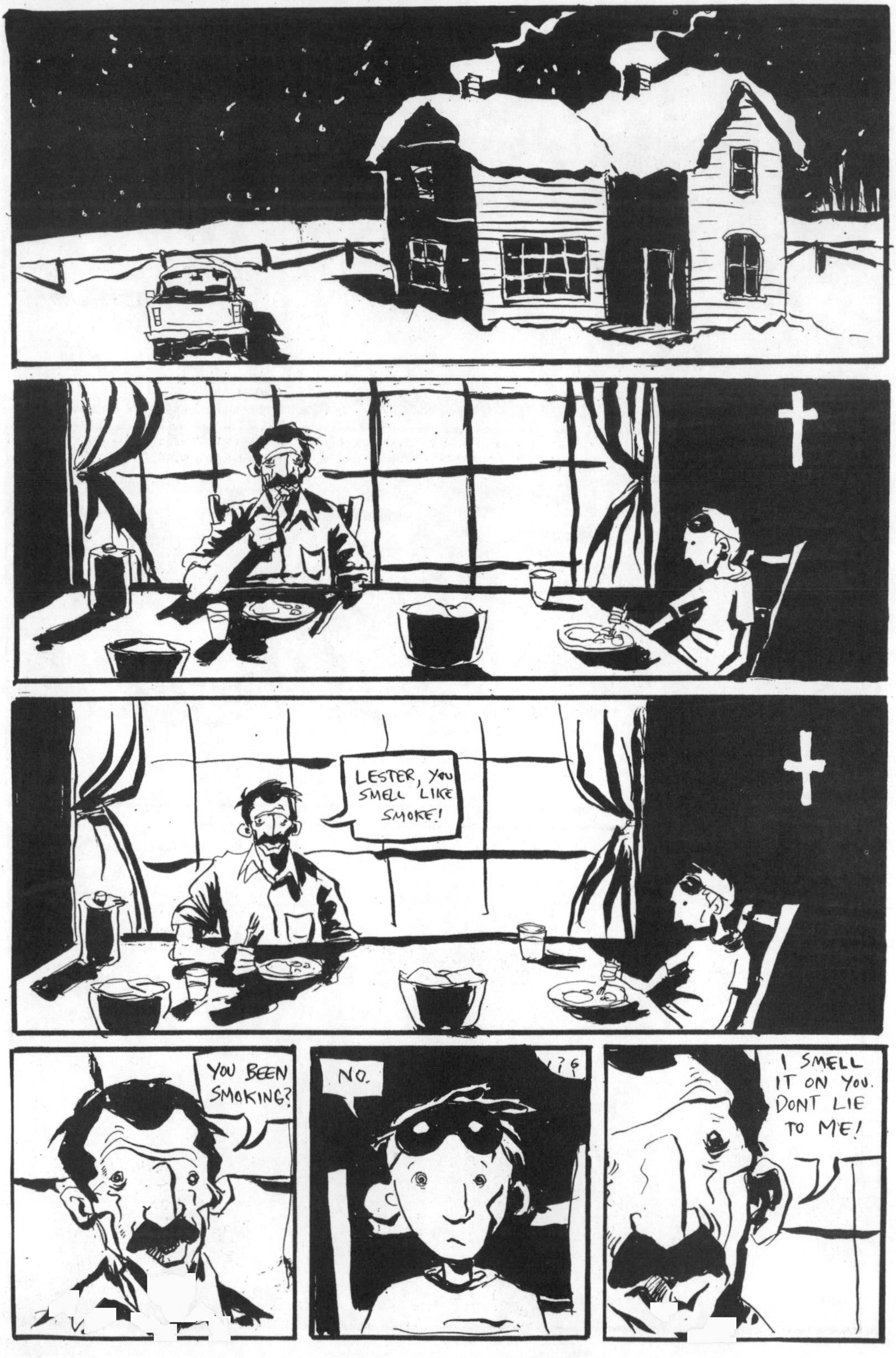

LESTER, YOU SMELL LIKE SMOKE!
YOU BEEN SMOKING?
NO.
I SMELL IT ON YOU. DONT LIE TO ME!

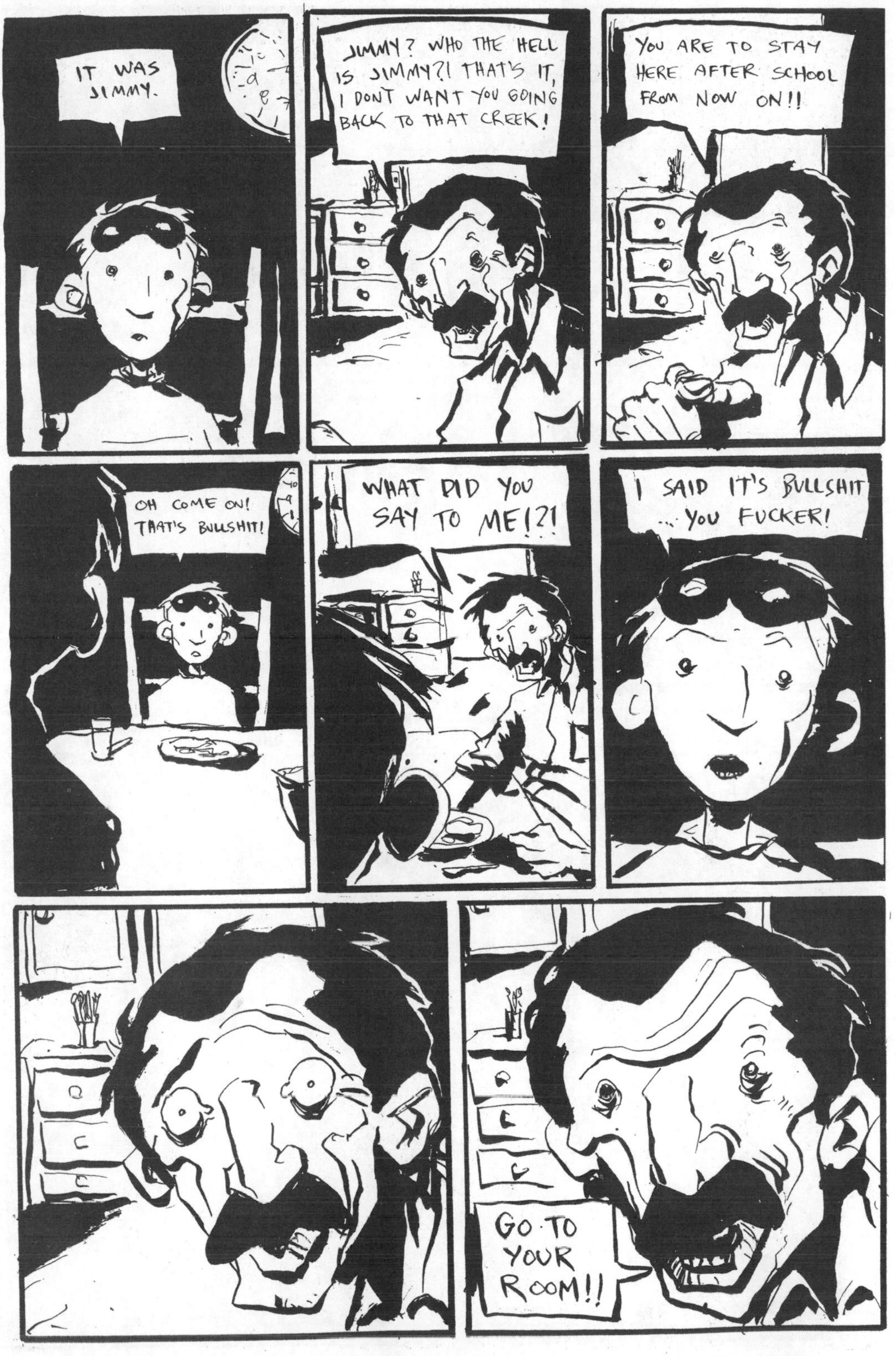
IT WAS JIMMY.
JIMMY? WHO THE HELL IS JIMMY?! THAT'S IT, I DON'T WANT YOU GOING BACK TO THAT CREEK!
YOU ARE TO STAY HERE AFTER SCHOOL FROM NOW ON!!
OH COME ON! THAT'S BULLSHIT!
WHAT DID YOU SAY TO ME!?!
I SAID IT'S BULLSHIT ... YOU FUCKER!
GO TO YOUR ROOM!!

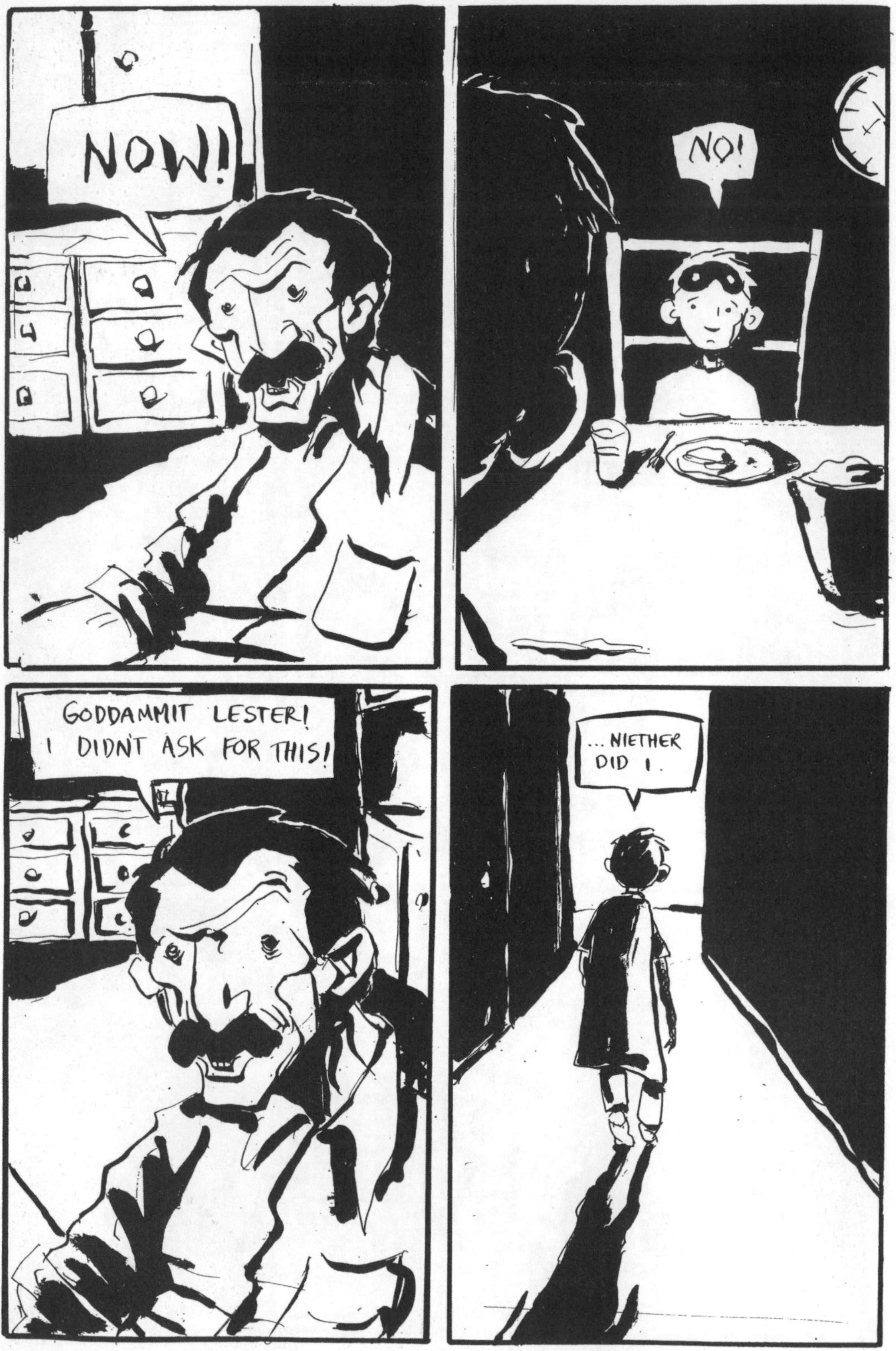
NOW!
NO!
GODDAMMIT LESTER! I DIDN'T ASK FOR THIS!
...NIETHER DID I.

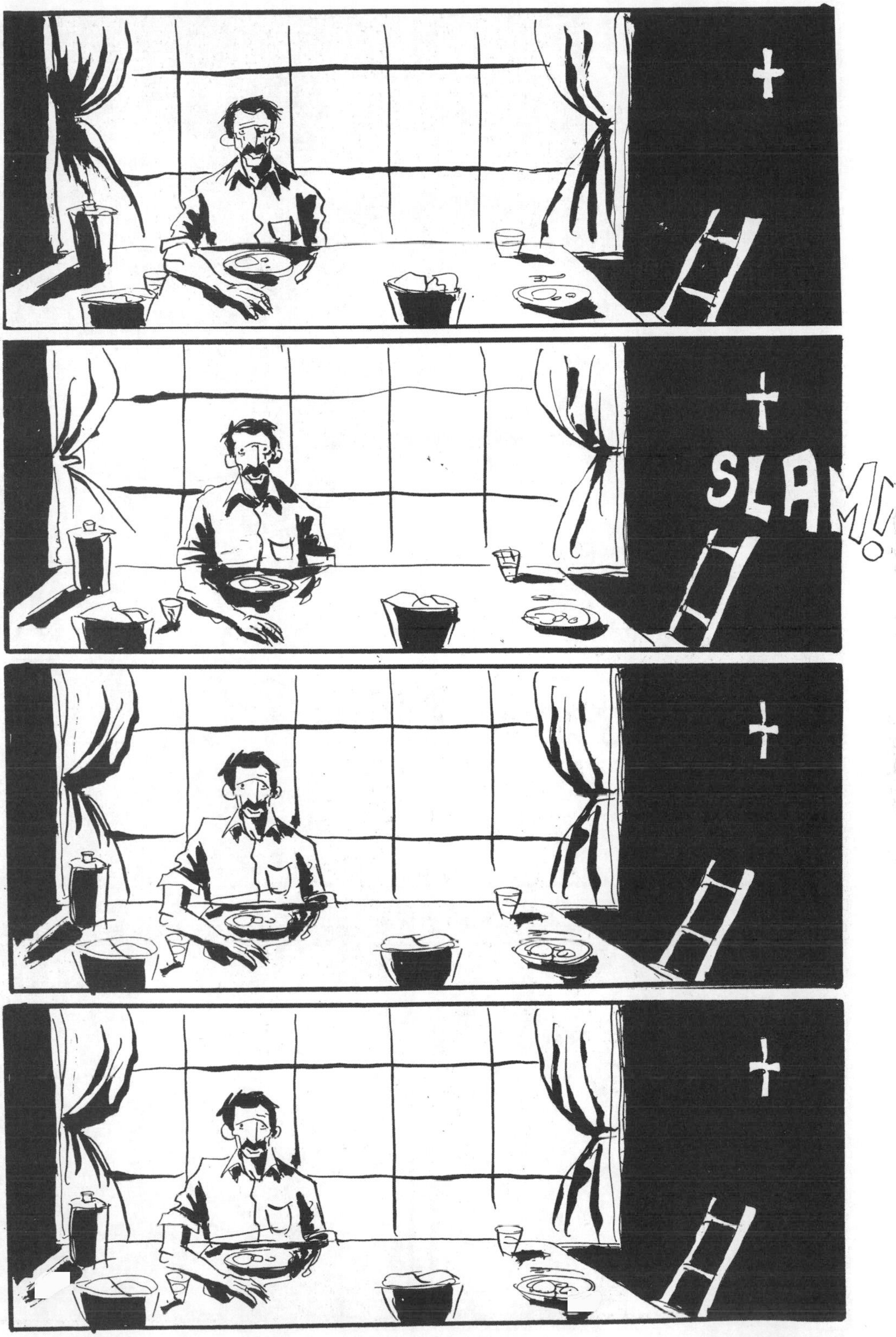
SLAM!

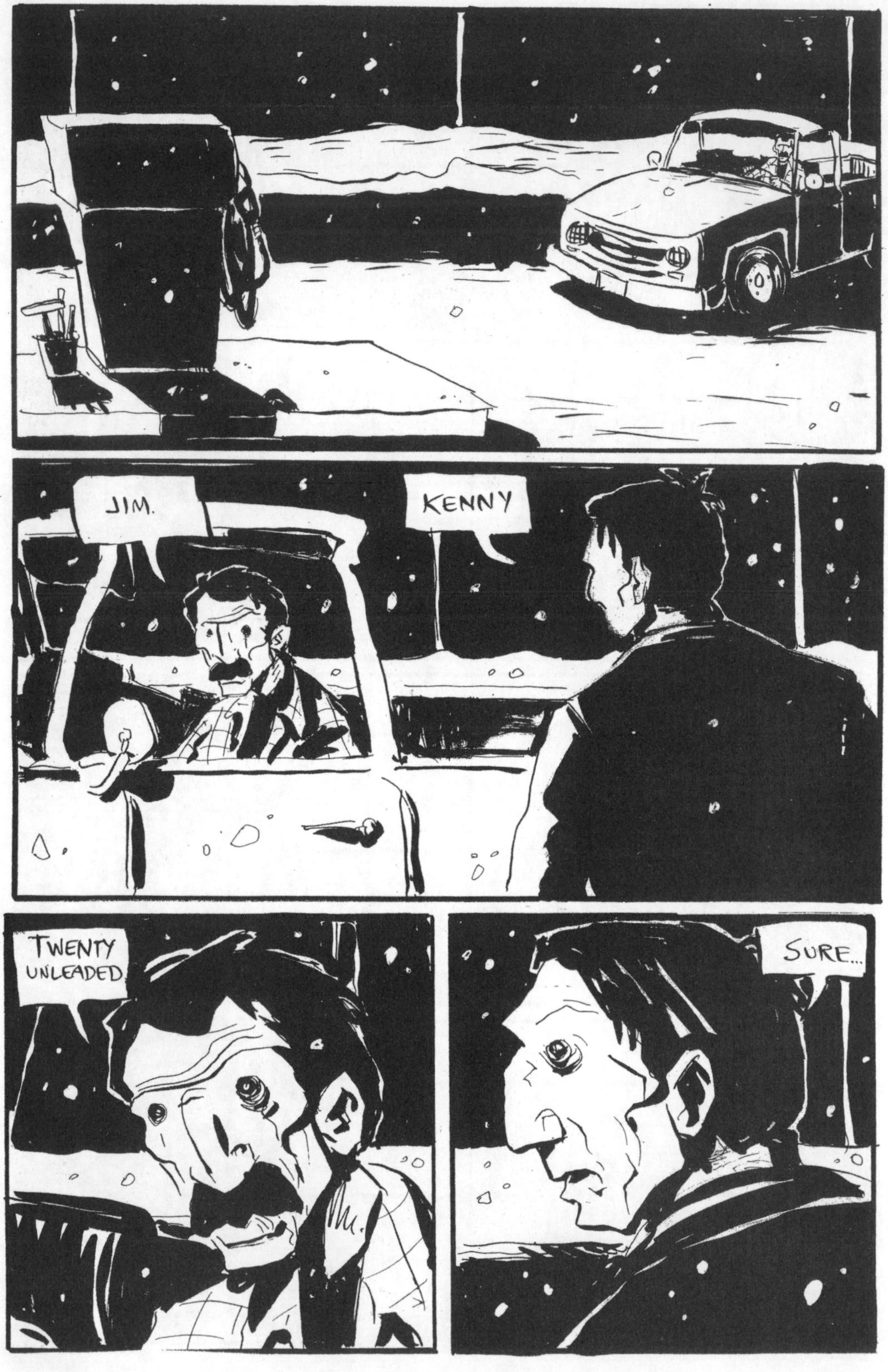
JIM.
KENNY
TWENTY UNLEADED
SURE...

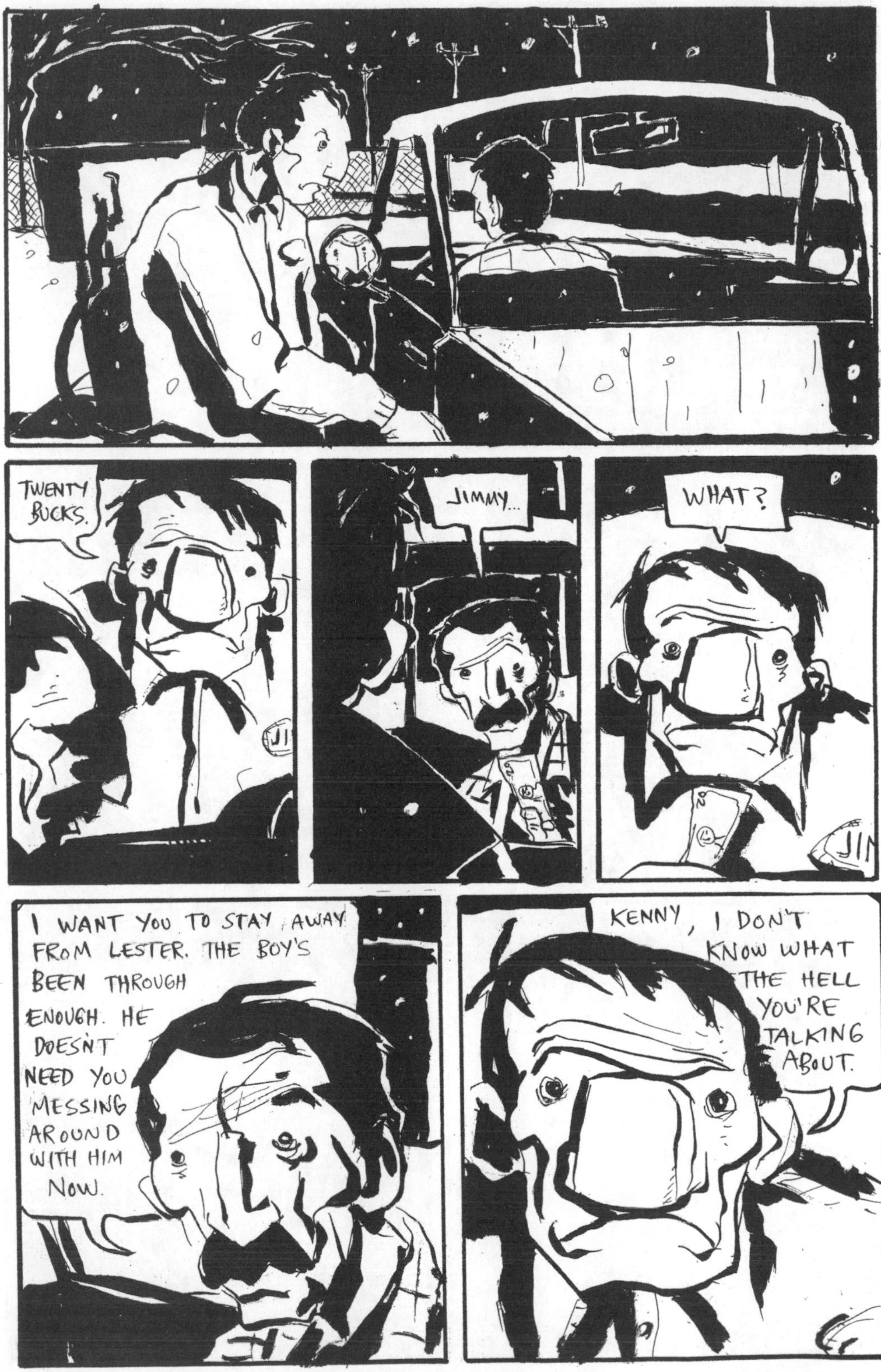
TWENTY BUCKS.
JIMMY...
WHAT?
I WANT YOU TO STAY AWAY FROM LESTER. THE BOY'S BEEN THROUGH ENOUGH. HE DOESN'T NEED YOU MESSING AROUND WITH HIM NOW.
KENNY, I DON'T KNOW WHAT THE HELL YOU'RE TALKING ABOUT.

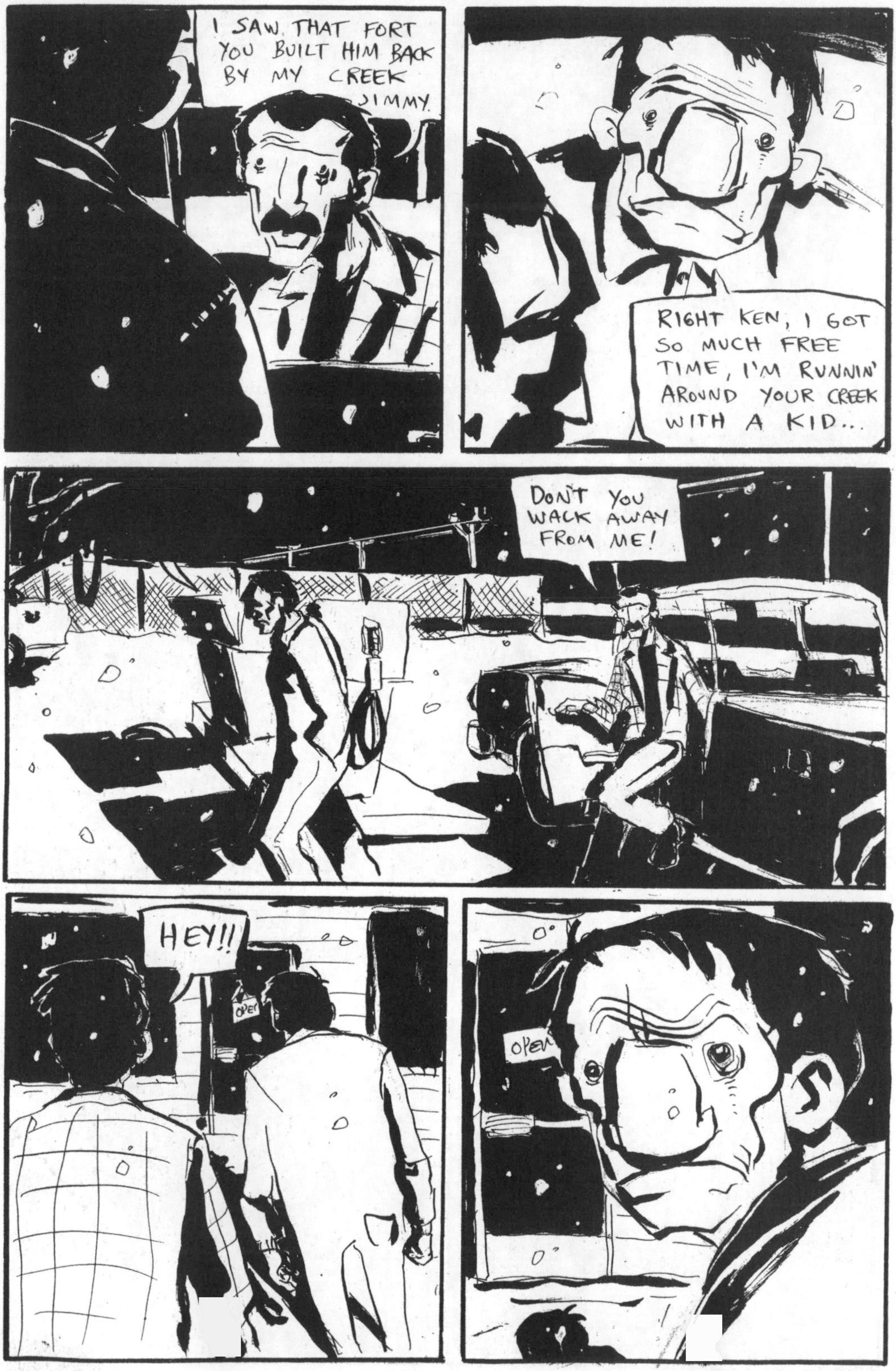
I SAW THAT FORT YOU BUILT HIM BACK BY MY CREEK JIMMY.
RIGHT KEN, I GOT SO MUCH FREE TIME, I'M RUNNIN' AROUND YOUR CREEK WITH A KID...
DON'T YOU WALK AWAY FROM ME!
HEY!!
OPEN
OPEN

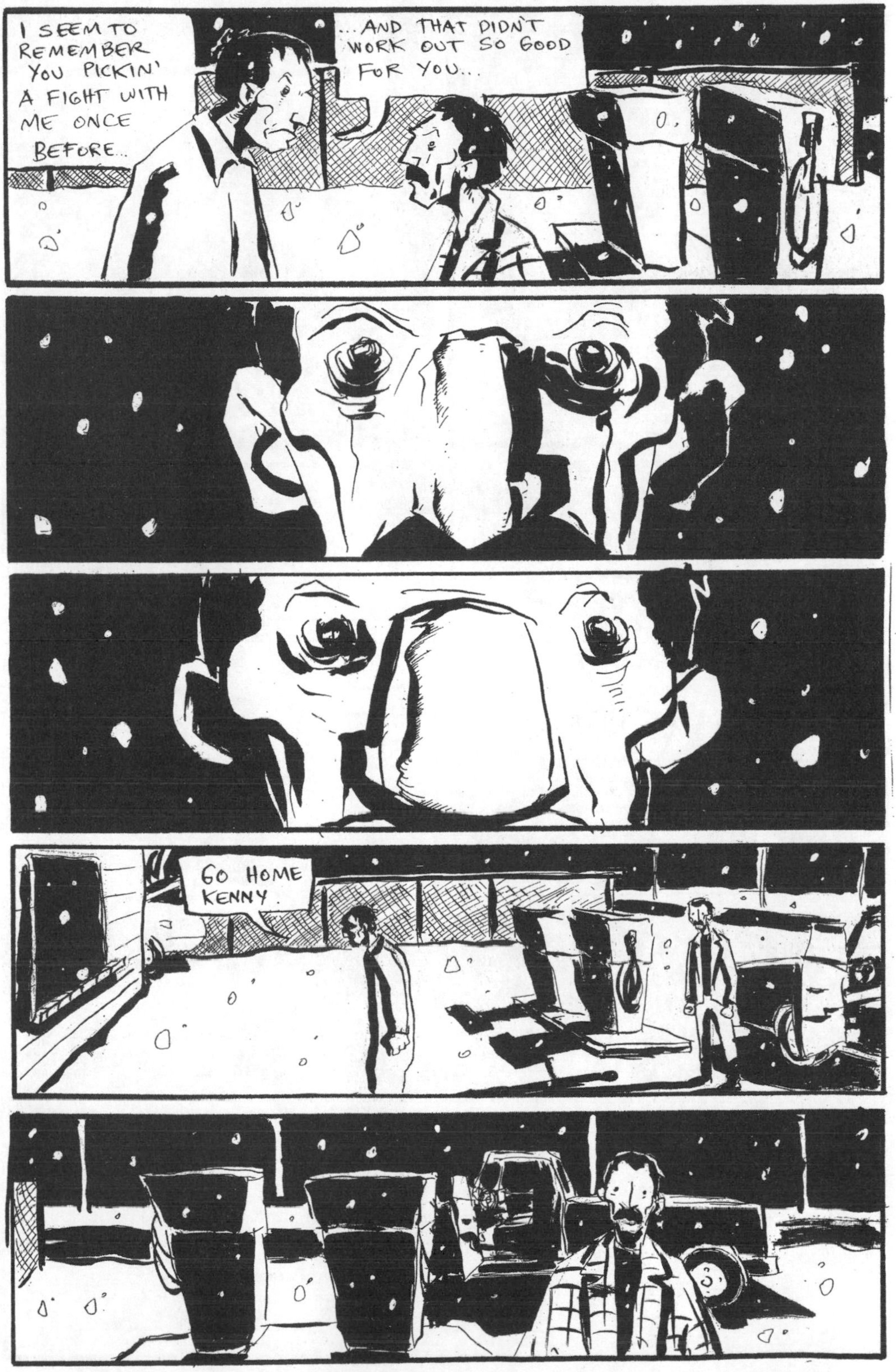
I SEEM TO REMEMBER YOU PICKIN' A FIGHT WITH ME ONCE BEFORE...
...AND THAT DIDN'T WORK OUT SO GOOD FOR YOU...
GO HOME KENNY.

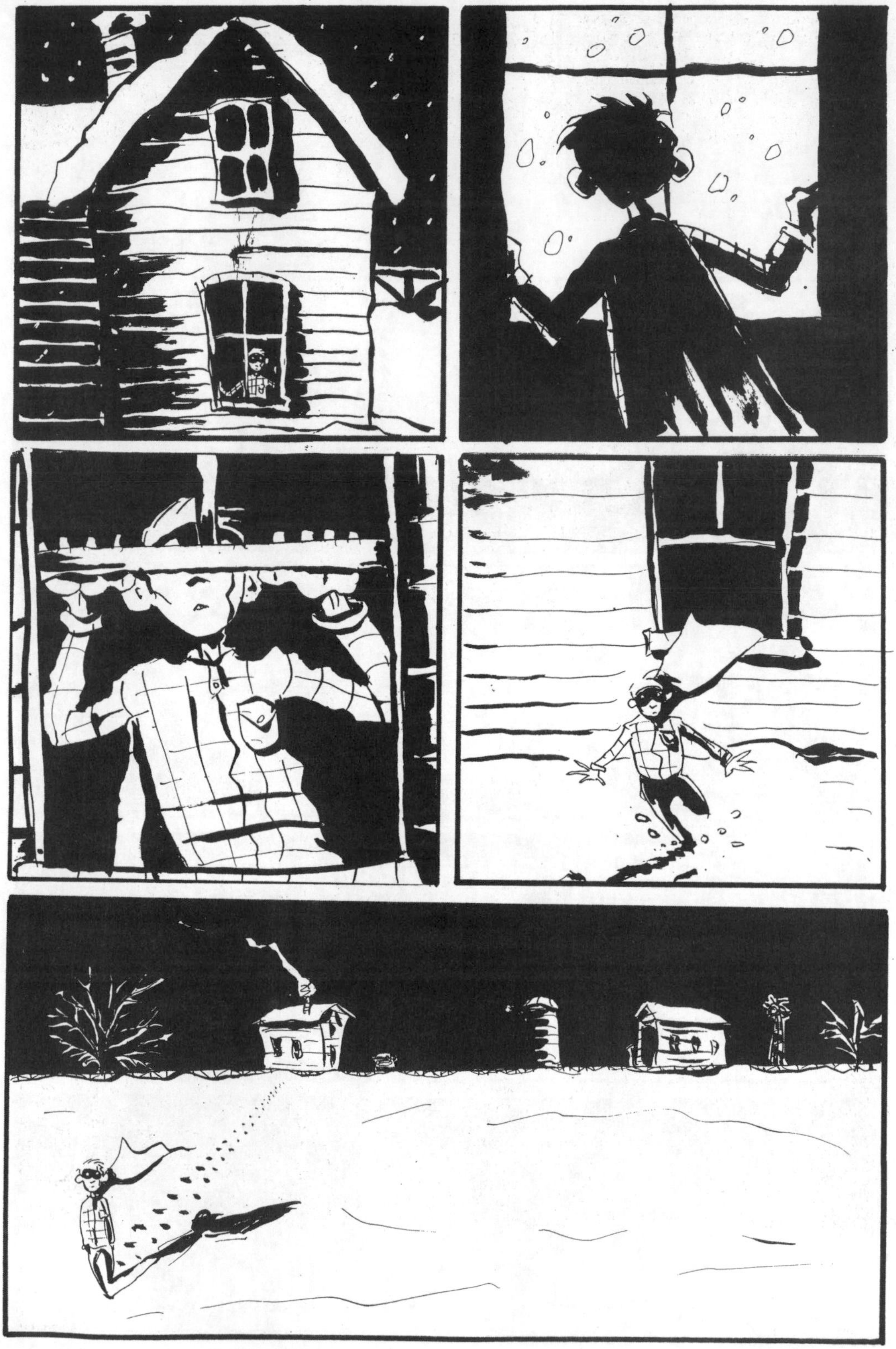

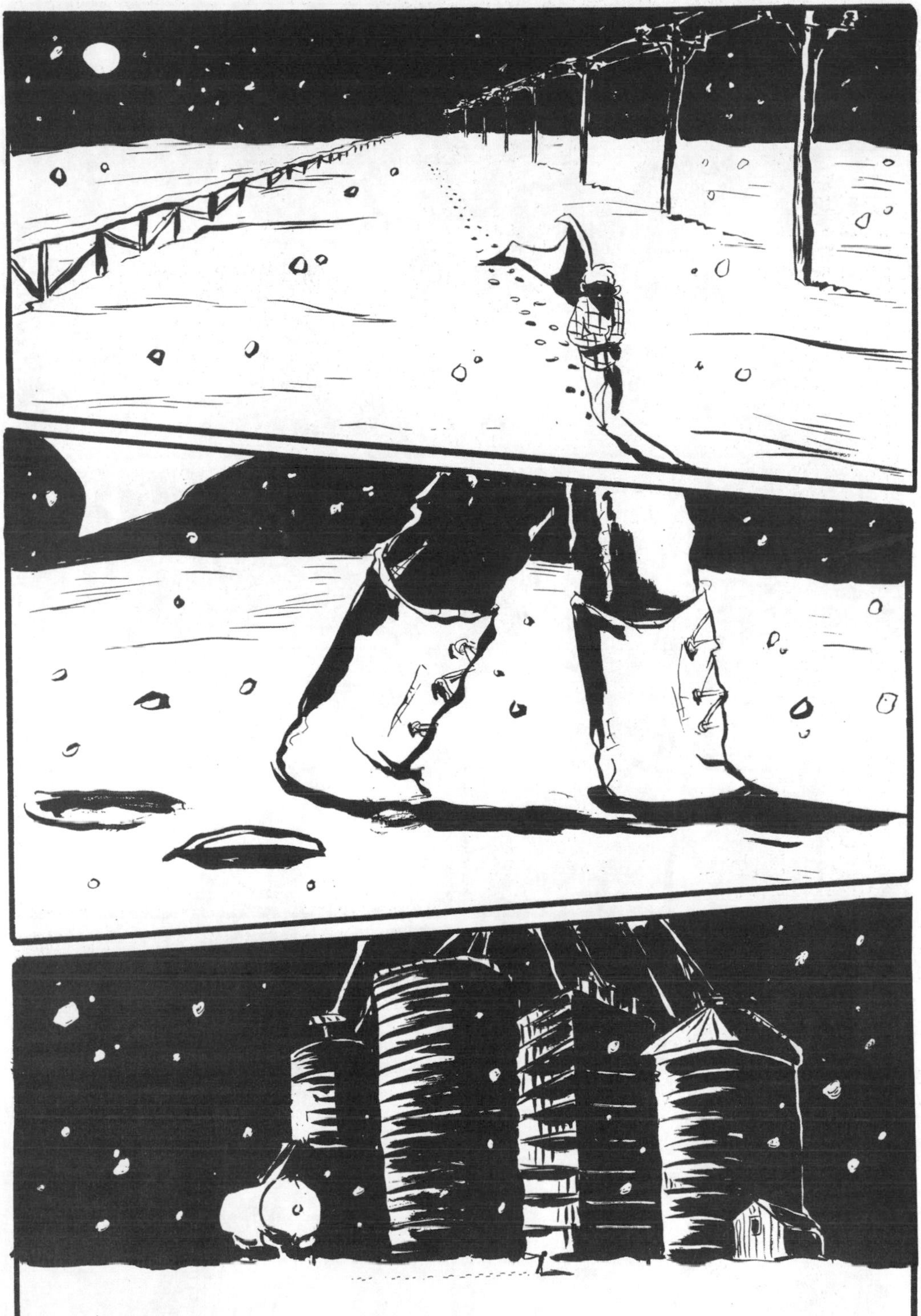

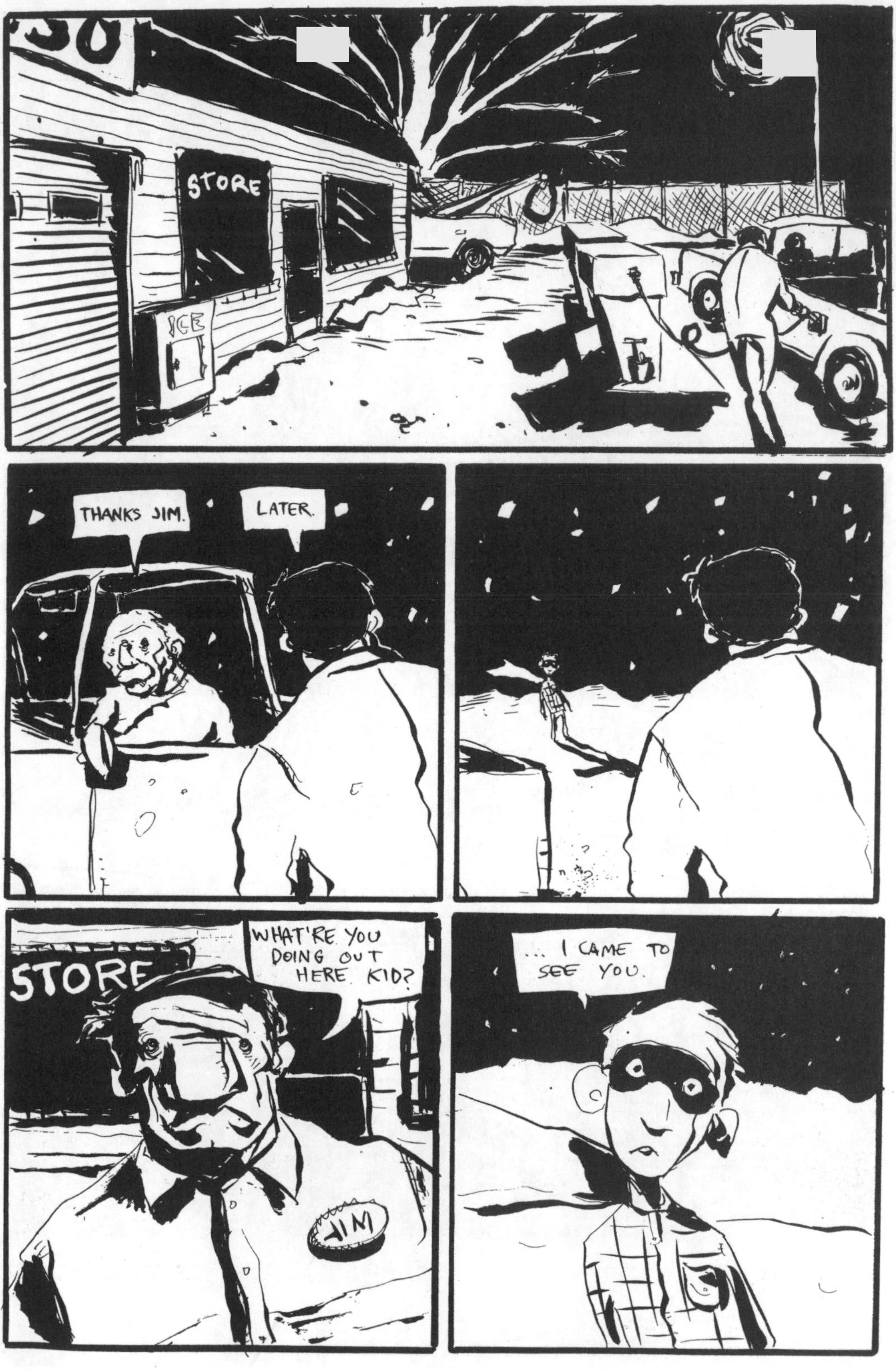
STORE
ICE
THANKS JIM.
LATER.
STORE
WHAT'RE YOU DOING OUT HERE KID?
... I CAME TO SEE YOU.

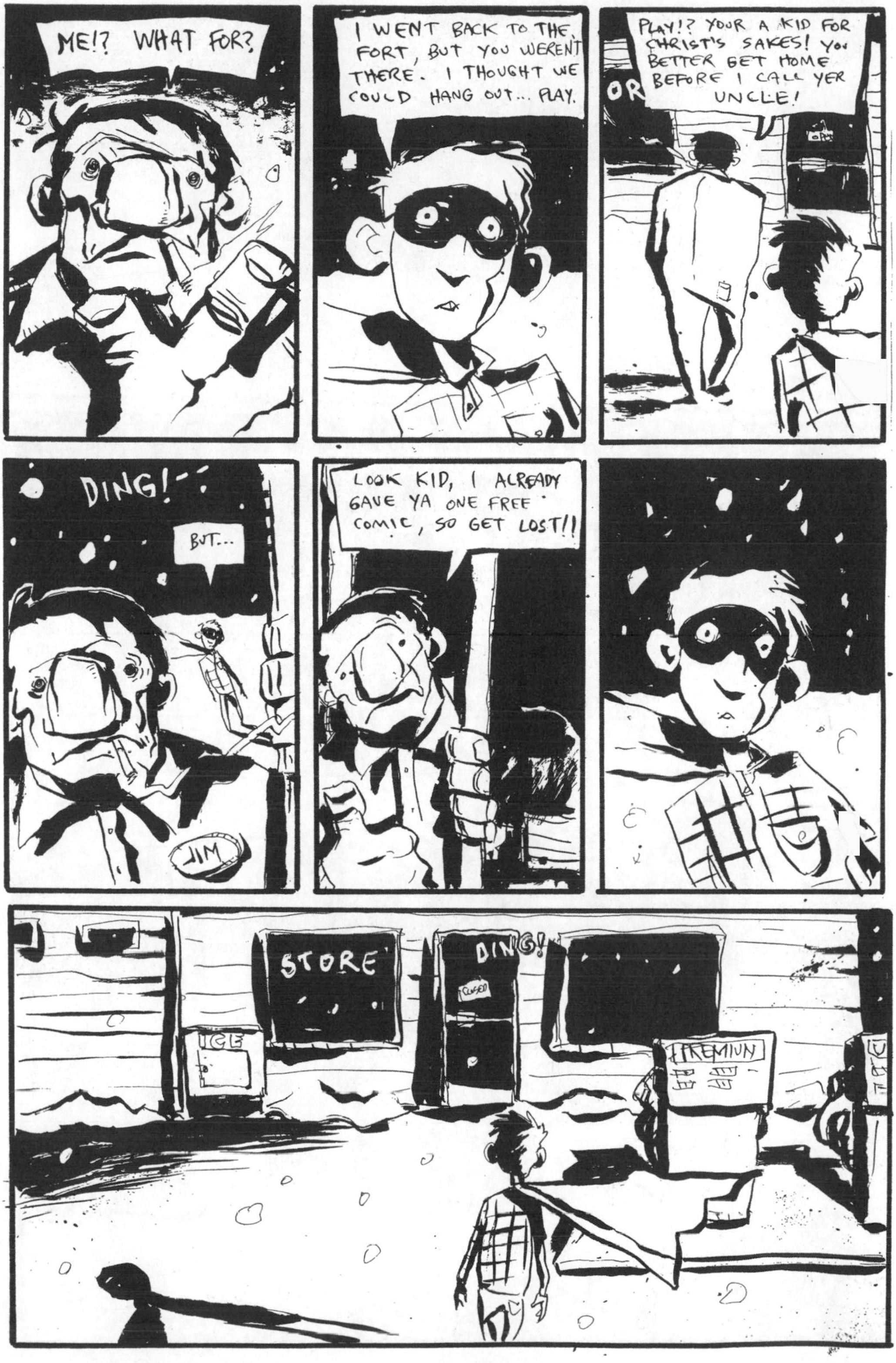
ME!? WHAT FOR?
I WENT BACK TO THE FORT, BUT YOU WERENT THERE. I THOUGHT WE COULD HANG OUT... PLAY.
PLAY!? YOUR A KID FOR CHRIST'S SAKES! YOU BETTER GET HOME BEFORE I CALL YER UNCLE!
DING!
BUT...
JIM
LOOK KID, I ALREADY GAVE YA ONE FREE COMIC, SO GET LOST!!
STORE
DING!
CLOSED
ICE
PREMIUM

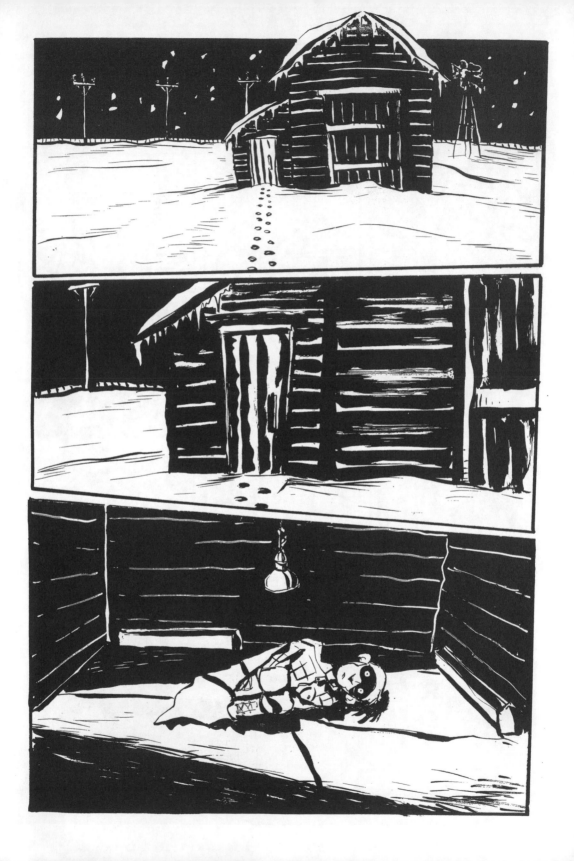

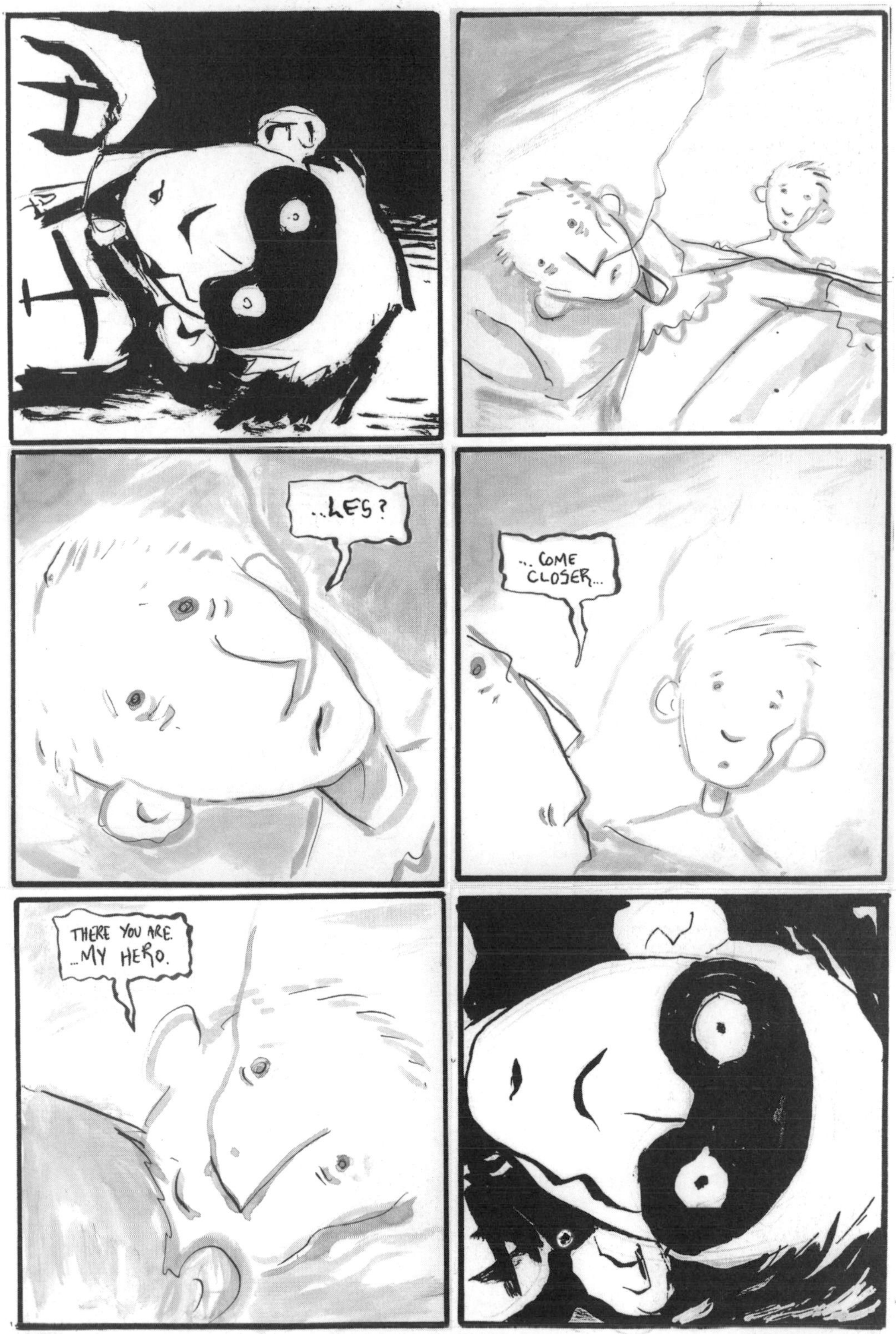
...LES?
... COME CLOSER...
THERE YOU ARE.
...MY HERO.

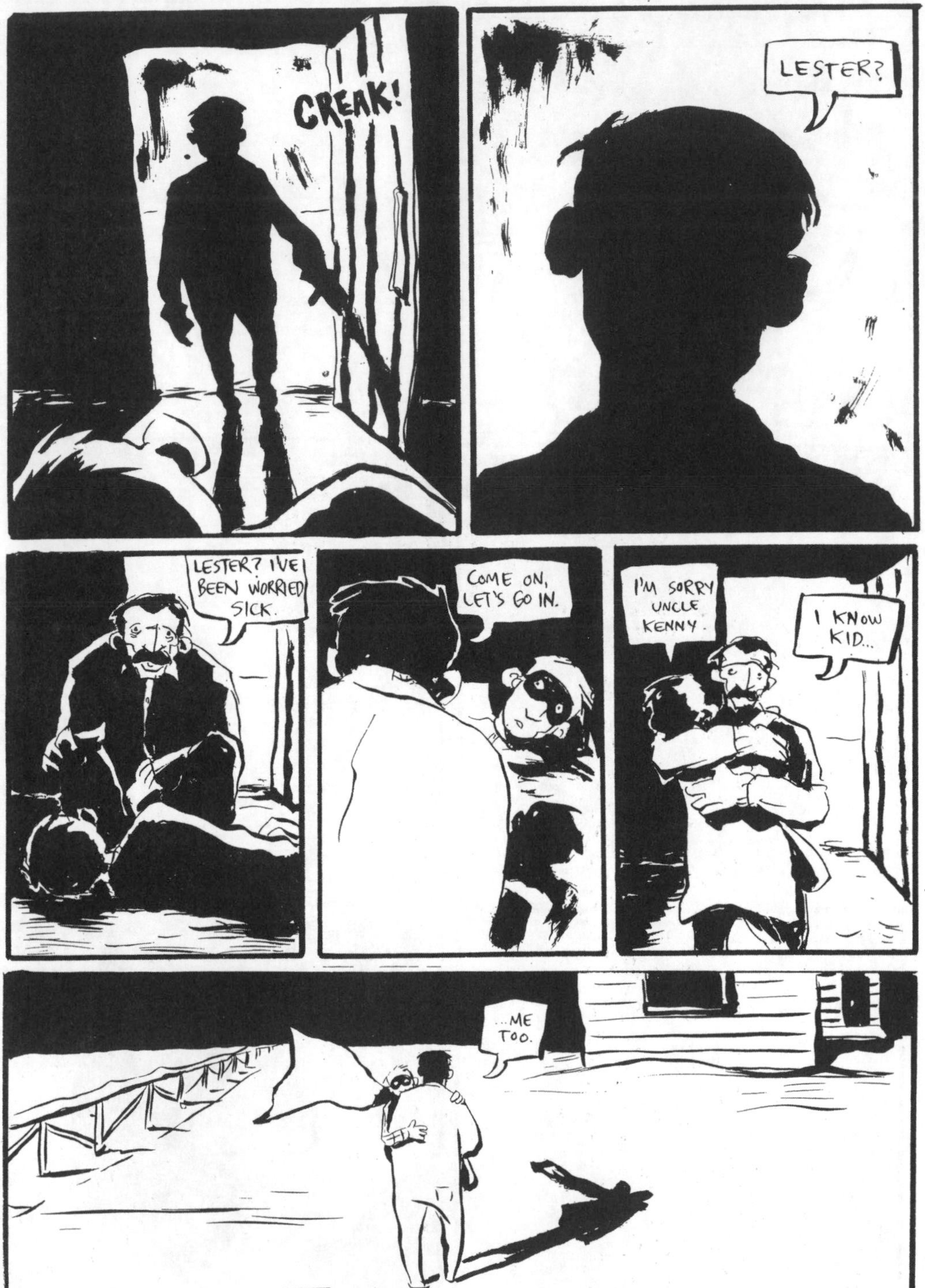
CREAK!
LESTER?
LESTER? I'VE BEEN WORRIED SICK.
COME ON, LET'S GO IN.
I'M SORRY UNCLE KENNY.
I KNOW KID...
...ME TOO.

SPRING

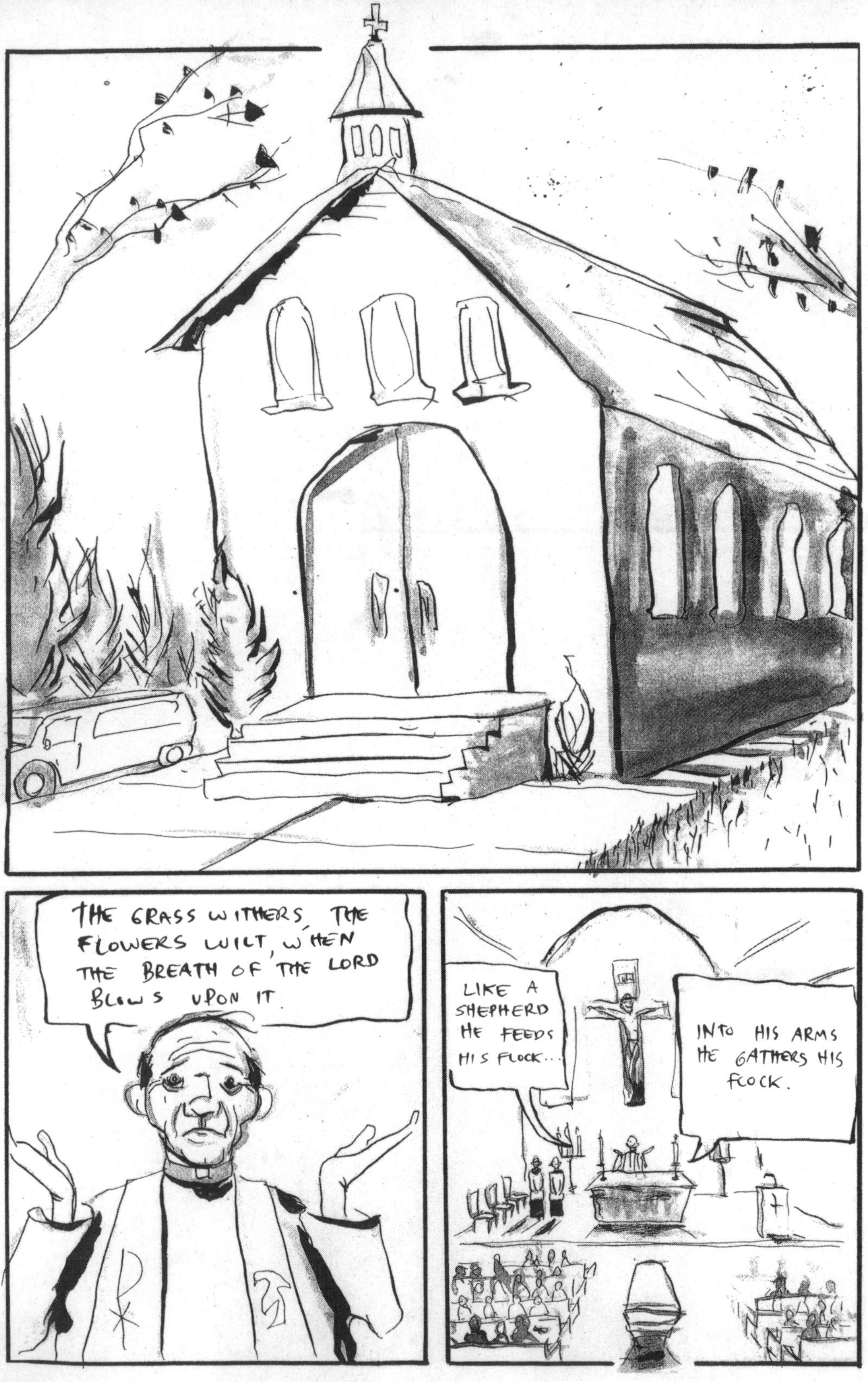
THE GRASS WITHERS, THE FLOWERS WILT, WHEN THE BREATH OF THE LORD BLOWS UPON IT.
LIKE A SHEPHERD HE FEEDS HIS FLOCK...
INTO HIS ARMS HE GATHERS HIS FLOCK.

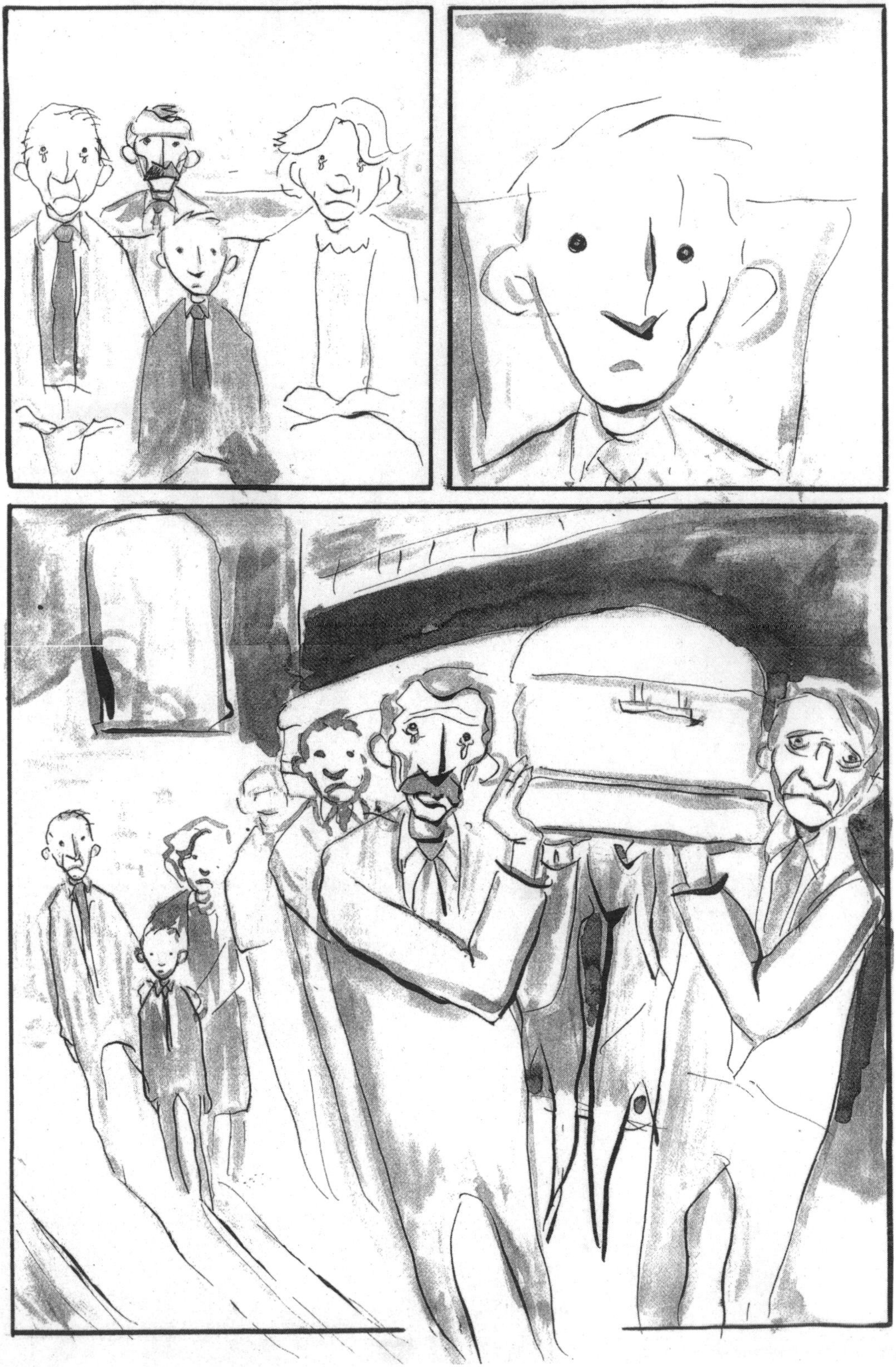

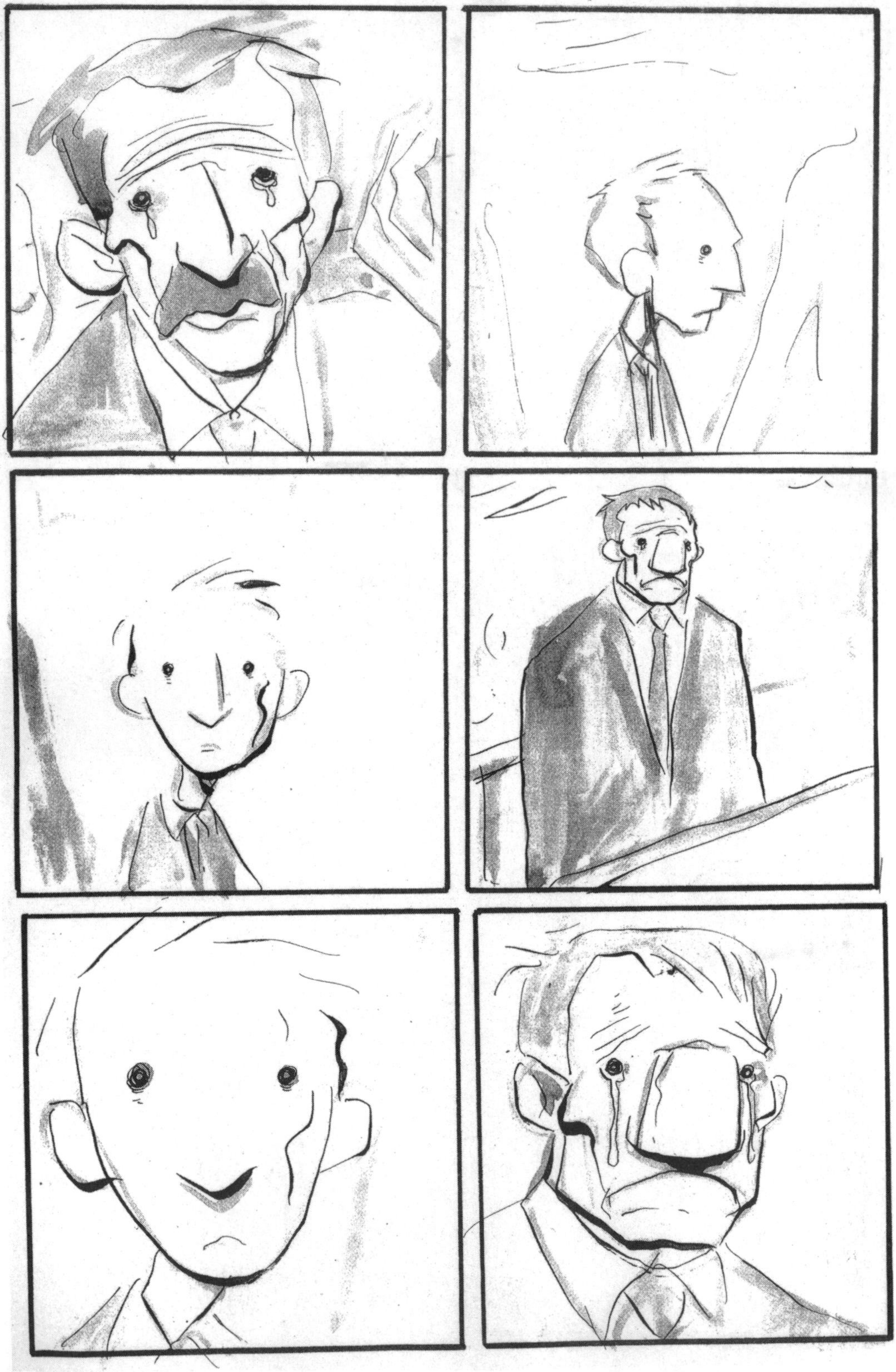

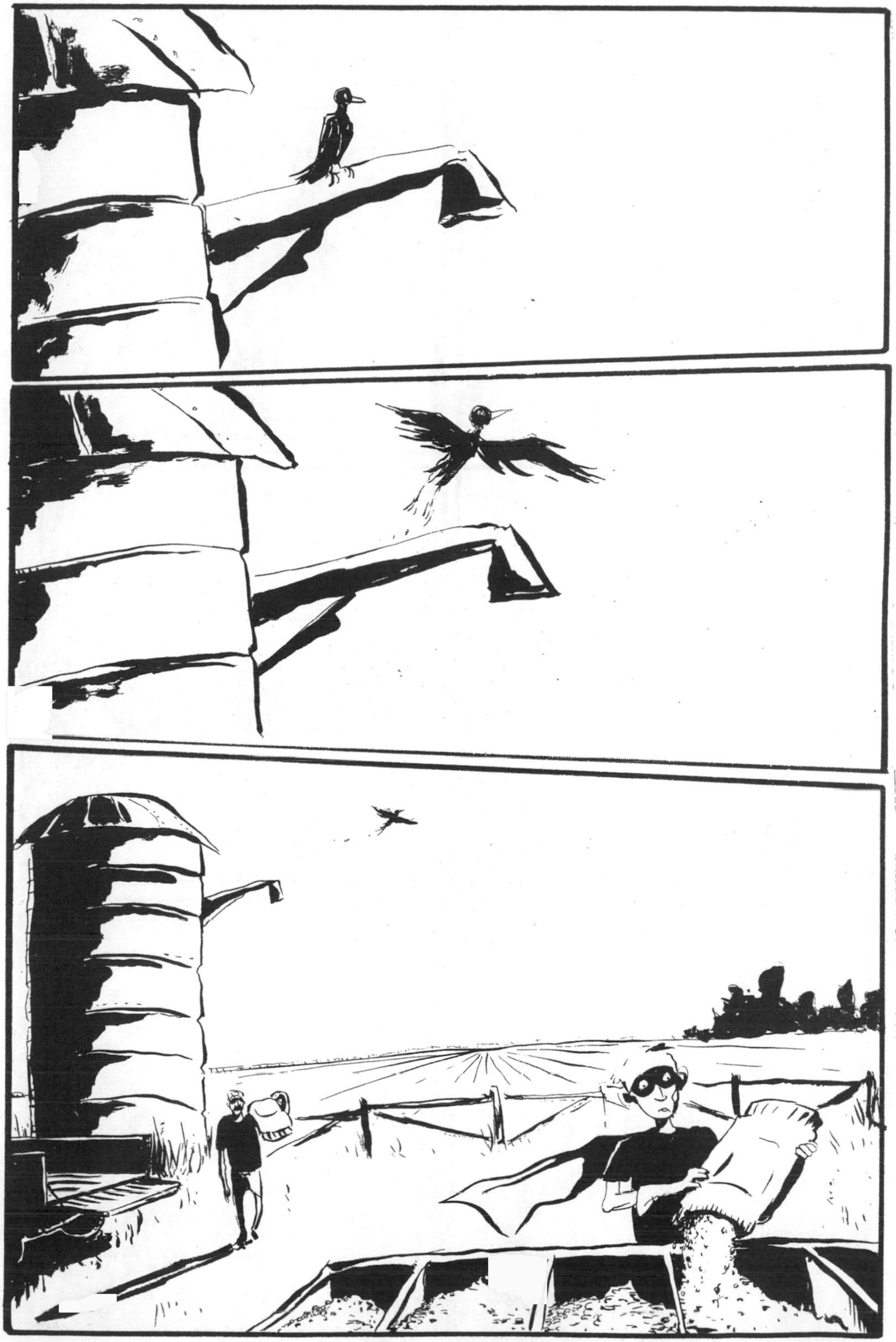

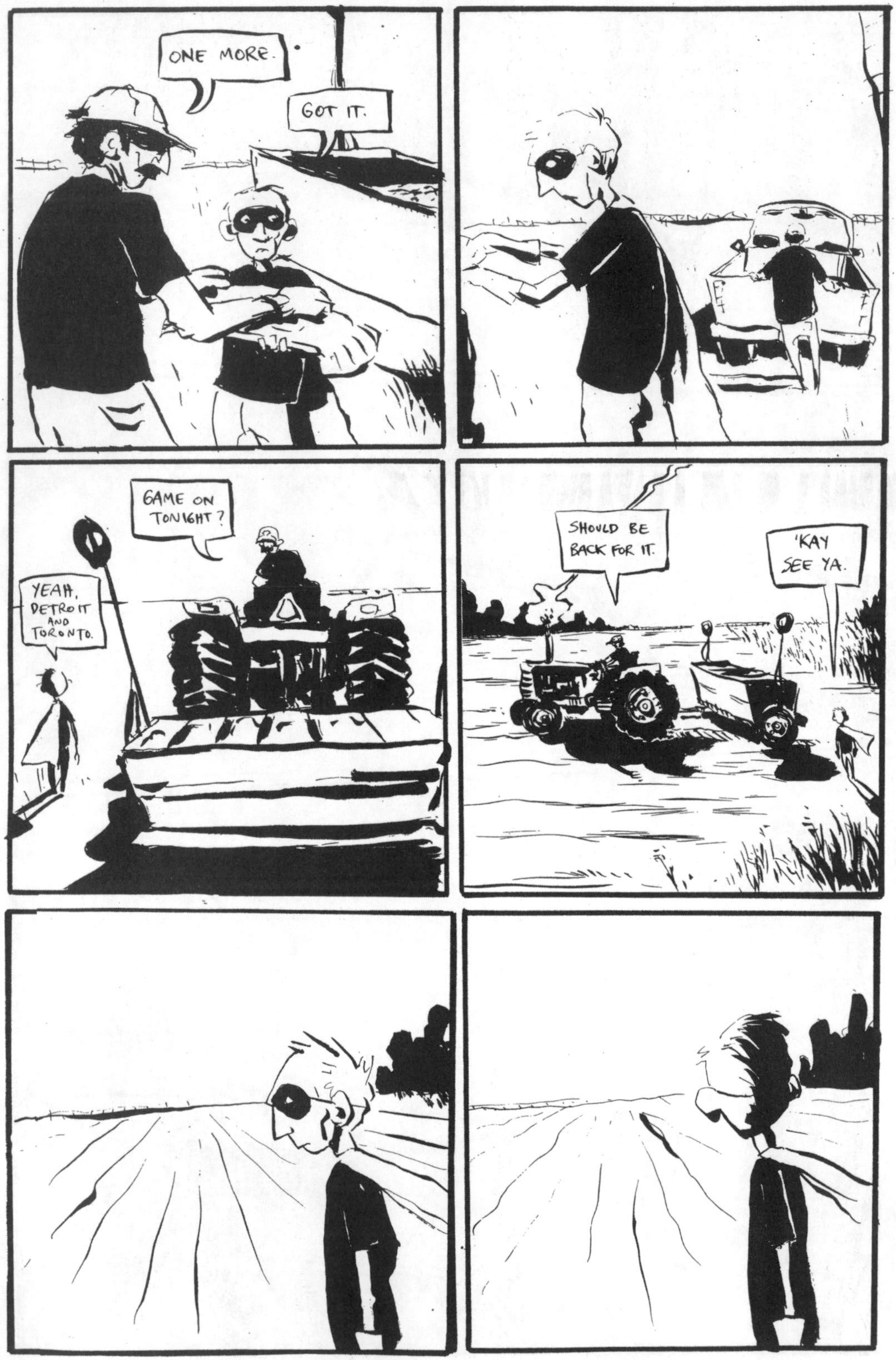
ONE MORE.
GOT IT.
GAME ON TONIGHT?
YEAH, DETROIT AND TORONTO.
SHOULD BE BACK FOR IT.
'KAY SEE YA.

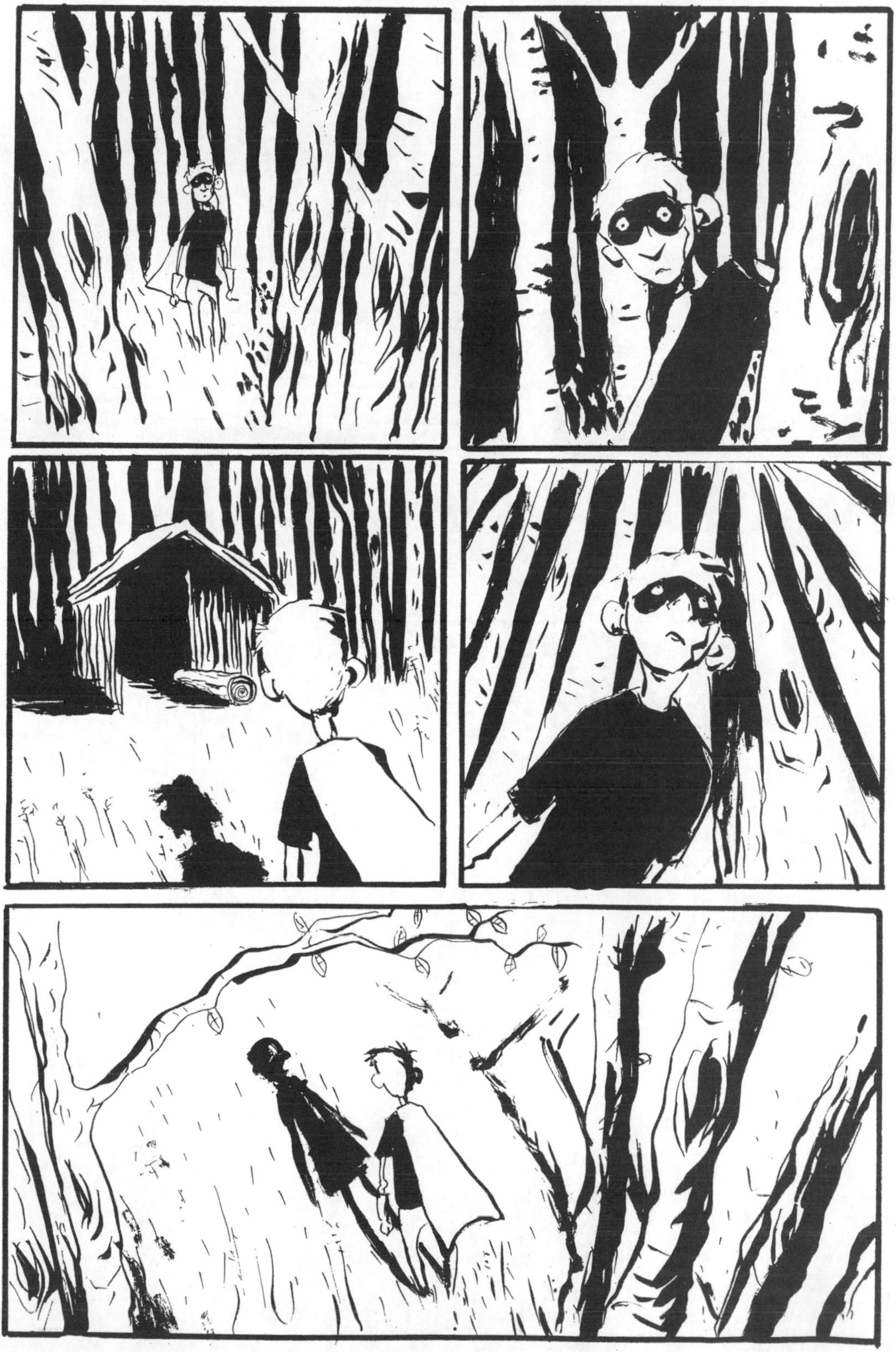

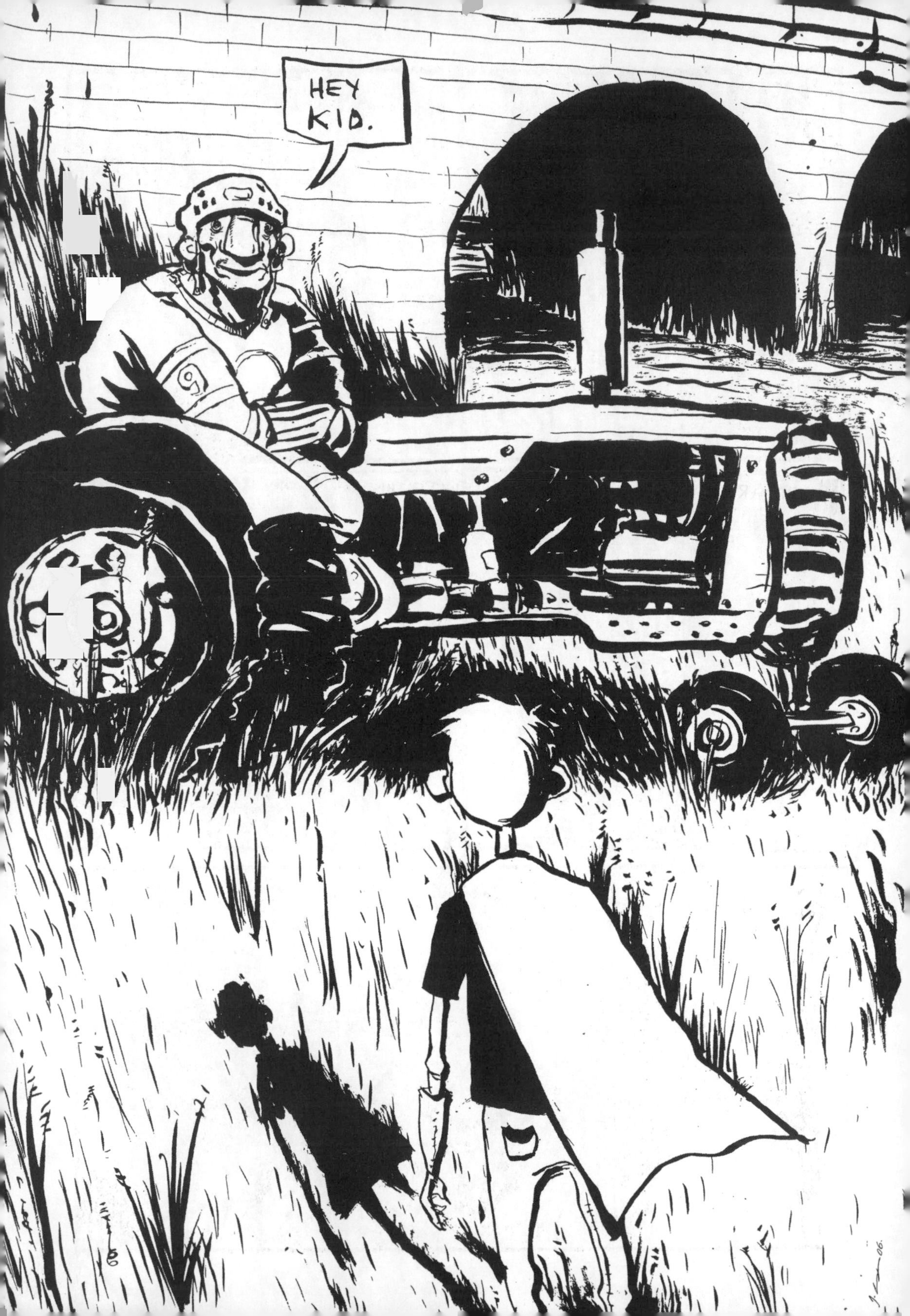
HEY KID.

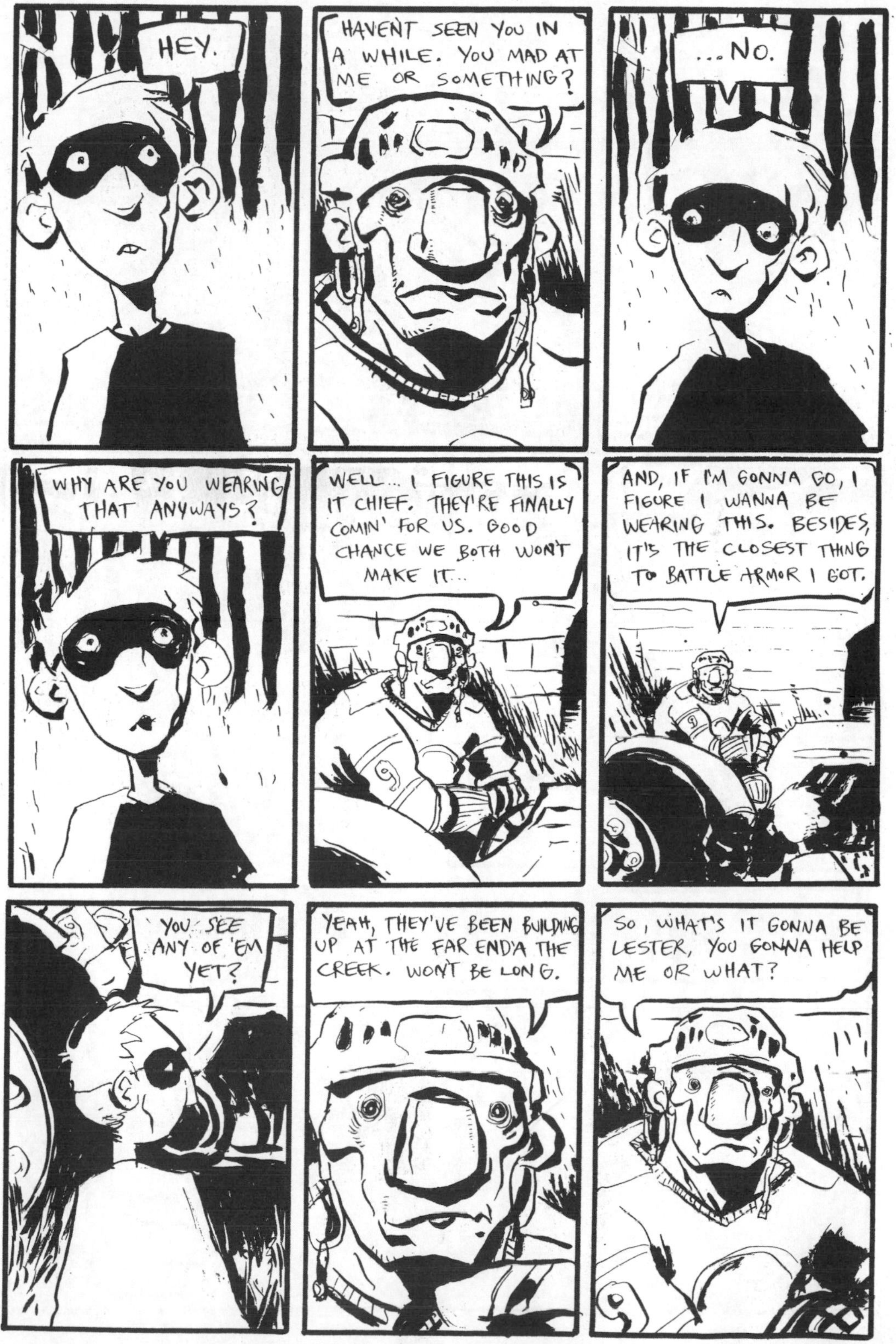
HEY.
HAVEN'T SEEN YOU IN A WHILE. YOU MAD AT ME OR SOMETHING?
...NO.
WHY ARE YOU WEARING THAT ANYWAYS?
WELL... I FIGURE THIS IS IT CHIEF. THEY'RE FINALLY COMIN' FOR US. GOOD CHANCE WE BOTH WON'T MAKE IT...
AND, IF I'M GONNA GO, I FIGURE I WANNA BE WEARING THIS. BESIDES, IT'S THE CLOSEST THING TO BATTLE ARMOR I GOT.
YOU SEE ANY OF 'EM YET?
YEAH, THEY'VE BEEN BUILDING UP AT THE FAR END'A THE CREEK. WON'T BE LONG.
SO, WHAT'S IT GONNA BE LESTER, YOU GONNA HELP ME OR WHAT?

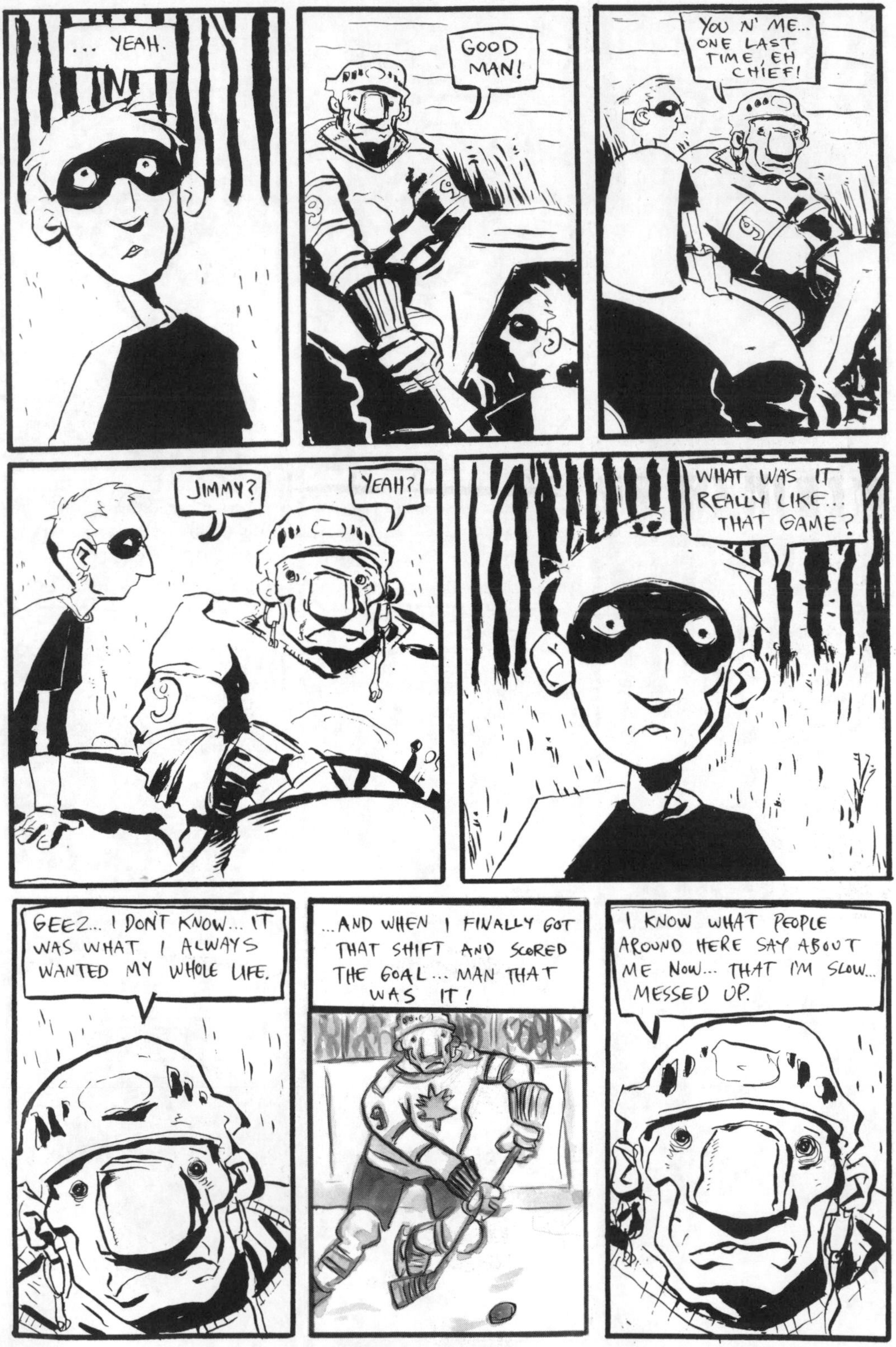

... YEAH.
GOOD MAN!
YOU N' ME... ONE LAST TIME, EH CHIEF!
JIMMY?
YEAH?
WHAT WAS IT REALLY LIKE... THAT GAME?
GEEZ... I DON'T KNOW... IT WAS WHAT I ALWAYS WANTED MY WHOLE LIFE.
...AND WHEN I FINALLY GOT THAT SHIFT AND SCORED THE GOAL... MAN THAT WAS IT!
I KNOW WHAT PEOPLE AROUND HERE SAY ABOUT ME NOW... THAT I'M SLOW... MESSED UP.

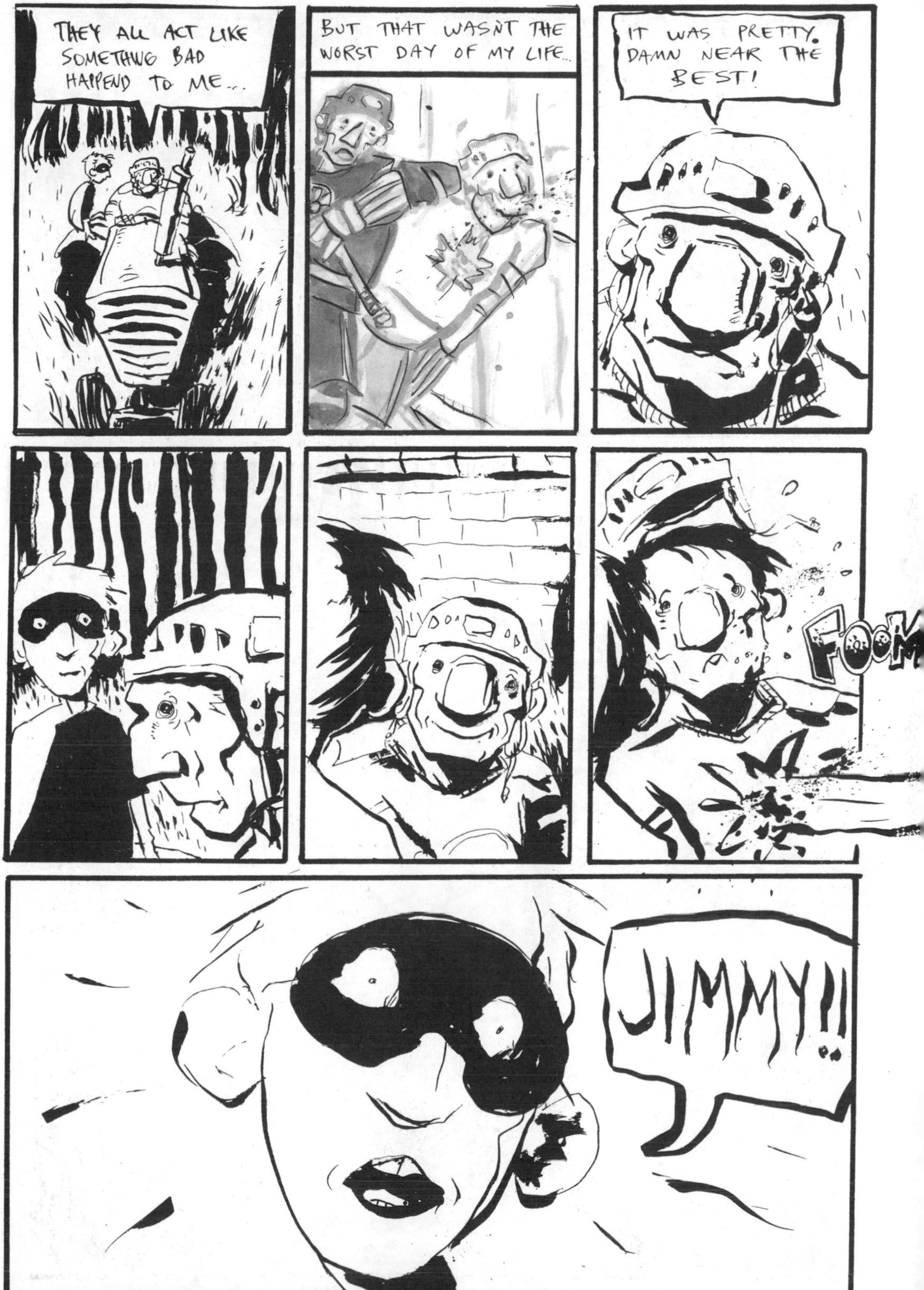
THEY ALL ACT LIKE SOMETHING BAD HAPPEND TO ME...
BUT THAT WASN'T THE WORST DAY OF MY LIFE...
IT WAS PRETTY DAMN NEAR THE BEST!
FOOM
JIMMY!!

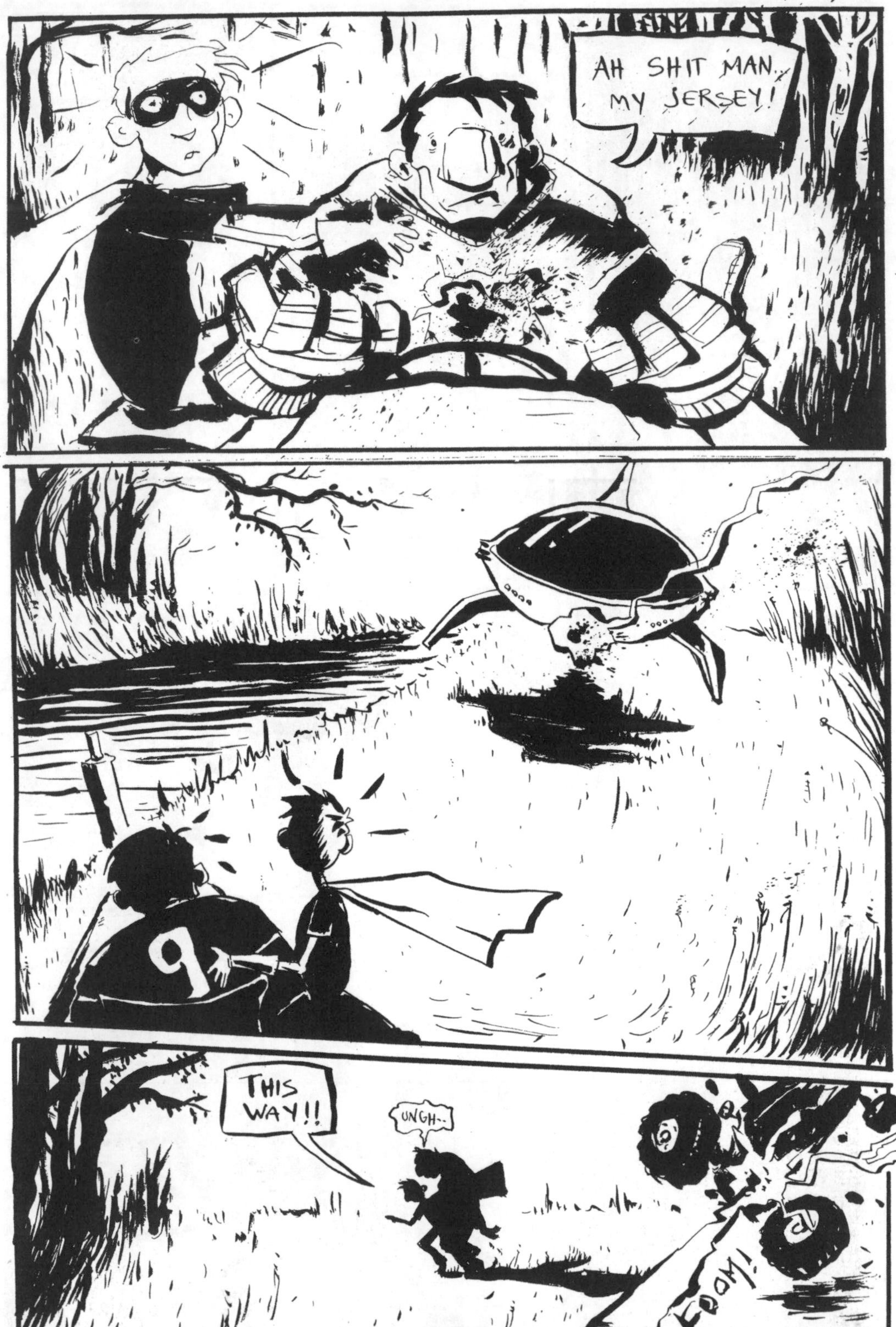
AH SHIT MAN, MY JERSEY!
9
THIS WAY!!
UNGH--
FOOM!

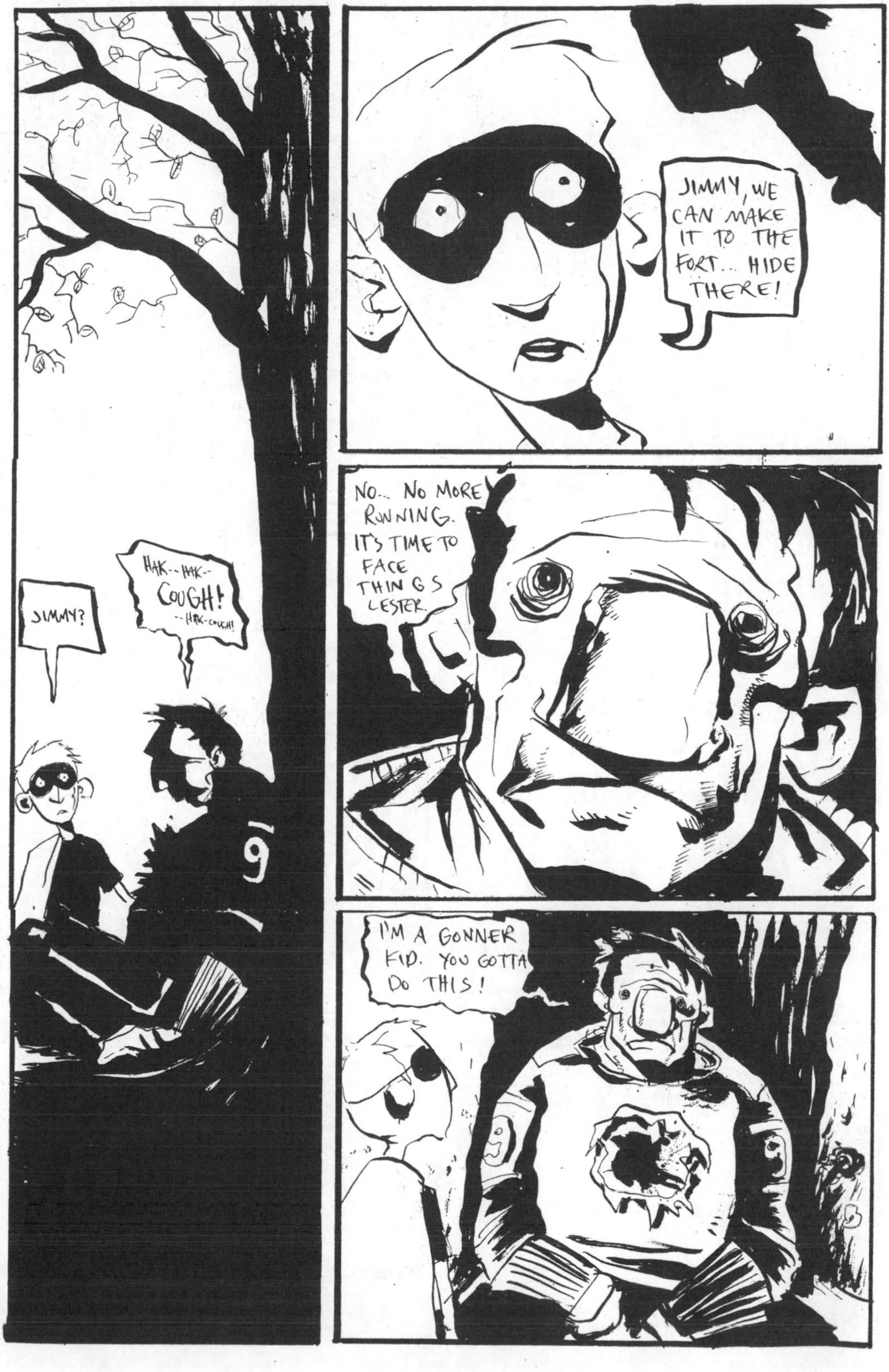
JIMMY, WE CAN MAKE IT TO THE FORT... HIDE THERE!
NO... NO MORE RUNNING. IT'S TIME TO FACE THINGS LESTER.
JIMMY?
HAK--HAK-- COUGH! --HAK-COUGH!
I'M A GONNER KID. YOU GOTTA DO THIS!

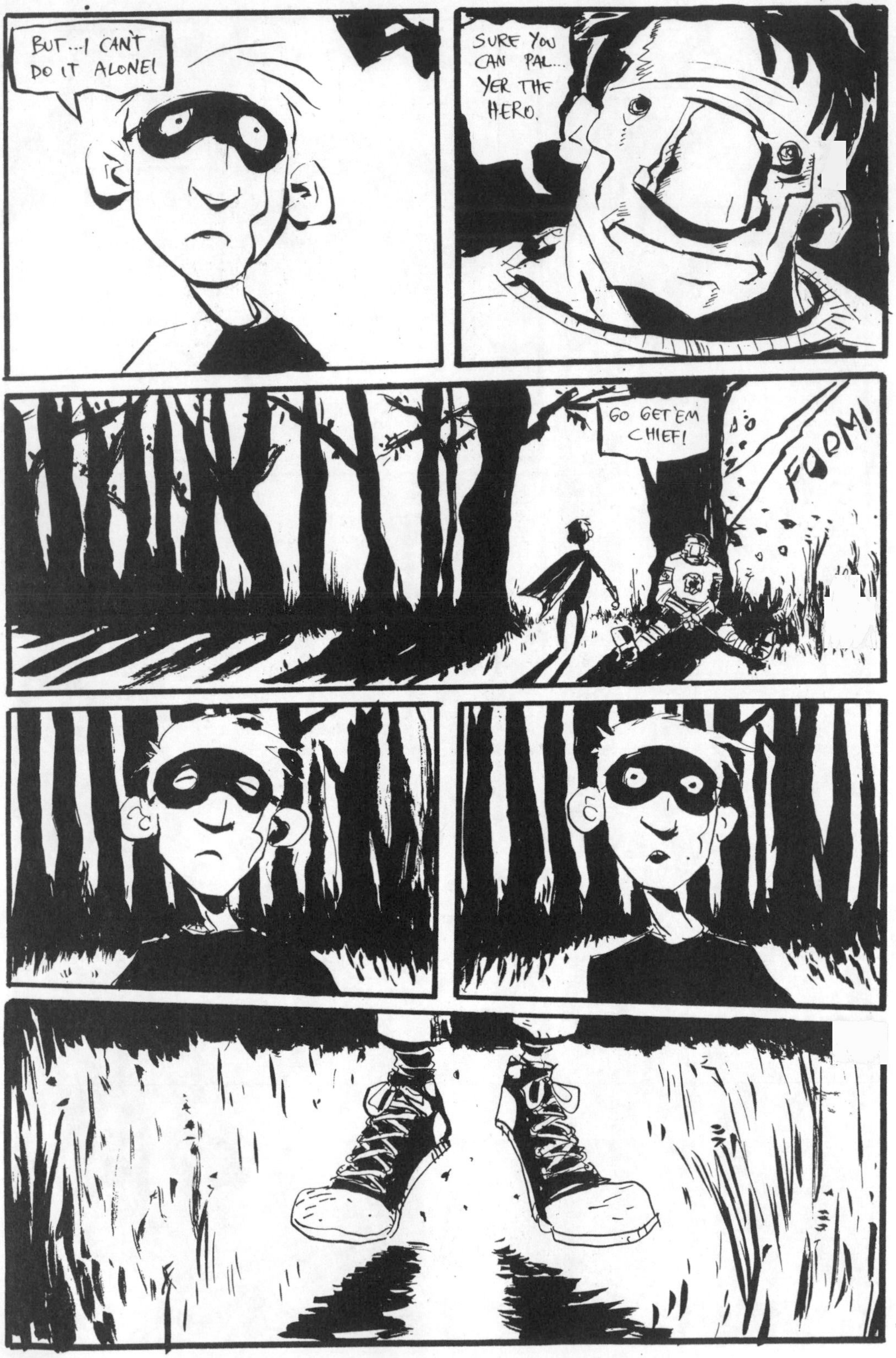
BUT...I CAN'T DO IT ALONE!
SURE YOU CAN PAL... YER THE HERO.
GO GET'EM CHIEF!
FOOM!

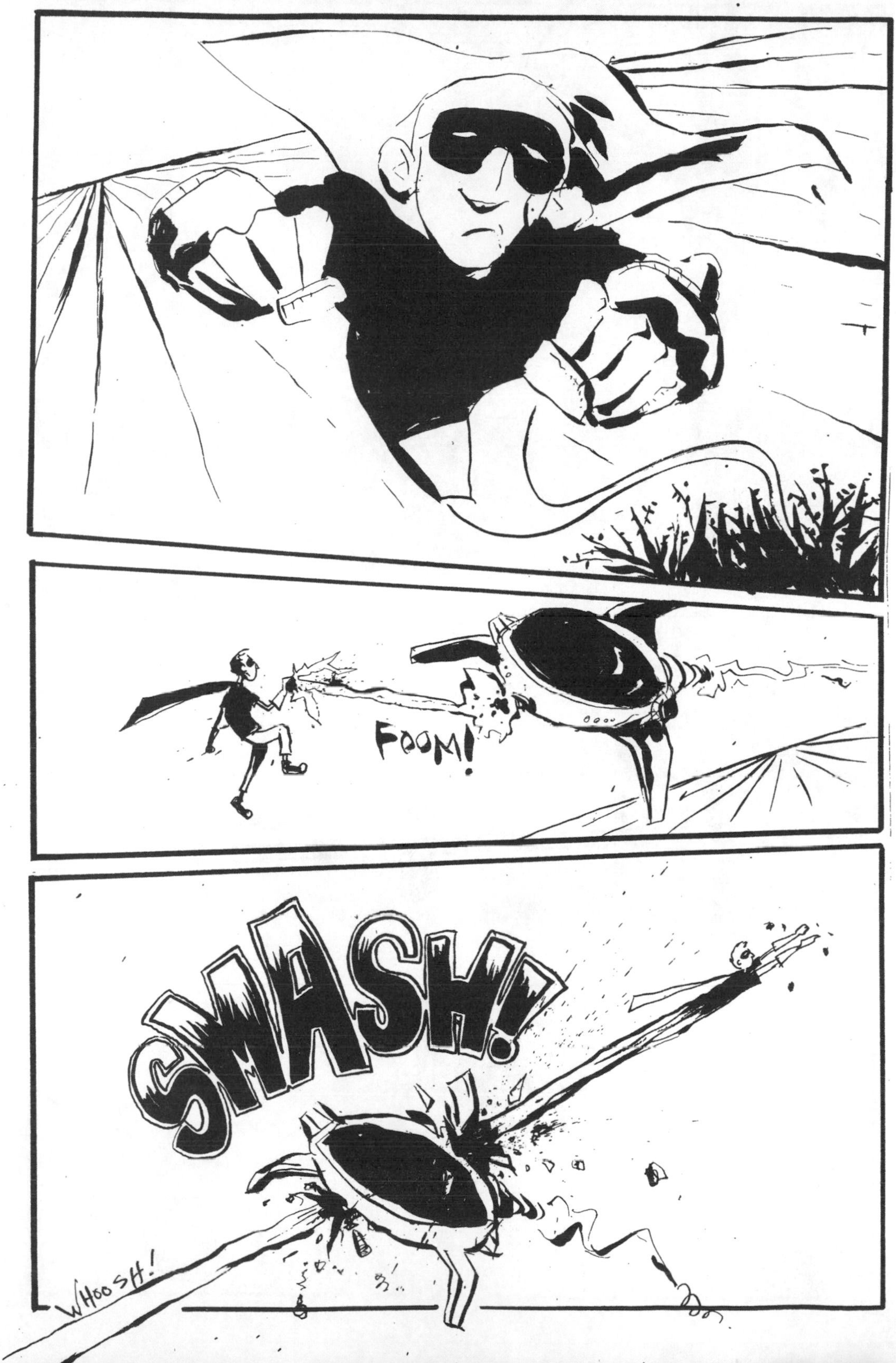
FOOM!
SMASH!
WHOOSH!

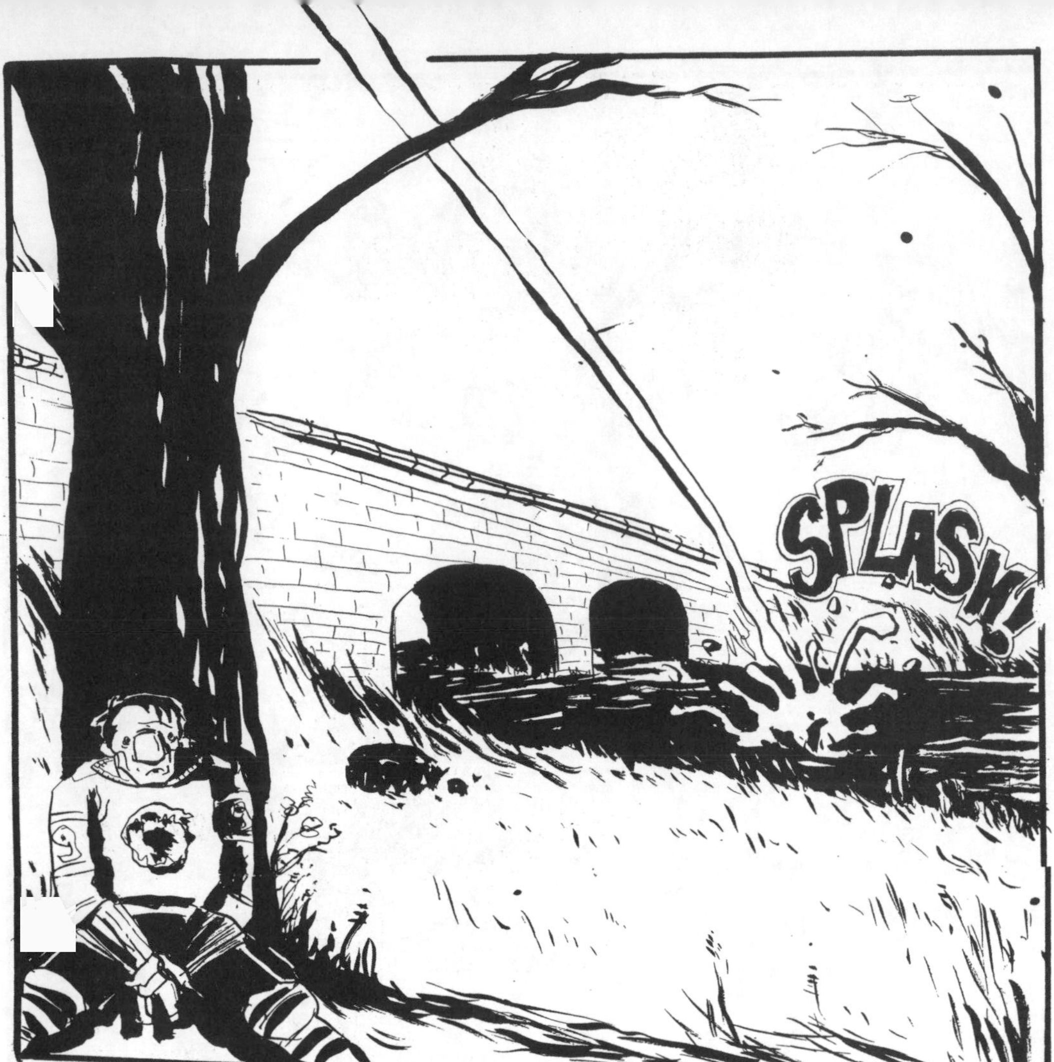
SPLASH!

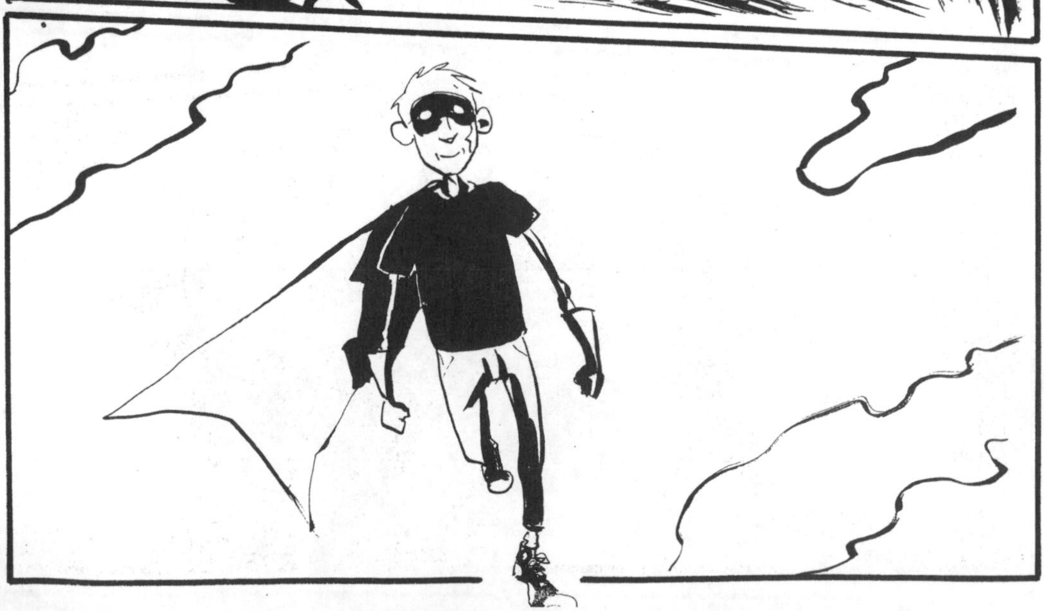

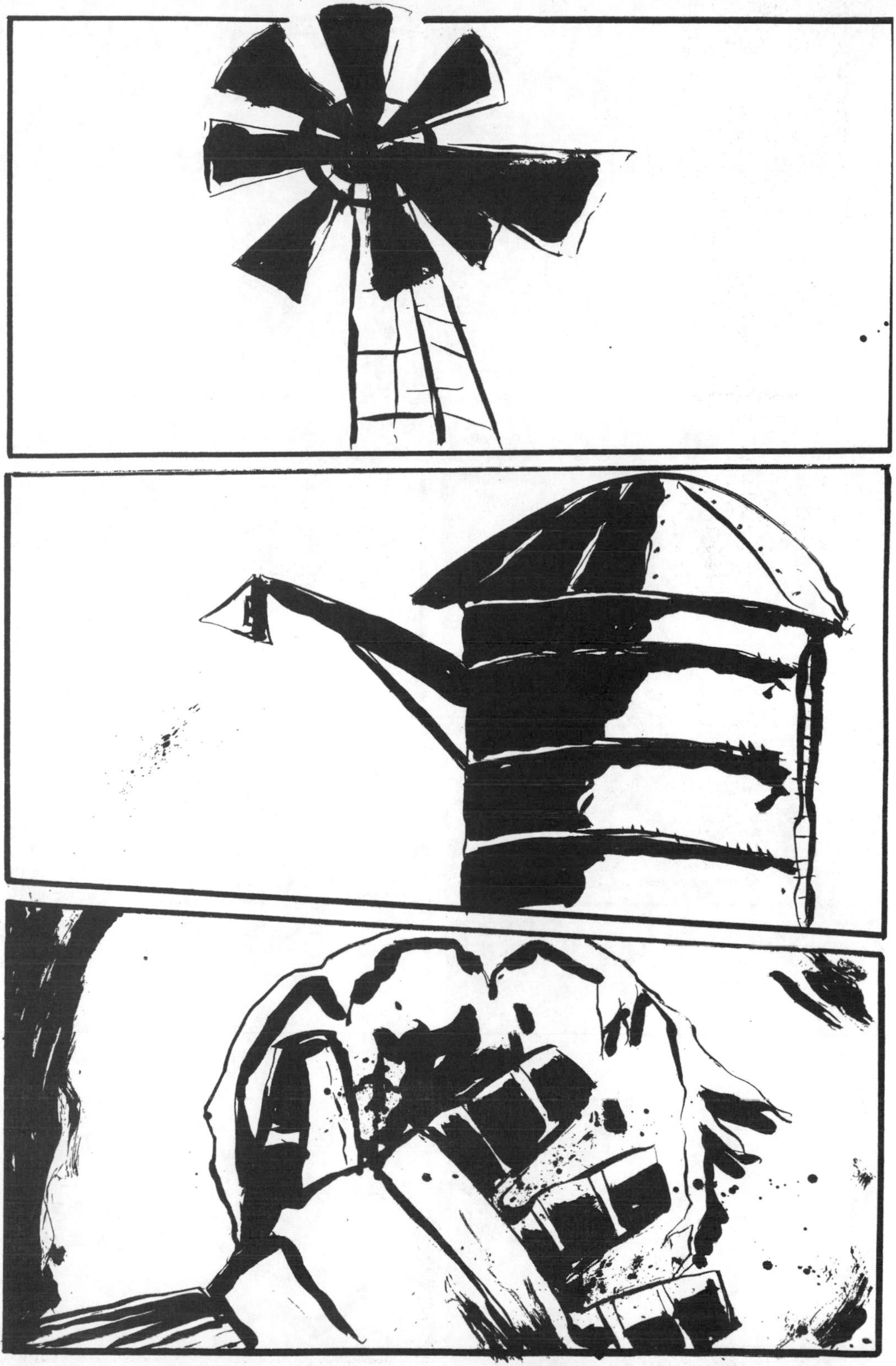

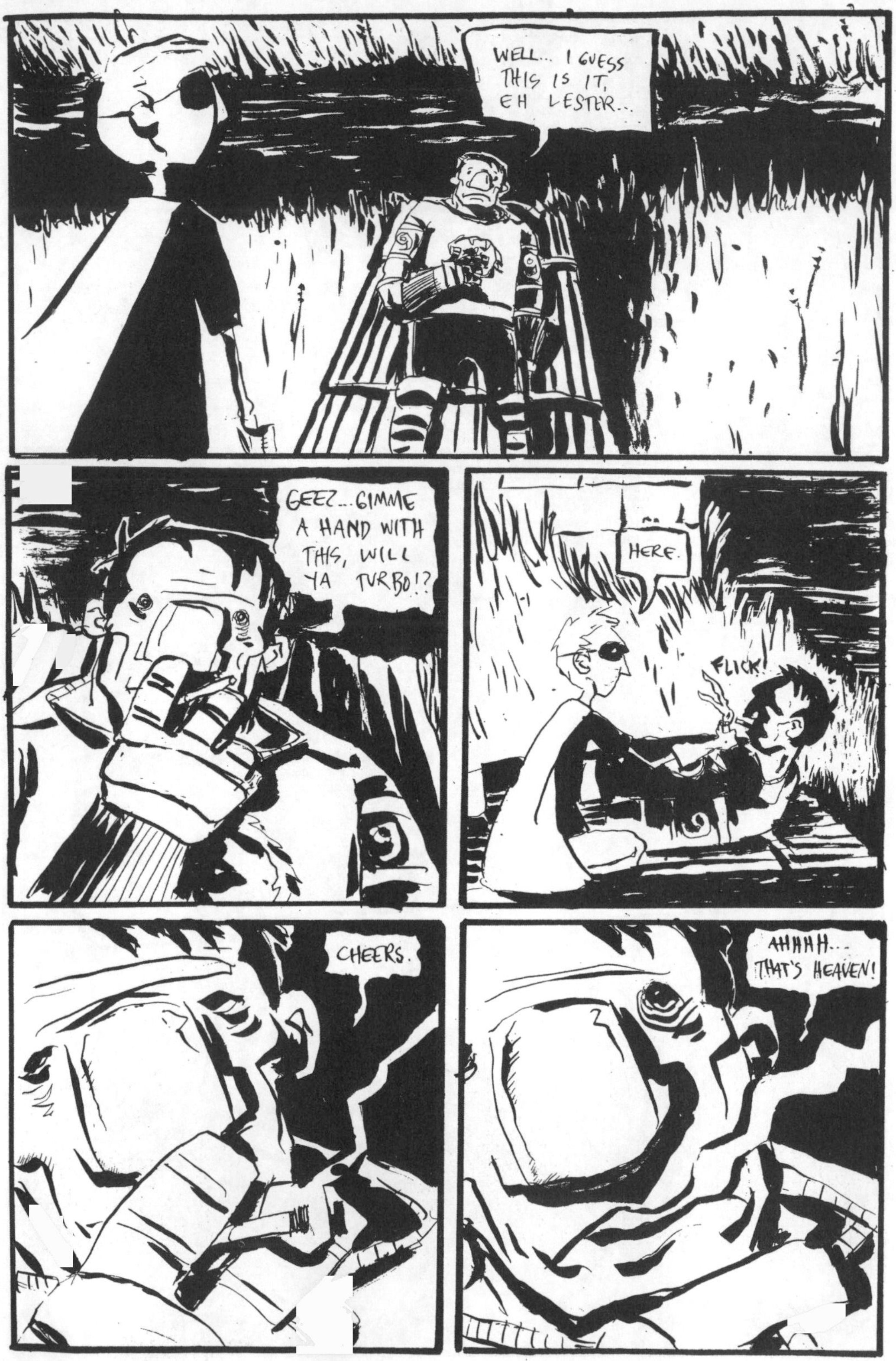
WELL... I GUESS THIS IS IT, EH LESTER...
GEEZ...GIMME A HAND WITH THIS, WILL YA TURBO!?
HERE.
FLICK
CHEERS.
AHHHH... THAT'S HEAVEN!

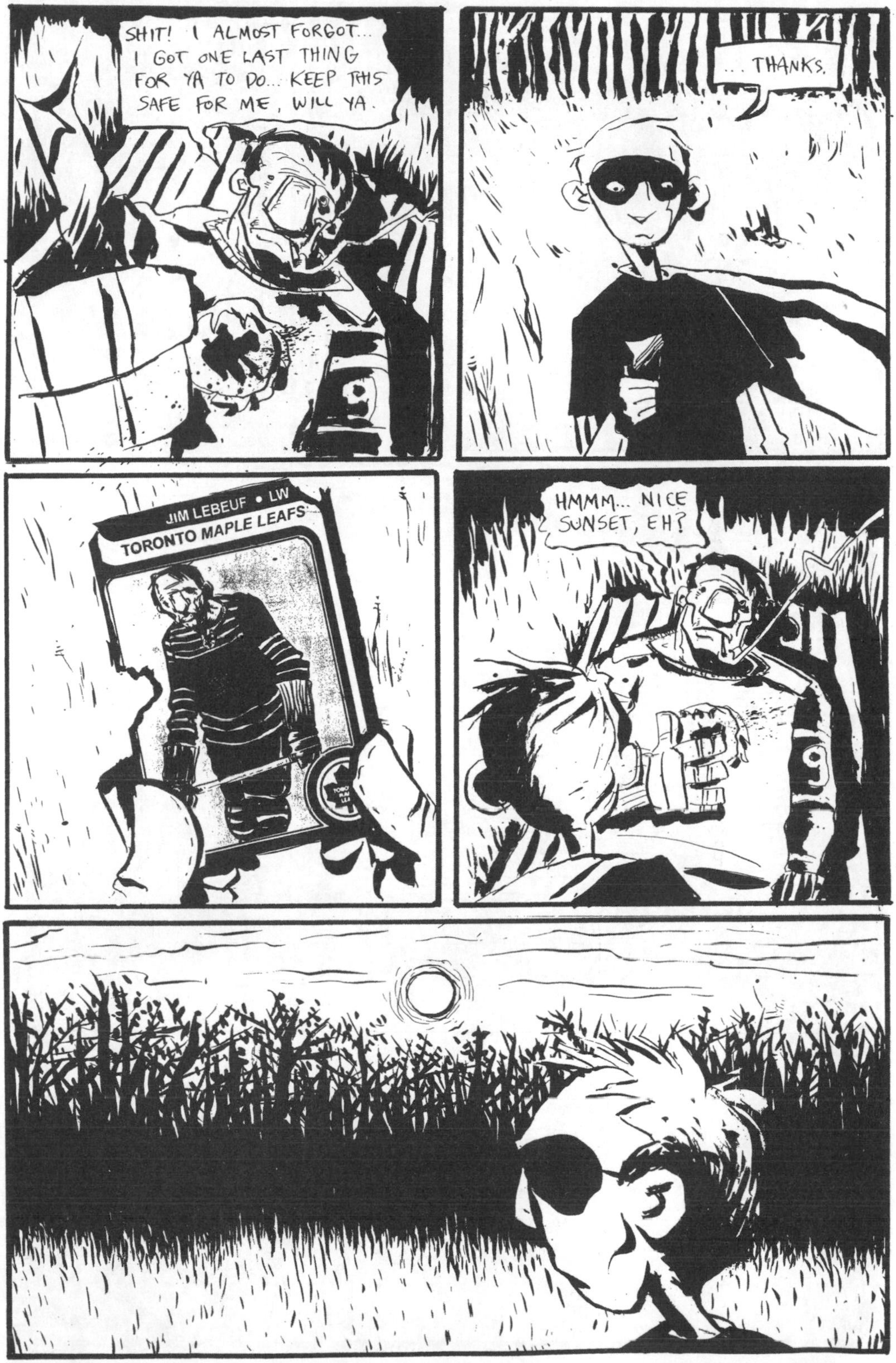

SHIT! I ALMOST FORGOT... I GOT ONE LAST THING FOR YA TO DO... KEEP THIS SAFE FOR ME, WILL YA.
...THANKS.
JIM LEBEUF • LW
TORONTO MAPLE LEAFS
HMMM... NICE SUNSET, EH?

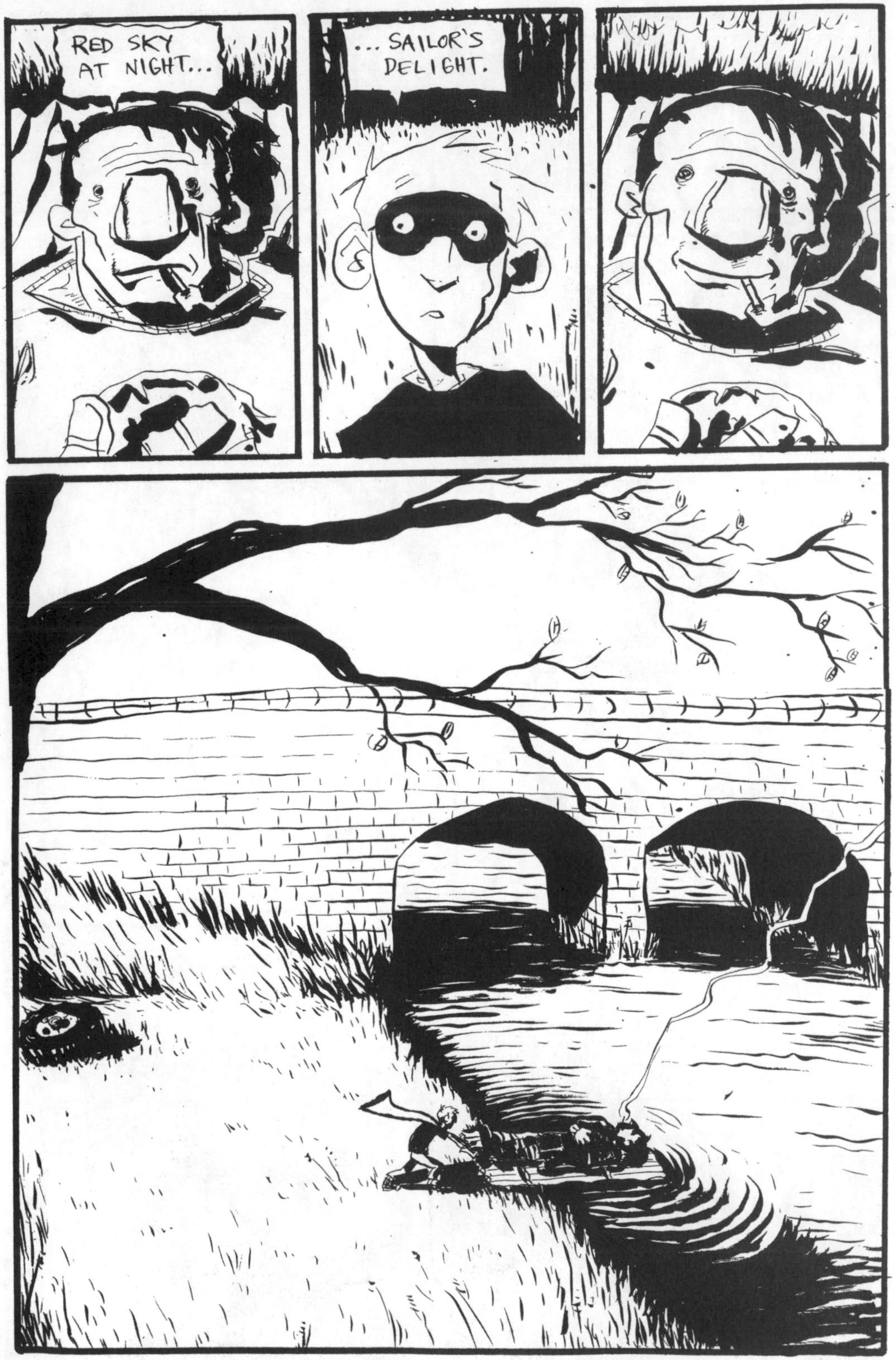
RED SKY AT NIGHT...
... SAILOR'S DELIGHT.

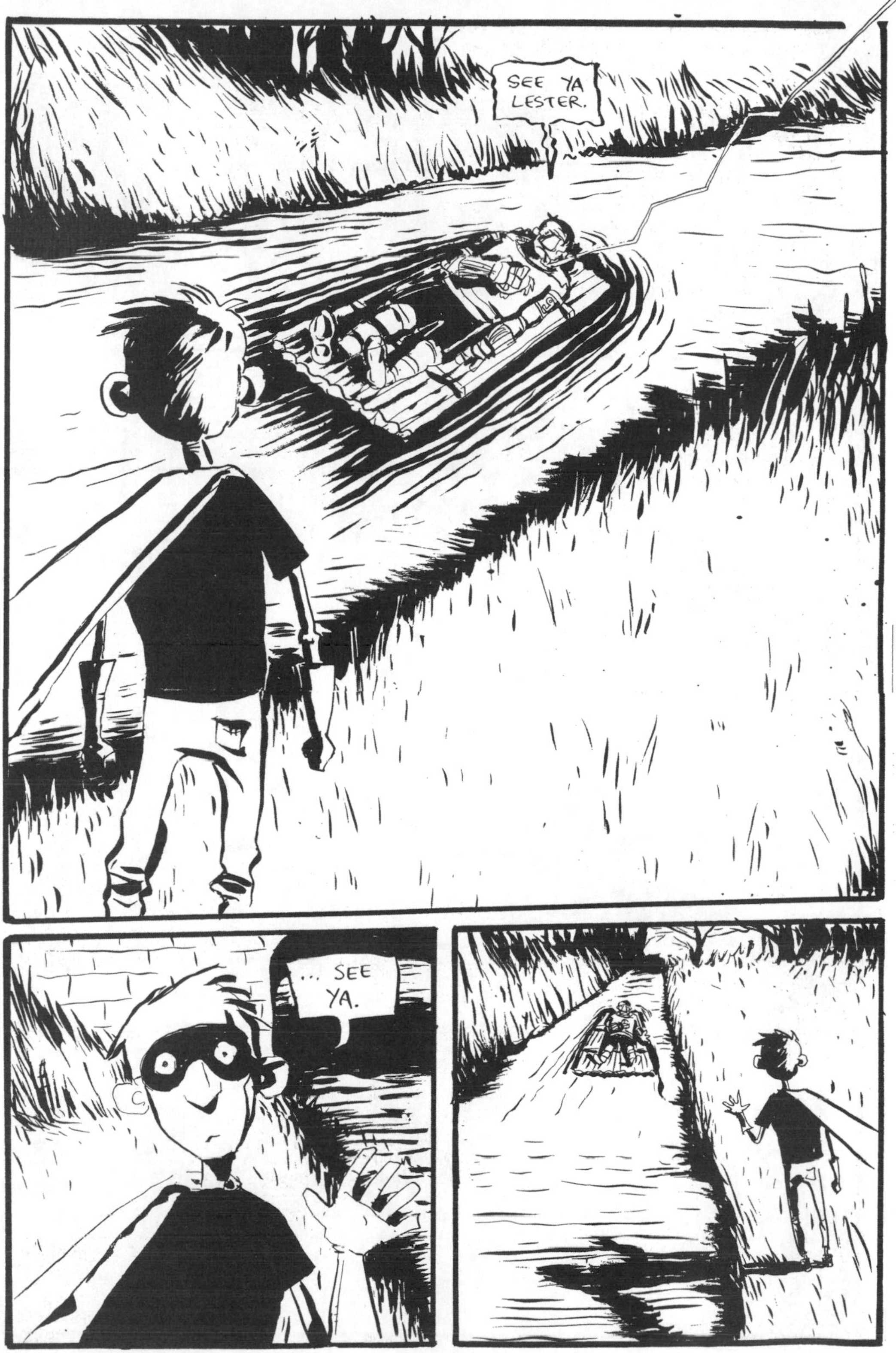
SEE YA LESTER.
... SEE YA.

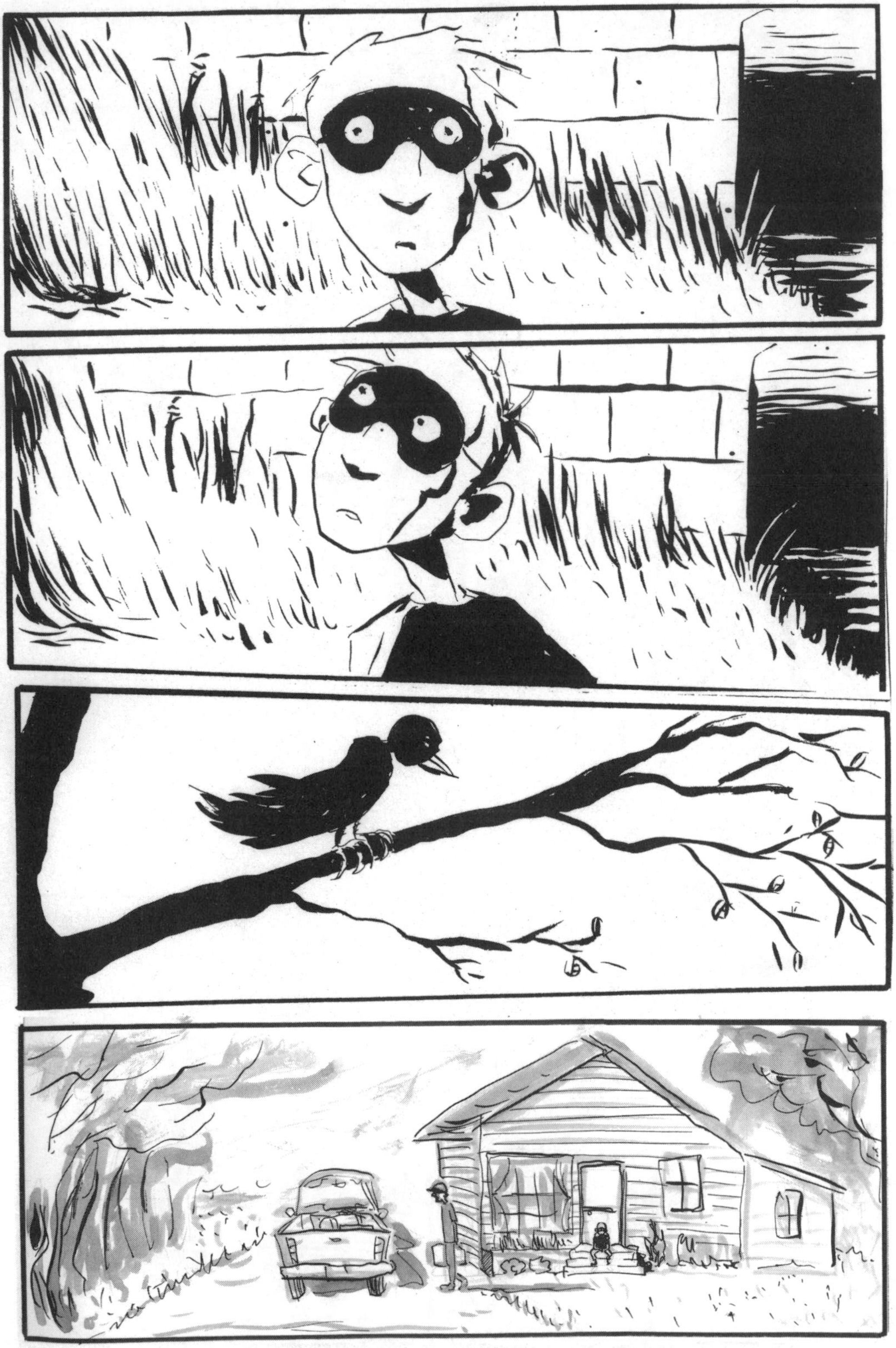

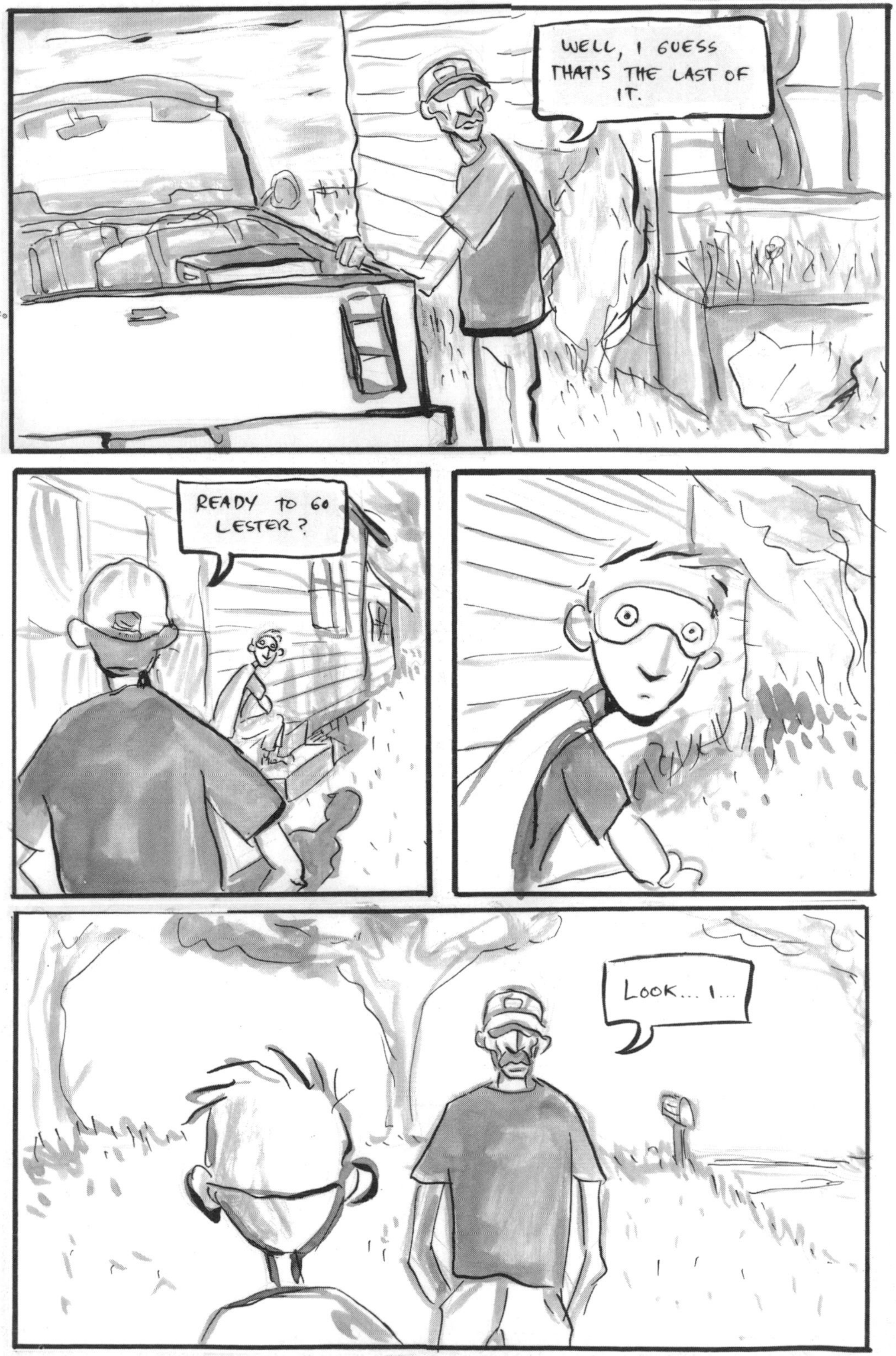
WELL, I GUESS THAT'S THE LAST OF IT.
READY TO GO LESTER?
LOOK... I...

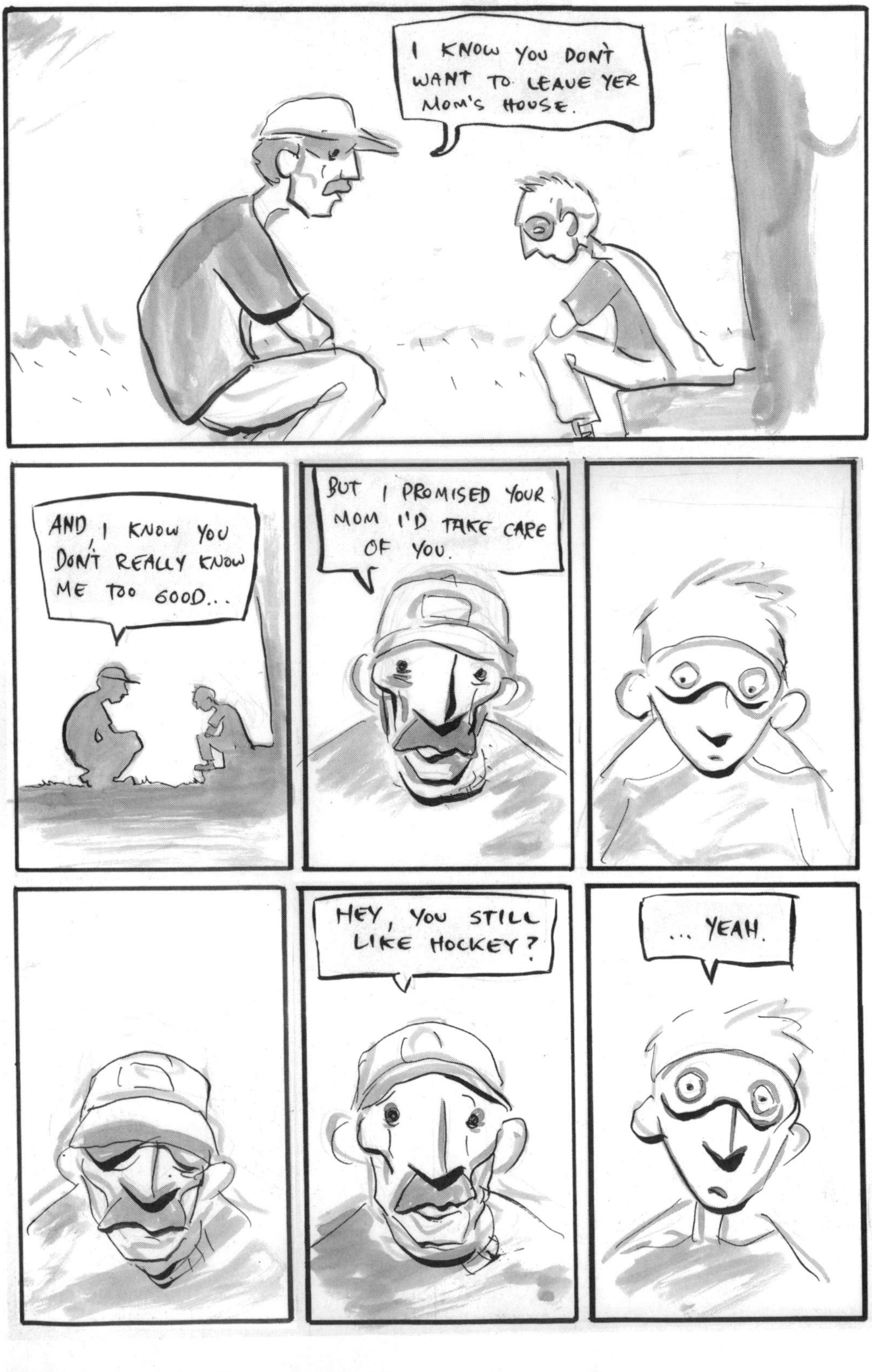
I KNOW YOU DON'T WANT TO LEAVE YER MOM'S HOUSE.
AND I KNOW YOU DON'T REALLY KNOW ME TOO GOOD...
BUT I PROMISED YOUR MOM I'D TAKE CARE OF YOU.
HEY, YOU STILL LIKE HOCKEY?
... YEAH.

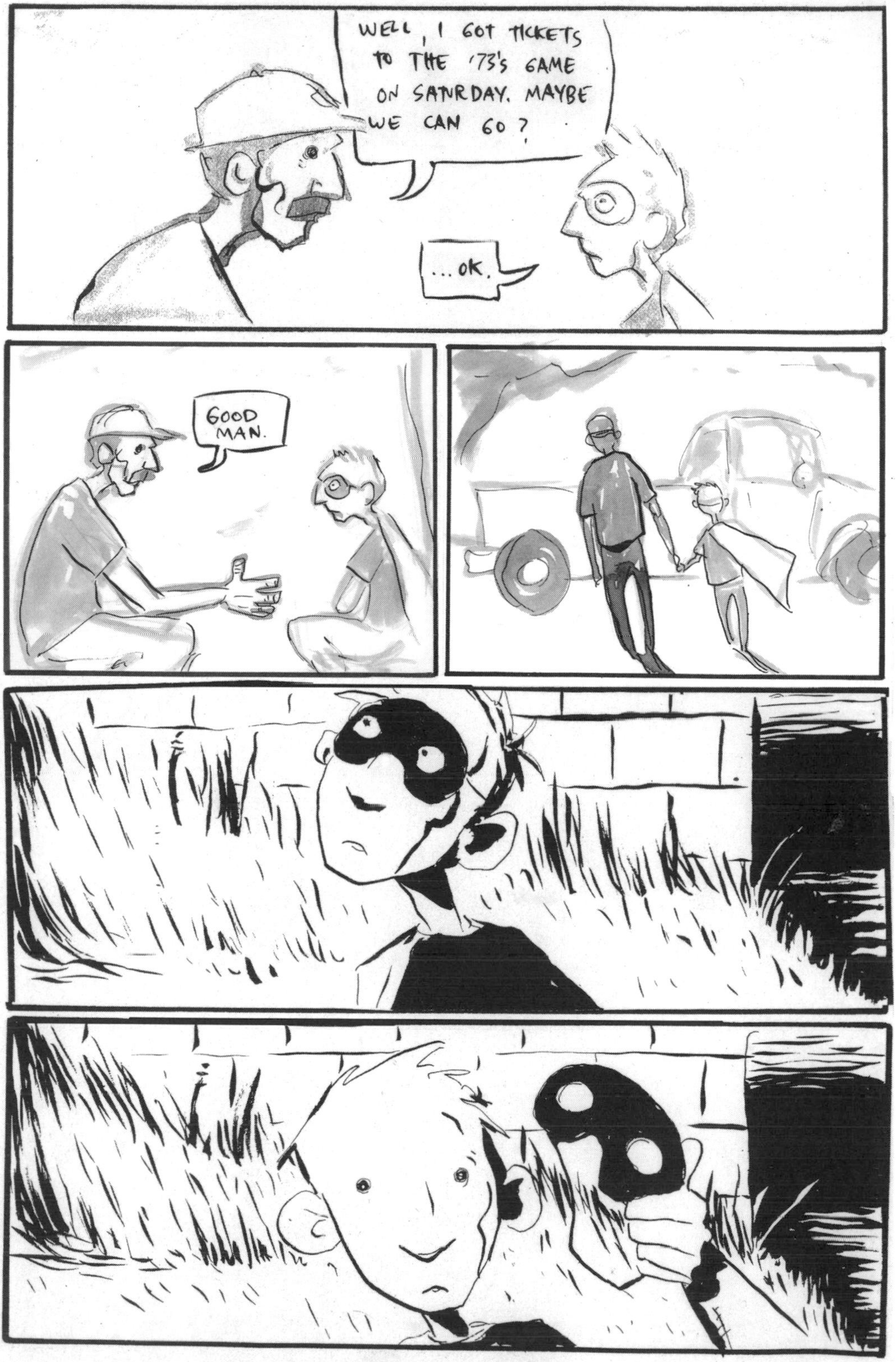
WELL, I GOT TICKETS TO THE '73'S GAME ON SATURDAY. MAYBE WE CAN GO?
...OK.
GOOD MAN.

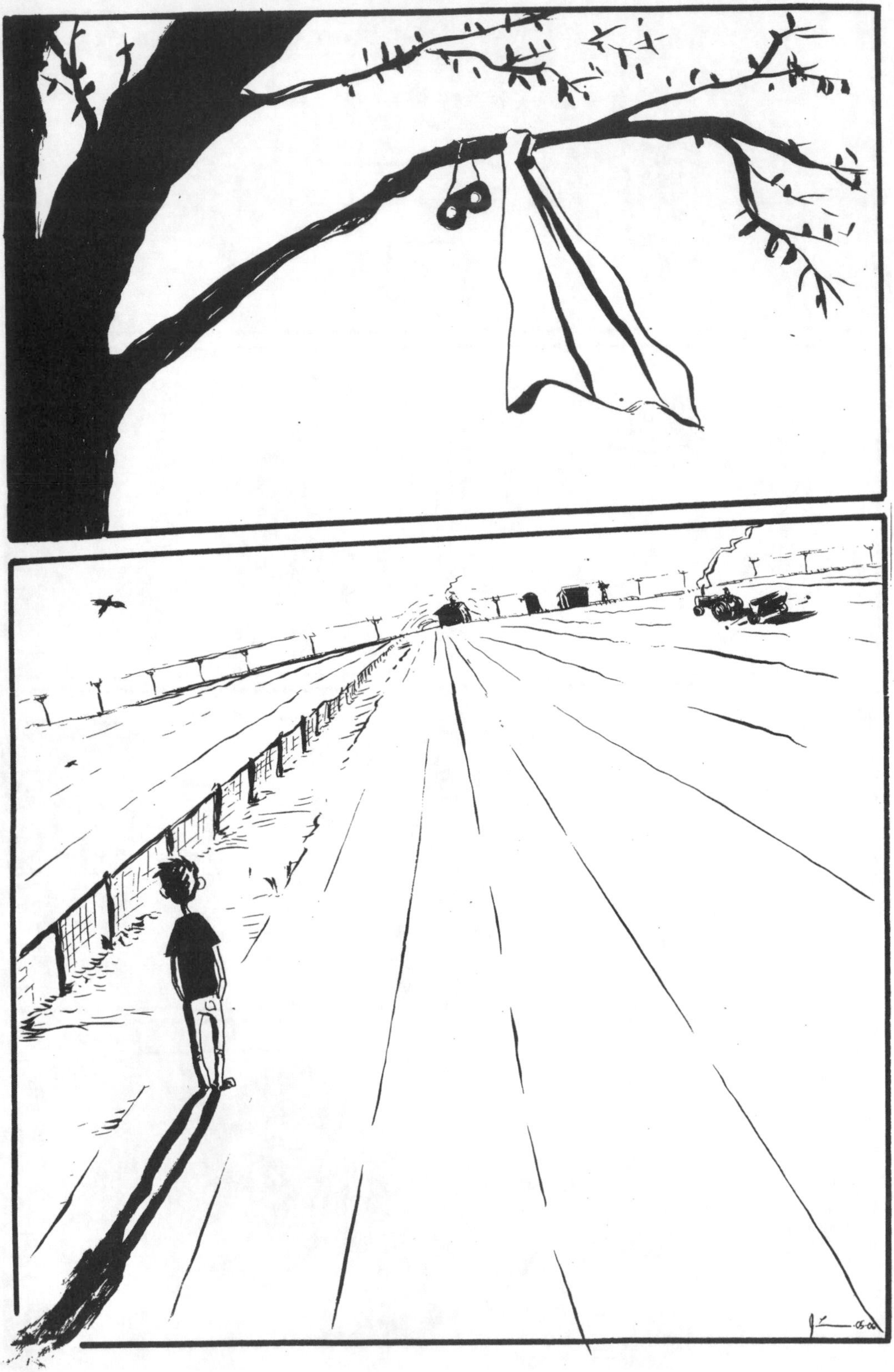

GLOSSARY OF TERMS

NHL
The National Hockey League (NHL). It is the premier professional hockey league in the world.

TORONTO MAPLE LEAFS
The Maple Leafs are an immensely popular tean across Canada and around the world, boasting one of the largest fan bases in hockey.

ESSEX COUNTY
Essex County is located in Southwestern Ontario and covers an area at the southernmost tip of Canada. The largest city is Windsor, which shares its border with Detroit, MI. Otherwise it is made up of smaller farming communities, such as Loamington, Woodslee, and Kingsville.

The author would like to thank the following for their support and encouragement... Chris Staros and Brett Warnock, Lesley-Anne Green, Ted and Mary Ellen Lemire, Dawn, Scott, Abby and Cole Herdman, Kelly and Steve Greff, Roger and Kathy Green, Mike Green and Rebecca French, Dwayne Maillet, Julie Stewert, Erin Burke, Kirk Prior, Dev Singh, Alex Grunwald, Zach Worton, Ryan Oakley, John King and Dragon Lady Comics, Chris Butcher and The Beguiling, Kevin Church, The Flying Burritos Hockey Club, and everyone at La Hacienda Restaurant.

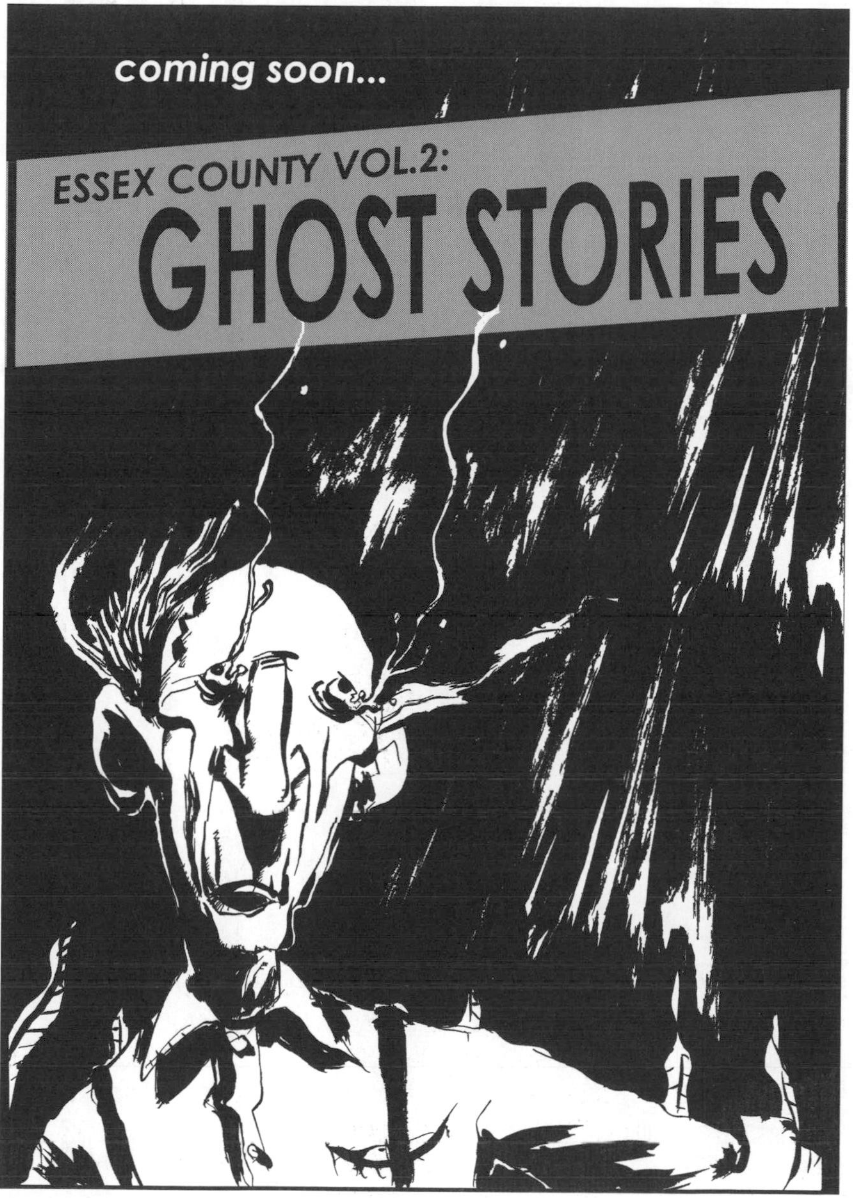
coming soon...
ESSEX COUNTY VOL.2:
GHOST STORIES

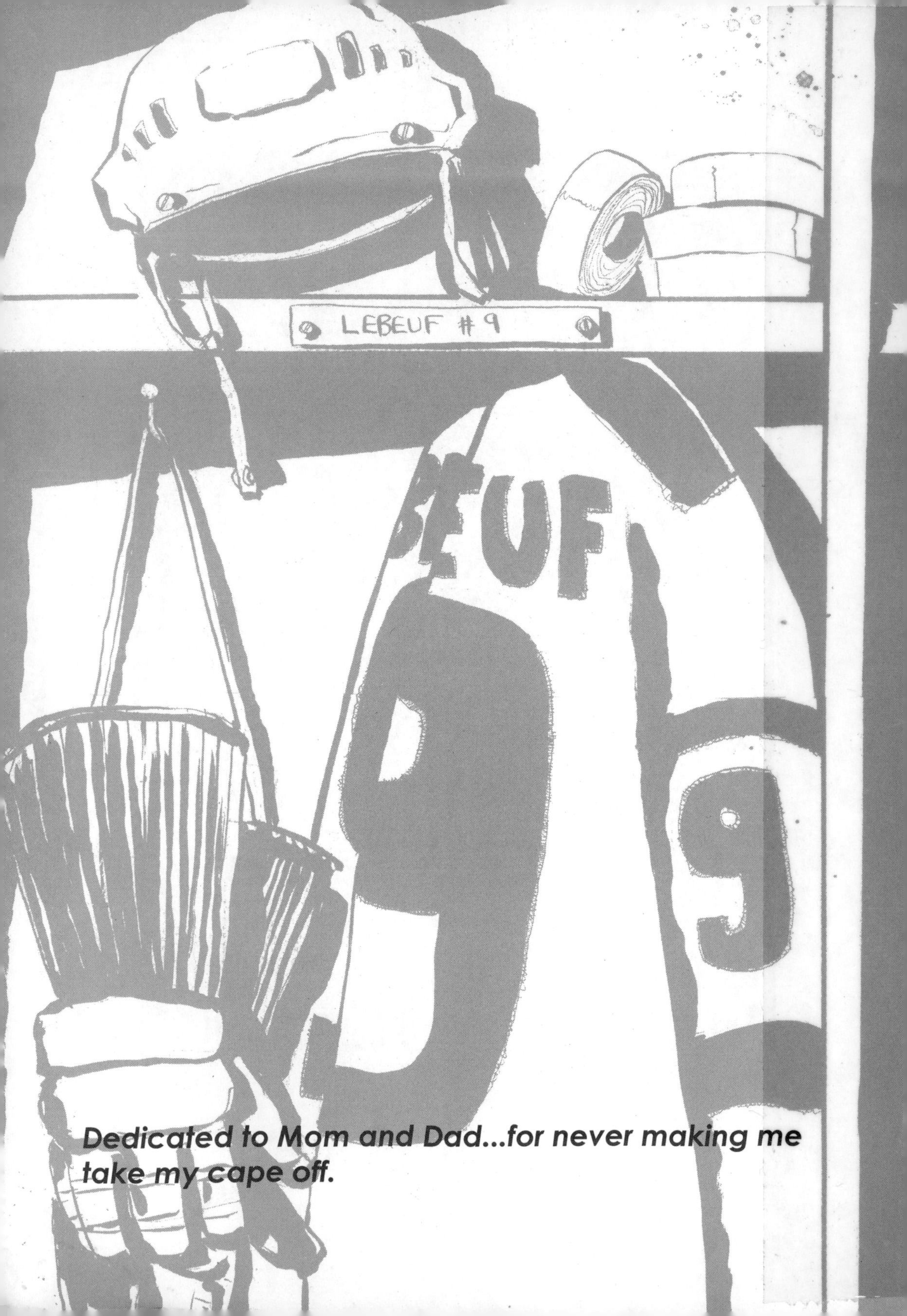
LEBEUF # 9

Dedicated to Mom and Dad...for never making me take my cape off.